D0904129

THE ECONOMICS OF THE SHORT PERIOD

THE ECONOMICS
OF THE SHORT
PERIOD

RICHARD KAHN

Emeritus Professor of Economics, University of Cambridge
Fellow of King's College, Cambridge

St. Martin's Press   New York

First published in the United States of America in 1989

Printed in the People's Republic of China

ISBN 0–312–02516–5

Library of Congress Cataloging-in-Publication Data
Kahn, Richard F. (Richard Ferdinand), 1905–
The economics of the short period / Richard Kahn.
p.   cm.
Bibliography: p.
Includes index.
ISBN 0–312–02516–5: $40.00 (est.)
1. Economics.   I. Title.
HB171.K26   1989
330—dc 19   88–23363
                                                    CIP

CONTENTS

PREFACE

The *raison d'être* of this Preface is to be found in the College Regulations. The Candidate has to provide a general statement of 'the sources from which his information is taken, the extent to which he has availed himself of the work of others, and the portions of the dissertation which he claims to be original'. To the tyro in economic writing such a task involves considerable embarrassment. Economics is a subject in which, perhaps more than in most subjects, the inexperienced writer requires much daring to assert a claim to originality; 'he has availed himself of the work of others' to a greater extent, very often, than he is consciously aware.

It is, of course, evident that the foundations of the treatment of the short period were laid by Marshall. In particular his conception of quasi-rent and the discussion on the short period in Chapter V of Book V of the *Principles* have provided, together with the additions of later economists, the material that I have tried to elaborate a little.

Where I think that I have departed furthest from the traditional treatment is at the position of prominence that I have assigned in the later stages of the dissertation to the imperfection of the market. I refer to the attitudes of some economists towards this subject in Chapter 5, § 28, and in Chapter 7, § 2. Chapter 7 derives its inspiration from an article by Professor Sraffa, and I have had the benefit of Professor Sraffa's criticisms on a first draft of this chapter. But the mathematical conclusions of Chapters 8, 9 and 10 I imagine to be new. And it is on widening these conclusions and on furthering their practical verification, with which a very small beginning is made in this dissertation, that I place the greatest hope for further development.

I have had access to the literature and statistics issued by the now defunct Cotton Yarn Association. Though these were issued confidentially and are not intended for publication, I have been permitted to make use of them for the limited purposes of this study. I have also had an interview in Manchester with two officials of the Association, Captain John Ryan and Mr L. J. Tattersall, to whom I should like to express my thanks. This contact with the cotton industry, which I have found extraordinarily useful, I owe entirely to the influence of Mr Keynes. But this represents only a very small part of my complete debt of gratitude to Mr Keynes for his constant stimulation and advice. It is difficult, also, to make sufficient acknowledgment of the advantage that I have derived through having been taught by Mr Shove. Much of what I now believe to be my own must in reality belong to him.

RICHARD KAHN

ACKNOWLEDGEMENTS

I owe the first publication of my fellowship dissertation to Professor Dardi of the University of Florence. It was published in Italian with a most interesting introduction by Professor Dardi.[1]

For this English edition I am indebted to Professor Maria Cristina Marcuzzo of the University of Calabria and to Dr Geoffrey Harcourt of the University of Cambridge for taking the initiative and for scholarly assistance. I am also indebted to Mr T. M. Farmiloe of the Macmillan Press Ltd, and to his colleagues, for the care with which it has been prepared.

Professor Dardi's initiative in undertaking an Italian translation of my fellowship dissertation came to me as a flattering surprise. The dissertation had been submitted to the Electors to Fellowships of King's College, Cambridge, on December 7, 1929, and secured my Election in March 1930.

I had taken my first degree in mathematics and physics in June 1927. I then began my study of economics and in June 1928 was placed in the First Class of Part II of the Economics Tripos. Some months passed before I selected the subject of my dissertation. Keynes, who in addition to Gerald Shove,[2] was my teacher when I was working for the Tripos, tried to secure for me access to the statistics of the Midland Bank, with a view to my making something of them. Keynes at that time was still a staunch believer in the Quantity Theory of Money, as an expression of causation.[3] From the first I had never been able to conceive of the theory as more than an identity. I was puzzled by the passages about it in Keynes's *Tract of Monetary Reform* (1923) and in his university lectures, and still more puzzled by Dennis Robertson's *Banking Policy and the Price Level* (1926), in the writing of which Keynes had collaborated.

I cannot conceive what use I could have made of the Midland Bank's statistics. But I was young and inexperienced, and unwilling to resist Keynes's influence.

Keynes took me along to meet Reginald McKenna, the Chairman

---

[1] *L'Economia del Breva Periodo* (Turin: Boringheri, 1983).

[2] See my entry on Shove in the *New Palgrave Dictionary of Economics*, edited by John Eatwell, Murray Milgate and Peter Newman, Macmillan Press, London, 1987.

[3] See my *The Making of Keynes's General Theory*, Cambridge University Press, 1984, pp. 50–59.

of the Midland Bank, who was easily persuaded by Keynes. I was then taken to his own room by the Head of the Intelligence Department of the Bank, A. W. Crick. He bluntly informed me that if anybody was going to make use of their statistics, it was he and his staff, and not I. Crick's attitude towards me is partly attributable to the fact that Keynes, as Editor of the *Economic Journal*, had rejected an article submitted by him in April 1928. I tremble to think how my career would have developed had he taken a conciliatory line. It was a miraculous escape from disaster.

Keynes then left me to choose my own subject. Under the influence of Marshall's *Principles*, I chose the *Economics of the Short Period*. In making my choice, I was encouraged by Shove and Piero Sraffa. Keynes happily acquiesced. Neither he nor I had the slightest idea that my work on the short period was later on going to influence the development of Keynes's own thought. But there are no traces of Keynesian thought in the dissertation itself.

In the writing of the dissertation I received enormous help from Shove, and Keynes exercised a stimulating influence on my progress. Fortunately for me he had since 1926 acted in an advisory capacity to the Lancashire cotton-spinning industry. His interest continued after the breakdown at the end of 1927 of a short-lived cartel, which he had supported.[1] Keynes presented me with a mass of statistics for the industry over this period. It will be seen that these played a creative role in an important section (Chapter 9) of my dissertation.

At King's College each Fellowship Elector (always a Fellow of the College) tries to make his own assessment of each dissertation. Among the Electors were Keynes, Pigou, Clapham (the economist and economic historian), Lowes Dickinson, Patrick Blackett, who had taught me physics, Frank Ramsey (the brilliant mathematician and mathematical philosopher), two classicists, the Professor of Music, Wollaston (mountaineer and explorer), a historian, an English scholar, and a chemist.

I was told that reliance was placed on Frank Ramsey (who under Keynes's influence had written two important articles on economics) for 'vetting' my so-called mathematics. But he died tragically at the

---

[1] Roy Harrod discusses the apparent conflict between his support of a cartel and 'the traditional Liberal Policy of hostility to monopoly in all its forms'. (R. F. Harrod, *The Life of John Maynard Keynes*, London, Macmillan, 1951, p. 385, and for an account of Keynes's connection with industry, pp. 379–86.) For more details see under *Cotton Industry, Lancashire*, the Index to Part II of vol. XIX of the Royal Economic Society Edition of Keynes's writings.

age of 26 on January 19, 1930, after a short illness, very shortly after my submission.

My dissertation is to be regarded mainly as of historic interest. It was written at a time of deep economic depression. Its analysis has little applicability to normal economic conditions. However, for some years now – and it is to be feared for some time to come – economic depression has prevailed throughout the world. My analysis conducted in 1929 perhaps has some practical usefulness today.

Having in 1983 read it for the first time for fifty years, I was impressed by it as a contribution made *at the time* – only two and a half years after I had embarked on the study of economics. Looking back, I feel that I made a mistake in failing to secure publication, in a shortened form. But I cannot recall any suggestion that I should do so. Indeed, the dissertation has not – as far as I know – until very recently, been read by anybody, apart from the Electors, Dennis Robertson, who was one of the referees,[1] Joan Robinson, and Nicholas Kaldor and, more recently, a number of academic scholars.

In the course of the following three or four years I did rewrite seven chapters, intending them for publication. On looking at them I am amazed to find that they are almost entirely confined to conditions of perfect competition; whereas the importance of my dissertation largely rested on its treatment of imperfect competition, and of the particular case of duopoly.

The other striking feature of these fragments, intended for publication, is the literary dreariness of the drafting, compared with the spontaneous enthusiasm and liveliness of some of the passages in the dissertation. The result is that I now strongly advise a young author of a striking but incomplete piece of work to publish it, or at least sections of it, after seeking advice, without delay. Published reviews and private comments will then be helpful in the writing of a substantial book, the completion of which is usually bogged down by teaching and administrative duties.

Among the fragments of my abortive book there is one important

---

[1] See *The Collected Writings of John Maynard Keynes*, London, Macmillan, vol. XIII, Part I, p. 121.

passage, extracts from which I can usefully quote, because its argument is not to be found in the dissertation:

> The whole usefulness of the device of the Short Period is based on the fact that the life of fixed capital is considerably greater than the period of production, greater that is to say than the life of working capital. It cannot be too strongly emphasised that this is a *fact*, which could not be deduced by *a priori* reasoning. In a different kind of world in which, for example, the plough wore out after a single season's use (or, better still, in which crops took as long to reach fruition as ploughs to reach decrepitude), quite a different kind of analysis would be appropriate.

Then, having taken die-castings as an example of fixed capital with a life much shorter than most machinery, I enquired what the position would be if:

> there were a complete range of continuous variation in the lives of different kinds of capital, from the coal in the locomotive at one extreme to the railway embankment at the other extreme . . .

The answer is that there could then be no 'economics of the short period'. Marshall's analysis is based on the fact that in nature there is a clear dichotomy based not on theory but on fact. I continued:

> The short-lived drill or die-casting is a rare phenomenon in industrial processes. Between raw materials, on the one hand, and productive plant, on the other hand, there is a desolate and sparsely populated area. As a general rule, the life of physical capital is illustrated either by the mayfly or by the elephant . . . If the life of productive plant varied over the whole range that is *a priori* conceivable, the concept of short-period equilibrium would have ruthlessly to be thrown overboard. Before the level of output had time to adjust itself to changed conditions of demand, the technique of production would have suffered an appreciable alteration.

The concept of the 'short period' is one of Marshall's most fruitful contributions. But he realised that it depended on a peculiarity of the world in which we live, as is indicated by his statement that 'there is no hard and sharp line of division between "long" and "short" periods. Nature has drawn no such lines in the economic conditions of actual life'.[1] By the same token the words *Natura non facit saltum*, which appear on the title-page of his *Principles*, contradict the facts of nature on which analysis of the short period depends.

Equally, the distinction between 'fixed' and 'working capital' is not one which can logically be made. In practice, it is possible to make the same fairly clear, but arbitrary, distinction to which I am referring. The distinction is useful in economic analysis provided that it is appreciated that it has no logical foundation: it is possible to make it as a result of this strange dichotomy in the world in which we happen to live between the time required to produce a finished product – wrongly called the 'period of production' – and the life of fixed equipment and buildings, including the gestation period.

Even with short gestation periods, when it is a question of statistical measurement rather than abstract thought, it must be laid down for working purposes which drills, die castings, etc., are included in working capital and which in fixed capital.

It is remarkable that this vital point was overlooked by Sraffa, so anxious in his *Production of Commodities by Means of Commodities*,[2] to erect a logically watertight structure of thought. The introduction of fixed capital into his system involves circular (as opposed to linear) processes of production. He drew a distinction between 'durable instruments of production', with a life of several years (typically four) and 'such means of production (e.g. raw materials) as are entirely used up in the course of a year' (p. 63). Sraffa did not conceive the possibility that ploughs might have a life of only one year, or one and a half years.

The logic of the distinction between fixed and working capital is seldom questioned. It is commonly supposed that the concept of 'gross output' is firmly based but not that of net output – precisely contrary to logical validity.

And yet Marshall had been made aware of the problem, by Ricardo. He referred to Ricardo as making the distinction between 'fixed' and 'circulating' capital turn on whether the goods comprised in them are 'of slow consumption or require to be frequently reproduced'. He wrote that Ricardo 'truly remarks that this is "a division not essential and in which the line of demarcation cannot be accurately drawn"'.[3]

---

[1] Later editions of Marshall's *Principles*, London, Macmillan, p. 378 (first edition, p. 416).

[2] Cambridge University Press, 1960.

[3] Marshall, *Principles*, in later editions, p. 75, note 2; in the first edition, p. 137, or in the second edition, p. 132.

Marshall then characteristically withdrew from this dangerous ground. He preferred to follow J. S. Mill in distinguishing *circulating capital* 'which fulfils the whole of its office in the production in which it is engaged, by a single use', from *fixed capital* 'which exists in a durable shape and the return from which is spread over a period of corresponding duration'. Marshall was quoting from Mill.[1] He defended his adoption of these shallow definitions (my words, not Marshall's) by the curious argument that 'Mill's modification of Ricardo's definition is generally accepted by modern economists'.[2]

Perhaps today the most interesting sections of my work are those in which Piero Sraffa's (1926) article is discussed, in the course of Chapter 7, my main chapter on 'Imperfection of the Market'. The development of my thinking on imperfection of the market is attributable mainly to Sraffa's article, as well as to my extensive talks with him (Shove also had an important influence). Of particular interest is my exposure of a serious error in Sraffa's exposition, to which Section VII of Chapter 7 is devoted. The character of the error is explained in § 5 of that chapter.

I summarised Sraffa's argument by saying:

that for an industry consisting of firms which are similar and similarly situated the final position of equilibrium is the same as would be arrived at if the whole industry were controlled by a single monopolist. Provided only that the market in is to some degree imperfect, however minutely, the magnitude of the imperfection is, according to this proposition, irrelevant.

That Sraffa made a serious error is obvious, and, 'subject to a possible reservation', Sraffa admitted the force of my objection.[3]

I cannot remember whether I requested Sraffa to show me his

---

[1] Ibid; in later editions, p. 75; in the first edition, p. 134.

[2] Ibid; in later editions, p. 75, note 2; in the first edition, p. 137; in the second edition, p. 130. This, and the two previous learned footnotes, I owe to Claude Guillebaud's ninth (variorium) edition of Marshall's *Principles* (1961).

[3] An unpublished letter from Sraffa to Keynes (King's College, Cambridge, library) is of interest.

original Italian article and read me a translation.[1] I had, like many others, supposed that his English article 'was a sadly truncated' version of the Italian article. I now find that they differ very substantially. Although the dates of publication (1925 and 1926) are close, the Italian article must have been drafted considerably earlier than the English article. There is, of course, a great deal in the Italian article for which there was no room in the shorter English article. But it is in his English, and not in his Italian, article that Sraffa introduced his path-breaking emphasis on imperfection of competition as the factor which explains the possibility of equilibrium for an industry in which the average cost curves of the individual firms fall with an increase in their output. No passages in the Italian article correspond to the passages from the English article which I quote in Section I of Chapter 7.

To go back to Sraffa's error, I was not content with a simple exposure. It led me on to a discussion of the Theory of Duopoly, in Section VIII of Chapter 7, in the elaboration of which I received considerable help from Sraffa. I was able to include a lengthy reference to an article on duopoly by Edward Chamberlin.[2] 'In some respects Dr Chamberlin's treatment reveals an almost curious similarity to the treatment that has occupied the preceding pages but on at least one fundamental issue there is complete disagreement' (Chapter 7, § 31). I attributed to Chamberlin in one section of his article the assumption of my 'third case': that each firm imagines if it alters its price the other firms will neither keep prices unaltered (the Bertrand–Edgeworth hypothesis) nor continue to produce the unaltered outputs (the Cournot hypothesis) but 'all the complex possibilities that emerge when the business man realises that neither the outputs nor the prices of his competitors will remain constant if he alters his own price'. Chamberlin did not rely on any understanding – tacit or overt – between the firms, just as I rejected any reliance on what in one passage of his article Hotelling described as 'something of a tacit understanding' (§ 30 of my Chapter 7).

And yet Chamberlin arrived at the remarkable conclusion that

[1] Piero Sraffa, 'Sulla relazione fra costo e quantità prodotta', *Annali di Economia*, vol. II, no. 1 (Milano: Universitá Bocconi, 1925) pp. 277–378.

[2] Chamberlin's article was published in the United States in November 1929; my dissertation was submitted on December 7, 1929. Fifty years ago postal services, relying purely on ships and trains, were remarkably speedy. (Chamberlin's book on *The Theory of Monopolistic Competition*, Harvard University Press, was not published until 1933.)

'although the sellers are entirely independent, the equilibrium result is the same as though there were a monopolistic agreement between them'. This goes much further than Sraffa's proposition (which he withdrew in deference to my criticism). Sraffa's proposition was essentially linked to his emphasis on the fact that in the real world markets are imperfect. Chamberlin was working on the basis of the customary assumption that *markets* are perfect (as opposed to competition – imperfect because the number of sellers is small). It should, however, be conceded that Sraffa asserted that his result 'requires only a *very slight degree* of preference for a particular firm in each of the groups of customers' (my italics).

After December 1929 I wrote nothing more about the problem until I published an article on the subject in March 1937.[1] Readers of this article may be interested in comparing the two treatments. The text suggests that in drafting the article I did not actually read the treatment in my dissertation. But clearly I retained a fairly clear memory of my earlier line of thought.

The article, which consists of only twenty pages, is a clearer and more precise presentation. A serious defect lies in a failure to outline the historical development of thought on the subject. This is attributable to the editorial limit on length imposed by the editor of the *Economic Journal* (Keynes). At the opening of the article I referred to various solutions which have been published in the last two or three years by some of that vast host who have gathered in this field. The resemblances are, I think, not quite as close as may superficially appear. But in any full-dress treatment I should feel called upon to indicate in what respects my solution was related to, and in what respects it differed from, the work of others. I confined myself to a few references to recent work by Pigou, Harrod, Stackelberg, Coase, and A. J. Nichol.

The article – in remarkable contrast to the dissertation – reads like the work of an economist ignorant of the relevant history of economic thought. The works of Cournot and of Bertrand explicitly provide the basis of the article, but without a single bibliographic reference to them. I should at least, as a result of consulting my dissertation, have included, in one bibliographical footnote (or as an Appendix), reference to the work (in addition to that of Cournot and Bertrand) of Pareto, Wicksell, Edgeworth, Schumpeter, Pigou, Sraffa, Hotelling

---

[1] Richard Kahn, 'The Problem of Duopoly', *Economic Journal*, March 1937, vol. XLVII, no. 185.

and Chamberlin (my failure in the article to express my personal debt to Sraffa is inexplicable).

Perplexed by Professor Dardi's courage in publishing my dissertation, I find some justification in these historic references to the theory of duopoly, which seem to me still to have some interest. (Incidentally, it has taken about fifty years to bring me back to the history of economic thought. The Cambridge University Press have published my book, *The Making of Keynes's General Theory*, based on lectures delivered in June 1978 (rewritten by June 1979) under the Raffaeli Mattioli Foundation at the Universitá Luigi Bocconi of Milano.)

Naturally enough in my 1937 article my conclusions about duopoly were less tentative than in my 1929 dissertation. I insisted more emphatically that a determinate solution must be asymmetric even though the two sellers are alike. To explain my solution I used the concepts of *price leader* and *price follower*.[1]

If the two firms are very similar it is 'a matter of historical accident' which emerges as the leader and which as the follower. 'But if the firms are sufficiently dissimilar . . . one of the two alternative positions will be more profitable for *both the firms* than the other, and that one will then be selected' (in my 1937 article, pp. 14 and 15).

I proceed now to refer to two further passages in my dissertation which may be of interest. In § 24 of Chapter 7 I wrote that 'the question is not what actually happens when a firm alters its price but what the owner of the firm imagines is likely to happen'. In § 25 I wrote:

---

[1] Ibid, p. 10. In a footnote I stated that it might have been better to invent new terms. The terms (price leader and price follower) I had derived from A. J. Nichol (who had used them in two articles, 'A Reappraisal of Cournot's Theory of Duopoly', *Journal of Political Economy*, February 1934, pp. 80–105; and 'Edgeworth's Theory of Duopoly Price', *Economic Journal*, March 1935, pp. 51–66). But I expressed myself as 'anxious to avoid many of the associations with which the concept of *price leader* is connected'. I desired 'to abstract no more than the purest essence of Nichol's meaning'. Still less did I desire to use the terms in the sense in which they were used by E. H. Chamberlin. His *price leader* is able to rely on such loyalty and trust that he established the industry's monopoly price no matter how large the number of competitors (E. H. Chamberlin, *The Theory of Monopolistic Competition*, Cambridge, Massachusetts, and Oxford: Harvard UP, 1933, p. 5, note 11).

there are many industries in which firms fix their prices over long periods of time and alter them, at rare intervals, only in response to very appreciable impulses . . . In such an industry a business-man is entitled to believe that a small change in his own price will fail to react on the prices charged by his competitors.

In § 26 I wrote 'it is the method of trial and error that must in many cases determine the business man's conception of his individual demand curve'. And then in § 28:

Suppose there are any number of sellers (more than two) all charging for the moment a certain price which happens, for some reason or another, to be in excess of the cost of production . . . Then a single firm may well be aware that if it were to lower its price in an attempt to increase its output, each of the other firms would be forced in self-defence to lower its price by an equal amount . . . For this reason the price may be prevented from moving downwards. If, on the other hand, a single firm decides to raise its price, its output will drop to zero; but there will be nothing to induce the other firms . . . to raise their prices . . . The equilibrium price is any and every price, and the price is where it is for no other reason than it happens to be so.

It is just possible – I rely for my claim on a conversation with E. H. Chamberlin – that I can claim priority for the important concept of the 'kinked demand curve' – the phrase introduced by Robert Hall and C. J. Hitch,[1] whose treatment is considerably more far-reaching than mine (they of course were unaware of my work). I continued:

Conversations with business men lead me to think that this conclusion – absurd though it may appear – has some bearing in practice. It applies more particularly in those industries where policy determines the price that a firm shall charge rather than the level of its output, where the price is fixed for fairly long periods at a time, where custom or convenience dictate that a change of price shall be substantial in amount, and where the number of

[1] R. L. Hall and C. J. Hitch, 'Price Theory and Business Behaviour', *Oxford Economic Papers*, May 1939, no. 2 (actually the second issue of this new journal), reprinted in T. Wilson and P. W. S. Andrews (eds) *Oxford Studies in the Price Mechanism* (Oxford UP, 1951. The book was reviewed by me in the *Economic Journal*, March 1952, vol. LXII, no. 245.)

firms is not too large . . . But it is important to note that while there can be equilibrium in any position, the equilibrium is unstable for changes in a downward direction.

Here my treatment becomes open to criticism. It is primitive and incomplete. Lacking is the concept of *price-leadership*, introduced in my article on duopoly.

In the dissertation much space – far too much, the reader will be ready to argue – is devoted to painstaking analysis of various cases of imperfect competition – and especially of imperfect markets. Perhaps of most interest is the treatment based on the distinction between *transport* and *preference imperfection* (described in Section V of Chapter 7). There is nothing in itself original in the importance which I attach to imperfection of the market. My debt to Sraffa – both to him personally as a friend and to his article – is made clear. I feel that I should have written more about Shove, one of my teachers. And I referred to Marshall (§ 2 of Chapter 7).

The importance of the dissertation rests largely on the analysis of the influence of imperfection of the market on the manner in which, at a time of depression, an industry's output is distributed between the individual firms.[1] I opened Chapter 7 by asking why most of the firms in the cotton-spinning industry, in which the degree of competition was regarded as high, work short-time, instead of those enjoying the lowest prime costs working to capacity. While the obvious answer is 'imperfection of the market', until 1930 it was seldom given. In § 4 of that chapter I developed the theme in general terms. In Chapter 8 the discussion acquired precision by being based on the assumption of ⌐-shaped prime-cost curves for each individual firm (the ⌐ is a reversed capital L).

It so happens that the short-period cost curves of a cotton-spinning mill approximated closely to the reversed L. A mill worked at full capacity on some days, and closed down on others. Both the analytical treatment and the arithmetical demonstrations were based on the relevant statistics for recent years of the Lancashire cotton-spinning industry which Keynes had handed over to me.

---

[1] *Establishment* is a better word than *firm*, for a firm often consists of a number of establishments, differing in efficiency. (By the same token, *plant* is often a still better word.) To avoid confusion I adhere to the word *firm* used in the dissertation.

It is for my readers to decide whether this elaborate analysis was justified. It impressed the Electors in 1929 and, for my own part, I find it impressive today.

Statistical confirmation of theory is not confined to § 24 of Chapter 9. I then proceeded to estimate the elasticity of aggregate supply of the industry. The result of the theoretical analysis is compared with the facts in § 26. A theoretical figure of 5 is compared with an experimental figure of 3.6.

In my Preface I wrote that

It is on widening the conclusions [mathematical] of Chapters 8, 9 and 10 and on furthering their practical verification, with which a very small beginning is made in this dissertation, that I place the greatest hope for further development.

I am inclined to the view that while further development would have proved fruitful, it is fortunate from my own selfish point of view that I did not make the attempt.

I find it extremely difficult to judge the extent to which my dissertation, written over fifty years ago, is of interest to-day. My advice to any reader is – at any rate in the first instance – to skim it, and avoid becoming bogged down in the algebra and geometry. If I were in his place I would read it superficially, bearing in mind when it was written.

The argument is unduly meticulous. The scrupulous care with which alternatives are examined – cases, or types, (a), (b), (c) in Chapter 3, § 6 – may perhaps in some passages be impressive. But excessively taxonomic treatment prejudices easy reading.

The publication of this book represents an act of gross impertinence on my part. Professor Dardi shares the blame. I admire him for his courage.

A further acknowledgement is due to Maria Cristina Marcuzzo. With characteristic care and energy she has provided a remarkable Bibliography which appears at the end of this book.

I am also indebted to my secretary, Mrs Marlene Gibbson, for her skill in deciphering my handwriting; also to James Trevithick and Terence O'Shaughnessy of King's College, Cambridge, for most

useful advice and help; as well – I repeat – to Maria Cristina Marcuzzo
and Geoffrey Harcourt.

RICHARD KAHN

INTRODUCTION

'The long run in which we are all dead has no terrors for this economist. The intricacies of the short period and the parochial view are relegated to a position of minor importance. Sometimes, I am inclined to think, exception might be taken to this attitude.'[1] In these words the London Professor of Economics reminds a former occupant of his Chair of Mr Keynes's taunt, which has now become classical. And what is true of Professor Cannan is true of most other economists. The long run and ultimate tendencies have provided their main preoccupation. Though 'the explicit introduction of the element of Time as a factor in economic analysis is mainly due to Marshall' and 'the conceptions of the "long" and "short" periods are his',[2] yet even in the pages of Marshall's *Principles* the references to the short period are not very numerous and are so intermingled in the theory of long-period value, which, one feels, is the real business of the *Principles*, that it is difficult to separate them. Possibly this entanglement of the short period with the long period can be attributed to Marshall's desire to trace 'a continuous thread running through and connecting the applications of the general theory of equilibrium of demand and supply to different periods of time'.[3] But Marshall himself stated that: 'The central part of the problem of value under competitive conditions is that scarcely any important result is true in regard to both short periods and long: a great part of the many barren controversies, that have raged on the matter, results from attempts to refute statements relating to long periods by others relating to short periods, or conversely.'[4] It is then at first difficult to see why, in common with most other economists, Marshall devoted so little space to the short period and treated short-period effects, for the most part, as mere modifications of long-period tendencies.

One reason that can be suggested is that, owing to the general tendency towards expansion which persisted in most industries throughout the greater part of the last century, the difference between the short period and the long period did not appear so fundamental

---

[1] L. Robbins, *Economic Journal*, September 1929, p. 412.
[2] J. M. Keynes, *Economic Journal*, September 1924, p. 351.
[3] *Principles*, p. 660, quoted by J. M. Keynes, *Economic Journal*, September 1929, p. 412.
[4] *Industry and Trade*, p. 396.

as it is now seen to be. Until quite recently it was possible to write: 'So an industry may, and often does, keep tolerably active during a whole year or even more, in which very little is earned beyond prime costs, and the fixed plant has to 'work for nothing'.[1] A year was regarded as near the limit of the period over which an industry would remain in a state of severe depression. But now most of our staple industries have been severely depressed for eight years and there is every sign that they will remain depressed for several more years. Fluctuations that are large relatively to a rapidly upward moving trend may involve absolute depressions that are small both in duration and in intensity. It was because most industries happened to be in a state of fairly continual expansion that the period during which they were sub-normally active did not usually extend to more than a year or two. But it is only during periods of sub-normal activity that the deviations from the long-period norm are persistent and easily noticeable. The closer we approach a static state, as opposed to a state of progress, the more important does the study of the short period become.

It seems clear that Marshall was not relying entirely on a state of general expansion to secure the expression of long-period tendencies within a reasonably short space of time. The forces that induce the closing down of those firms that are working at a loss and the decay of that capital on which an insufficient return is being earned are parallel to the forces that induce the entry of new firms into an industry and the expansion of existing firms. It was always recognised that the former pair of forces, which are active in the case of a declining industry, are the very much weaker pair and much slower in action. But it, nevertheless, seems reasonable to suppose that the strength of these forces was overestimated. The tenacity with which industrial units may cling to a productive existence has, perhaps, been fully realised only as a result of the great post-war depression, which has thrown its shadow across most of the following pages.

There is an additional reason for the growing importance of short-period considerations. When an industry becomes depressed, the extent of the fall in price from its normal long-period value depends on the relative importance of overhead costs in that industry. When overhead costs are unimportant, the fall in price is small. Now, with the introduction of modern methods of manufacture, overhead costs are continually growing at the expense of prime costs. '*Betriebsbereit-*

---

[1] Marshall, *Principles*, p. 421.

sein ist alles; die eigentliche Ausführung der Arbeit macht dann wenig Mühe mehr.[1] This factor imbues the short period of sub-normal activity with an ever-increasing degree of terror for the employer class.

This essay is an attempt to trace the factors that combine in determining the price and output of the product of an industry in such a short period. To some extent I shall have in mind an industry that is depressed. But much of the treatment is of more general application.

---

[1] Schmalenbach, *Vossishe Zeitung*, June 1, 1928.

CHAPTER 1
DEFINITIONS

I THE SHORT PERIOD

1 In any enterprise there are some features of the productive process
that are amenable to change, and are in fact changed rapidly and
frequently, and others that are less easily changed. The most stable
element is usually the fixed plant. Next to this, the whole complex
that is covered by the term 'organisation' is the element that in fact,
and frequently by necessity, conforms most closely to a stereotyped
form, while conditions in the industry may alter fairly substantially.
Fixed plant and organisation both change gradually, but over a
sufficiently short period of time the change is inappreciable. The
short period for an industry is one in which the fixed plant and
organisation of all, or nearly all, the firms can be assumed to remain
constant.

Over such a short period, a certain portion of a firm's cost of
production persists unchanged at a level that is independent of its
output. This portion is generally referred to as the overhead cost.
The rest of the cost of production, which is responsive to changes in
output, is known as the prime cost. On the whole, it may be said,
overhead cost is incurred in respect to fixed plant and organisation.
But for our purposes more accurate definition is necessary, and it
will be attempted in the next section of this chapter. Meanwhile the
nature of the short period will be given further consideration.

2 It is at once clear that the length of the period for which an industry
satisfies the conditions of the short period varies enormously with
the circumstances of the industry. In general it depends on the rate
of growth and on the rate of decay of fixed plant and organisation;
but the rate of growth is a very different thing from the rate of
decay, and often, though not invariably, it is only one of these rates
that is really a relevant consideration.

3 We will begin by considering the growth and decay of fixed plant,
which constitutes the more obvious frontier to the realm of the short
period, and at the same time the more important one. The process
of decay of fixed plant is usually very slow; but, in the absence of

special difficulties, improvements in fixed plant, extensions, and additions are effected with considerable rapidity. So long as an inadequate return is being earned on its fixed capital by the preponderating portion of an industry, it is the rate of decay that sets the bounds to the short period; and the short period may run into decades. It is true that a technical improvement may make investment in a depressed industry profitable where it was not profitable before. But only a great improvement is likely to be profitable in an industry that is seriously depressed; and, even if such an improvement is a profitable one, it is difficult, both physically and psychologically, for a firm that is incurring a heavy loss to indulge in the new investment that an improvement involves. The fact, however, has to be faced that local improvements and additions to fixed plant are continually being adopted, though a general process of decay is in vogue. This is particularly so where, as in coal-mining, the conditions of production are very diverse. Coal-cutting machinery is being put into use and, even, new mines are being opened. But it may reasonably be hoped, with a view to such a study as this, that over the whole field of the industry these changes are not very appreciable. In any case, at the risk of venturing beyond the undisputed sway of the short period, we shall have to pay some attention to certain repercussions on the efficiency of fixed plant.[1]

On the other hand, if the industry is a prosperous and a growing one, and if the prosperity is thought to be more than a passing phase, so that improvements to fixed plant and additions, whether by the expansion of existing firms or the entry of new ones, are being undertaken continuously at a rate that is significant, considerations that are based on the short period are only applicable over a short space of time. This space of time may not, in some cases, extend over more than a year, or even less. As Mr Robertson has been heard to put it, 'the short period is not the same length at both ends – and never has been'. Fortunately, perhaps, for our purpose, the staple industries of this country are depressed, and have been depressed since 1920; and it is the long end of the short period from which they are suffering.

§ 4   It might at first appear that this conclusion as to the length of the short period when an industry is depressed is partially upset when organisation is given its place next to fixed plant as a factor that determines the length of the short period. For just as fixed plant

[1] See Chapter 3, §§ 20 to 27.

increases rapidly but decreases slowly, so organisation can be easily and rapidly cut down but can only slowly and with difficulty be enlarged. But this statement of the apparent difficulty itself contains a partial answer. It is the hope of the return of prosperity that sustains a firm through a period in which existence is possible only at the expense of a loss. The very fact that organisation could be restored only with difficulty, when prosperity returns, prevents a firm from cutting it down during the period of depression. Moreover, in the case of a joint-stock company, a decision to economise on organisation might cut of the means of livelihood of some of those who helped to procure the decision: it is, therefore, the more unlikely to be undertaken.

But it is not necessary to assume that everything that is covered by the word 'organisation' is kept completely rigid. It is sufficient if there is a rigid relation between the organisation of a firm and its output. It is not so much the organisation itself that we have to assume to be fixed, as the policy that relates organisation to output.

That this policy does in fact change cannot, however, be controverted. But it may be suggested that such changes are of a discontinuous rather than a progressive nature, and are not likely to be very frequent when the forces of depression have been at work for a considerable length of time. But just as in the case of fixed cost, repercussions on organisation will have to be given some attention.[1]

So far we have been concerned with the upper limits to the length of the short period. Certain lower limits must also be considered.

In the first place, the period is long compared with the period of production. Errors of forecasting, which arise when a manufacturer who is embarking on the production of a particular parcel of goods makes a wrong estimate of the price at which he will be able to sell them, are the subject of a different kind of study.

Second, market price is a quite different thing from short-period price. We shall be mainly concerned with a steady rate of production and its relation to a normal short-period price. The fluctuations of price that occur within still shorter periods in association with fluctuations in stocks are, for the most part, outside the scope of this essay.

A distinction that might, perhaps, be made to render good service is between the short period and what may be called the 'longer period'. The criterion of the longer period we postulate to be that in

---

[1] See Chapter 3, §§ 17 to 19.

it, as opposed to the short period, firms do not make a loss.[1] In the short period firms carry on at a loss in the hope of an improvement, but in the longer period such firms have closed down, either in despair or through necessity. We see, then, that in the short period profit is a quasi-rent that is simply maximised; in the longer period this quasi-rent is always positive; and in the long period it is not only positive but constitutes a normal return to the investor and to the entrepreneur.

In the treatment that follows it will frequently be found that considerations that belong to the longer period obtrude themselves into the short period. Indeed, in point of time these two periods are often hopelessly intertwined: firms may close down at an appreciable rate within quite a short period of time. But the complications that arise from this fact could possibly have been dealt with somewhat more coherently if greater use had been made in this essay of the conception of the longer period.

II   OVERHEAD COST, FIXED COST, PRIME COST, AND PRIME PROFIT

§ 7   Allusion has already been made to the general nature of the distinction between overhead costs and prime costs. Overhead costs are inherent in the inelastic elements of the productive machine: prime costs are associated with the more flexible elements, notably labour and raw materials. But accurate treatment demands more rigid definition than is usually attempted.

It is in the first place necessary to distinguish between costs in the ordinary sense of the term, which represent the actual money payments that have to be made by a firm and costs in the economic sense, which control the growth and decay of firms and industries. In neither sense does the term include the *actual* profits that may be earned. In the second sense it includes *normal* interest and profits, but not in the first sense, except so far as they are represented by debenture and loan charges. The term 'overhead cost' will be retained to represent the more general second sense, and thus becomes identical with Marshall's 'supplementary cost'.[2] For the first sense

---

[1] For reasons that will appear later, it is only technical fixed cost (see § 17), not the whole of overhead cost, that must be reckoned in evaluating this loss.

[2] Overhead cost is discussed further in § 16.

the term 'fixed cost' will be employed; it represents actual money payments which a firm incurs, profits being regarded as a surplus or quasi-rent left over after all other charges have been met.

Instead of defining fixed costs by setting out a list of those items of expenditure of which it is comprised (management, rent, upkeep, and so on), it is both more natural and more desirable to define it quite simply as that portion of the total cost which is fixed, in the sense that it does not vary with the output under the short-period conditions that are relevant to a particular problem. We consider a single firm, pursuing a certain policy and bound by the restrictions of the short period. Then a schedule can be drawn up to show the relation between its total cost and its output. As the output tends to zero, the total cost approaches a definite figure. This will be called the fixed cost.

It is the cost that *would* be incurred in producing an output of just about nothing. It is the cost of keeping the firm in running order when its output is zero; but it is not suggested that such a policy is usually resorted to for any length of time. It follows that, on certain assumptions,[1] fixed cost is identical with the 'stopped cost' of cotton spinning and other industries.

Aggregate prime cost is now defined quite simply as the difference between total cost, at any level of output, and fixed cost.

It is clear that in a rough sort of way fixed cost covers the costs of management and upkeep, rent, rates, and such interest charges as are not covered by working capital; while prime cost is due to labour, materials, and interest on working capital.[2]

The excess of aggregate proceeds over aggregate prime cost is an entity to which it is convenient to give a name: 'prime profit' will serve as well as any other. Then profit *simpliciter* is the excess of prime profit over fixed cost. If a profit (prime or otherwise) is negative, it is called a loss.

III DEPRECIATION COST

The allocation of depreciation costs necessitates a somewhat

---

[1] See Chapter 5, § 19.
[2] If the funds necessary for increasing working capital are raised by selling investments, withdrawing money from deposit account, or withholding profits from distribution, the loss of interest that results must be regarded as a virtual money payment and so is included in the cost of production.

lengthy digression. Depreciation is defined by L. C. Cropper to be 'the diminution in the utility value of an asset due to natural wear and tear, exhaustion of the subject matter, effluxion of time, accident, obsolescence, or similar causes'.[1] It is important to observe that depreciation is not a money payment rendered in the course of the process of production. It has for instance to be carefully distinguished from the cost of repairs. It is true that if repairs are not undertaken, depreciation results. But in the normal way repairs represent that portion of the work of maintaining capital which is carried on steadily and continuously, and their cost must be included in the costs of production.[2] Depreciation, on the other hand, cannot be regarded as a cost in the same sense.

§ 11   When depreciation is taken into account in the books of a firm, the effect is that the value of the fixed capital is written down by the appropriate amount. The counterbalancing item is, in the first place, an equal reduction, on the liabilities side of the balance sheet, in the credit balance of the profit and loss account. If a profit is being distributed, the ultimate effect is likely to be that the amount distributed is decreased and that cash and investments are increased by the amount of depreciation. The effect is therefore not dissimilar to that of placing profits to reserve. When the time comes to make good the depreciation, the increase in cash and investments is available to meet the necessary expenditure. Profits are reduced by the amount required to maintain the value of the capital, if they were not so reduced, the firm would be distributing its capital under the guise of profits.

If, however, the firm is prevented from distributing a profit (most generally because it is making a loss), the allocation of depreciation becomes a mere bookkeeping transaction. Fixed capital is written down and the credit balance of the profit and loss account is decreased by an equal amount (or the debit balance on the assets side is increased, or reserves on the liability side are decreased). But it is perfectly evident that no manipulation of depreciation can in this case have the slightest effect on the amount of cash and investments, and therefore on the real position of the firm as a productive enterprise.[3] When money is spent on making good the depreciation,

---

[1] *Higher Book-keeping and Accounts*, p. 41.

[2] In general the item of repairs is comparable with that of depreciation. Thus for a cotton mill the former is £1,800 per annum, while the latter may be estimated at £5,000 per annum.

[3] This is a point that many business men fail to realise. Much time and ink have

the same decrease in cash and investment must be sustained as would result if no account had been taken of depreciation. (Instead, however, of being a burden on the profit and loss account, the sum appears in the balance sheet as an increase in the value of the fixed capital on which it is spent.)

A sharp distinction must therefore be drawn between depreciation and the expenditure that results from depreciation. The latter may be called expenditure on renewals. It is an actual money payment rendered in the course of the process of production and must be included in the cost of production (fixed cost or prime cost, as the case may be), even in the restricted sense in which we use the term cost. So long as expenditure on renewals follows a uniform course,[1] there is no difficulty and the distinction between renewals and repairs becomes somewhat arbitrary. Suppose, for instance, that a firm owns 200 machines, ten of which have to be renewed every year; and assume that it is the policy of the firm to maintain its productive capacity. Then each machine depreciates on the average by a twentieth of its value every year and the total annual depreciation is just made good by the renewal of ten machines. In this case the amount of depreciation and the cost of renewals are equal and the value of the capital is just maintained. But more typical is the case where all the machines are of the same age and none of them are renewed over a long course of years. Depreciation then goes on unimpeded by any expenditure on renewals. At the end of twenty years the question arises whether the whole plant is to be replaced. But here we arrive quite definitely at the bounds of the realm of the short period, and we need not consider the allocation of expenditure on such replacement. It might logically be held that we had already crossed the frontier when we assumed, in dealing a few sentences back with the firm whose machines are of all ages, that 'it is the policy of the firm to maintain its productive capacity'. The possibility of a different policy being adopted is one which cannot be ignored, even in an essay that purports to deal exclusively with the short period: it is considered in Chapter 3, § 20, below.

---

been wasted in attempts to show how the cotton industry would be more prosperous if, with the object of reducing the cost of depreciation, the book values of the mills were written down.

[1] The same is true if the course, not being uniform, is however perfectly arbitrary in its irregularity. Some method of averaging the expenditure evenly must then be applied (such a method is available in the form of a 'repairs and renewals reserve fund').

But in the practical cases that will confront us there will be little difficulty. A cotton mill, to take an example, is usually made up of plant that is all of the same age. Doubtless from time to time renewals of essential pieces of machinery are necessary, since the mill could not be operated without them. These are conveniently bracketed with repairs. But the bulk of the plant does not have to be renewed, except at long intervals.[1] Moreover, under the conditions that at present rule in the industry, the installation of new plant is unlikely to be lightly undertaken.

§ 13   When expenditure on renewals, following either a regular or a completely haphazard course, can be included in cost, in the restricted sense in which we use the term, it is allocated between fixed cost and prime cost according to the usual principle. Some expenditure may be necessitated even when a firm's output is zero. This portion appears in fixed cost and the rest is included in prime cost.

§ 14   It is when depreciation exceeds expenditure on renewals that the difficulties arise, and it is this excess that it is necessary to allocate. Like expenditure on renewals, depreciation can be divided into a fixed portion, that does not alter with the output, and a prime portion. When depreciation is largely due to obsolescence, as a result, for instance, of the action of the atmosphere or of technical improvements, it appears mainly in the fixed portion; when it is due to wear and tear, it appears in the prime portion. For a standard cotton mill the annual rate of depreciation may be assessed at £4,000 when the output is zero and at £6,250 when the mill is working full-time.[2] The fixed depreciation cost is therefore £4,000, while, for full-time working, the prime depreciation cost is £2,250.[3]

We are concerned, then, with the excess of fixed depreciation cost over fixed expenditure on renewals, and with the excess of prime depreciation cost over prime expenditure on renewals. These excesses may be termed the actual fixed depreciation and the actual prime depreciation. The fact that actual fixed depreciation does not represent a money payment rendered in the course of production justifies us in refusing to admit it within the category of fixed cost. Like interest, it must be relegated to overhead cost. But, for a reason that will immediately be made clearer, actual prime depreciation must,

---

[1] Of twenty years or more.

[2] Cotton Yarn Association, Circular of July 28, 1927.

[3] On the other hand, it seems that in the lace trade machines depreciate more rapidly when they are not working (L. C. Cropper, *Accounting*, p. 69) so that the prime cost of depreciation would appear to be negative.

properly considered, be included in prime cost, in spite of the fact that it does not represent an actual money payment.

The reason for this apparent contravention of our definition of the term cost,[1] set out in § 7, lies in the different uses that will be made of fixed cost and prime cost. Prime cost represents the sacrifice that production entails and so determines a firm's productive policy. This sacrifice must, in general, include burdens that will accrue only in the future as well as money payments that are due in the present. Fixed cost, on the other hand, is only important in helping to determine the amount of a firm's losses and so the extent to which its resources are being exhausted. As was shown in § 11, the actual cost of depreciation involves no drain on a firm's assets. Actual fixed depreciation is therefore not included in fixed cost.

But it is still necessary to take a step that appears even more arbitrary. The inclusion of actual prime depreciation in prime cost provides a correct basis for a firm's productive policy. The exclusion of actual fixed depreciation from fixed cost provides a means of arriving at a value of the loss that measures the rate at which financial resources are being exhausted. But the loss depends, not only on the fixed cost, but also on the prime profit; and the prime profit depends on the prime cost. If, therefore, the prime cost includes, as we have just found that it should include, the actual prime depreciation, the loss, determined by the equation:

$$\text{loss} = \text{fixed cost} - \text{prime profit}$$

exceeds the rate of exhaustion of financial resources by the amount of the actual prime depreciation. To get round this difficulty, it is sufficient to subtract the actual prime depreciation from fixed cost, as we have hitherto defined it, and consequently to include the whole of the actual depreciation, fixed and prime, in overhead cost.

Reasons will be adduced later[2] for believing that in depressed industries actual prime depreciation is, in point of fact, either wholly or partly omitted from prime cost, when prime cost is employed, consciously or unconsciously, as the basis of productive policy. The portion that is omitted is not then, of course, subtracted from the other elements of fixed cost, in order to arrive at the adjusted value of the fixed cost that has just been defined.

[1] That it is only apparent will appear at the end of § 15.
[2] In Chapter 3, § 29.

It can now be seen that the total cost of production is the actual money expenditure, just as it was defined in § 7. All that we have now done is to postulate that a certain amount, which is less than or equal to the actual prime depreciation, must be added to the aggregate prime cost of § 7 and an equal amount subtracted from the fixed cost.

IV THE DISTINCTION BETWEEN FIXED COST AND OVERHEAD COST

§ 16   The nature of the distinction – drawn quite arbitrarily – between the use of the terms fixed cost and overhead cost has already been set out. We are distinguishing two meanings of total cost, one of which we call fixed cost plus prime cost, the other overhead cost plus prime cost. In the former sense the word 'cost' includes only those items which represent actual money payments. But prime cost occurs equally in both senses, and it follows that the difference lies entirely between fixed cost and overhead cost. Overhead cost is equal to the whole of fixed cost, and in addition includes those elements which should (according to the economist) determine the growth and decay of capital in the long run but are irrelevant to the consideration of short-period variations: these elements are normal profits and interest on and depreciation of fixed capital.[1] But if fixed cost includes interest on fixed capital (in the shape of bank and debenture charges) and expenditure on renewals, the amount by which it falls short of overhead cost is decreased by the amount of these items.

V TECHNICAL FIXED COST AND FINANCIAL FIXED COST

§ 17   By eliminating the more transcendental elements from overhead cost we arrived at fixed cost. But another stage is necessary in the process of subdivision; failure to effect it is responsible for much confusion. In addition to the costs of factors that are essential to the

---

[1] It may be noted that if the 'Annuity Method' of providing for depreciation is adopted (see *Accounting* by L. C. Cropper, p. 71), the interest on the fixed capital is included in the amount written off each year, and this amount represents the whole difference between fixed cost and overhead cost, plus the amount of the prime depreciation. The method is, however, rarely employed.

life of a firm as a productive unit, fixed cost often includes elements that are accidental and unnecessary. The payment of interest on loans and debentures is a liability based on law rather than on technical necessity. It takes its origin in contracts undertaken in the past; and voluntary or compulsory processes of liquidation can reduce or extinguish such obligations without affecting the conditions of production. This portion of fixed cost will be referred to as financial fixed cost, while technical fixed cost will denote the remaining more tangible portion, which represents the payments that are necessary if the technical efficiency of production is to be maintained. Technical fixed cost includes all such elements as the costs of management and upkeep. It also includes rates, and the minimum rent that would be necessary to prevent the land from being turned over to another use. The surplus above this transfer rent (a very indefinite entity in the short period) is included in financial fixed cost; but the important element in financial fixed cost is of course debenture and loan interest (excluding that portion which, being covered by working capital, is included in prime cost).

VI TEMPORARY CLOSE-DOWN AND SHUT-DOWN COST

By definition the cost of running a firm as a going concern when its output is zero is its fixed cost. It has been stated that this corresponds to the term 'stopped cost' in certain industries. But it is clear that if it is intended to refrain from producing over a long period of time there are more economical methods of tiding over the interval. In fact the firm suffers what is called a temporary close-down. Certain expenses still have to be met: machinery has to be maintained in good condition, a nucleus staff has to be retained, although a large part of the organisation is allowed to lapse; and interest charges still continue. We shall denote these costs by Professor J. M. Clark's rather inelegant term 'shut-down cost'. Like fixed cost it can be divided into a technical and a financial portion, and it commonly includes a number of items in common with fixed cost. It is of course necessarily less than fixed cost.

VII PERMANENT CLOSE-DOWN

A temporary close-down is only resorted to if conditions in the industry are expected to improve. Otherwise the concern will be completely abandoned and the process may then be termed a permanent close-down. The distinction between a temporary close-down and a permanent one is not of course a perfectly rigid one. As long as money is expended on upkeep to some small degree, the close-down cannot be regarded as truly permanent, even though the probability of a reopening is regarded as very small. But on the other hand a truly permanent close-down, even if undertaken in all sincerity, cannot be said to have achieved permanency until sufficient time has elapsed for the processes of decay to arrive at a fairly advanced stage. A ship may be sold as scrap and find itself resuscitated at the hands of a foreign shipowner. Usually, however, there is little ambiguity. A coal-mine which ceases operations is either kept dry by means of pumping or water is allowed to penetrate the workings; and in the latter case the expense of reopening soon becomes exorbitant. Moreover if the plant is actually removed and scrapped, for instance if a ship is really broken up, the close-down is irrevocably permanent.

VIII   PERFECT COMPETITION: POLYPOLY AND PERFECT MARKET

§ 20   'Conditions of simple competition' are defined by Professor Pigou as 'conditions such that it is to the interest of each seller to produce as much as he can at the ruling market price, and not to restrict his output in the hope of causing that price to rise'.[1] It is then fairly obvious that three independent conditions must be fulfilled where competition is simple, or perfect:

(a) There must be a large number of separate firms, each producing an output which is small in relation to the aggregate output.

(b) There must be no agreement, however informal, among producers controlling a substantial portion of the aggregate output; and, in the absence of such an agreement, individuals must act each for himself, devoid of all feeling of corporate responsibility and business convention.

(c) The market in which the output of the industry is sold must be perfect. A perfect market is one in which differences of price (after costs of transport have been allowed for) cannot persist over an appreciable period of time. If a single firm raises its price

---

[1] *Economics of Welfare*, Macmillan, 3rd Edition, 1929, p. 215.

in a perfect market, either its output is rapidly reduced to zero or the other firm or firms raise their price.

It is clear that condition (c) may hold where conditions (a) and (b) do not hold. On the other hand, conditions (a) and (b) are often adequately satisfied in a market that is by no means perfect. The complexity of the conception of perfect competition is not, therefore, purely verbal in nature, and it is difficult to avoid some further terminological innovation. Condition (a) will be represented by the term 'perfect market'. When conditions (a) and (b) both hold, a state of 'polypoly'[1] will be said to exist.[2]

In the next chapters we shall examine the case of perfect competition, where polypoly and a perfect market can both be assumed. In Chapters 7 to 10, while polypoly will still be assumed to exist, the market will no longer be supposed to be perfect. Finally we shall examine the effects of the presence of various restraints, whose absence condition (b) postulates, when there are a large number of sellers in a perfect market, in other words, where conditions (a) and (c) are assumed to hold; and some consideration will have to be paid to the case where condition (a) alone holds.

---

[1] Monopoly represents the case of a single seller who acts solely in his own interest. Under duopoly there are two sellers, each of whom is actuated by purely individualist motives. So under polypoly there are many sellers (condition (a)), acting each for himself (condition (b)).

[2] Since I wrote the above I have found that Professor H. L. Moore many years ago set out categorically the 'hypotheses' 'implicit' in the 'blanket-term' of competition (*Quarterly Journal of Economics*, vol. xx, February, 1906, p. 213); but I find it difficult, on logical grounds, to accept Professor Moore's view (*Quarterly Journal of Economics*, p. 215) that 'there is room for maintaining that a perfect market is one in which competition is perfect'. I have also found that the word 'polypoly' was used many years ago by Umberto Ricci, though in an entirely different sense from that which I have, perhaps more logically, ascribed to it – *'una parola un po' bizzarra – polipolio – per designare un insieme* [i.e., a group] *di monopoli'*. (*Dal Protezionismo al Sindacalismo*, Laterza, Bari 1926, p. 131.)

CHAPTER 2

THE SUPPLY SCHEDULE OF A SINGLE FIRM UNDER PERFECT COMPETITION

1 THE PRIME COST CURVES

§ 1   The object of this chapter is to examine the nature of the short-period supply curve and the general conditions of equilibrium in an industry producing in a state of perfect competition. As in the case of long-period equilibrium, a satisfactory solution can be obtained only by subjecting to analysis the behaviour of the individual firm.[1]

We suppose it to be producing a single commodity, homogeneous and infinitely divisible, and we imagine that its output is capable of continuous variation. To conform to the conditions of the short period, it has to be supposed that the risks of price fluctuations during the period of production are absent or have been eliminated. (We may imagine, if we like, that the output is all sold by contract or that it is covered by sales of futures).

§ 2   Then, after a certain price has ruled in the market for a time equal to the period of production, the output of this firm will be so adjusted as to equate its marginal cost of production to this price. This marginal cost of production is determined by short-period variations, and is therefore, as a result of our definition of fixed cost,[2] equal to the marginal prime cost of production. Up to a limit, of which more will be said later, the individual supply curve is the marginal prime cost curve.

---

[1] Through failure to adopt this intimate method of approach, the same type of fundamental difficulty is likely to be unconsciously slurred over as in the case of increasing returns.

[2] See Chapter 1, § 7.

14

Round the point of equilibrium the marginal prime cost must of course rise with an increase of output. It will be demonstrated at the opening of Chapter 5 that it almost certainly begins, for small values of the output, by falling. The importance of the law that has just been enunciated depends upon how early in its course the marginal prime cost curve begins to rise. If it only begins to rise when the output is about normal, the law can have no reference to a firm whose output is less than normal. Such expectations of usefulness as the law may arouse will in fact suffer some disappointment when definite problems come up to confront us.

But consideration of the shapes of the prime cost curves and of the difficulties that emerge is deferred; and, for the present, curves

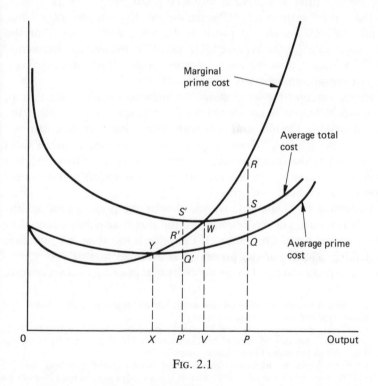

FIG. 2.1

of the general shape indicated in Figure 2.1 will be pictured, and the consequences followed up.

Meanwhile it is worth noting that, in the range over which the law of equality of marginal prime cost and price holds sway, the level of a firm's output is completely independent of changes in its fixed cost. The continual insistence in this essay on the relative irrelevance of fixed costs to short-period equilibrium is, here at any rate, justified up to the hilt.

§ 5   In Figure 2.1 are represented the curves (for a single firm) of average prime cost per unit of output,[1] average total cost, and marginal prime cost. The vertical distance between the prime cost and average total cost curves represents the average fixed cost, and it varies inversely with the output. By a well-known rule, the marginal prime cost curve cuts the average prime cost curve at its lowest point, Y. Since the marginal prime cost curve is also the marginal short-period total cost curve, it follows in the same way that it also cuts the average total cost curve at its lowest point, W.

Then, if PR is the price, OP is the output. RQ is the average prime profit, and RS the average profit. If the price, $P'R'$, is less than the minimum value of the average total cost, VW, the average fixed cost, $Q'S'$, is greater than the average prime profit, $Q'R'$; and there is a loss of average amount $S'R'$.

Hence emerges the interesting, if somewhat obvious, fact that an increase in output is associated with increasing average cost if the firm is making a profit, and only with decreasing average cost if the firm is making a loss.[2] The average cost is at a minimum, in the short period, when the firm is making neither a profit nor a loss.[3] All this depends, of course, on our fundamental assumption that marginal prime cost is equated to price.

§ 6   Returning to Figure 2.1, we see that as the price is reduced the supply is reduced in accordance with the supply schedule denoted by the marginal prime cost curve. If the price is less than WV, the firm is making a loss. For the present it is assumed that its policy is to minimise its loss, subject to the necessity of remaining a going concern:

---

[1] To avoid monotonous repetition, the word 'average' will in future be always used where 'average per unit of output' is meant.

[2] I have only once seen it categorically stated – in a dissertation submitted by Dr T. J. Kreps to the University of Harvard on 'The Economic Development of the Sulphuric Acid and Alkali Industries in the United States.'

[3] Dr Kreps quotes W. K. Lewis (*Chemical and Metallurgical Engineering*, vol. 28: 988, 1923), who points out how unreasonable it is to judge managerial efficiency by the level of unit cost. The business man who regards as the optimum level of output that level of output at which unit cost is a minimum will, of course, be producing too little if he is making a profit and too much if he is making a loss. This is merely a special instance of the general effects of failure to comprehend the marginal principle. How far the prevalence of such failure will affect the general conditions of supply is discussed in a later chapter.

the likelihood of its closing down, temporaily or permanently, will be considered later. So long as the price is greater than XY, a prime profit can be earned by producing.

When the price is XY and the output is OX, the prime profit is zero, and the loss is equal to the fixed cost. If the price is less than XY, the production of any output at all is attended by a prime loss. The loss is now a minimum when the output is zero; it is then equal to the fixed cost, which is the cost of running the firm when its output is zero. Y is therefore a critical point. If the price is less than XY, production can only be carried on at under prime cost. The marginal prime cost curve represents the supply schedule to the right of this point Y, but from this point we should expect the supply curve to drop discontinuously to zero, in the manner of the thick line in Figure 2.2B. (Figure 2.2A represents the case where the firm closes down, temporarily or permanently, because it is making a loss, at a point at which it is still capable of earning a prime profit.)

II   PRODUCTION AT A PRIME LOSS

But there are many reasons which prevent a firm from reducing its output entirely to zero, when such a policy is for the moment the most profitable. Even at the expense of an extra loss, commercial connections must not be destroyed and the services of particularly valuable workers must be retained. Sometimes less tangible factors have to be considered. Many employers are reluctant to cause undue distress to their workers, and an idle factory is too overt a recognition of failure: many a business man would rather lose more in order to appear to lose less. The divorce between ownership and control in the case of joint stock companies serves to intensify these tendencies. The managerial staff, which directs policy but suffers no pecuniary loss from the consequences of its policy, and particularly the selling side of the staff, feel that the maintenance of an output of goods which can be touched, seen, counted and weighed constitutes a more obvious justification of their own existence than a problematical reduction of the shareholders' losses.

A very important factor in the cotton industry takes its origin in a peculiarity of banking psychology. If a spinning mill reduces its output to nothing it is enabled, and in practice compelled, to reduce its overdraft by the amount of its working capital, which is substantial. But if later on it desires to restore the *status quo* its bank will refuse

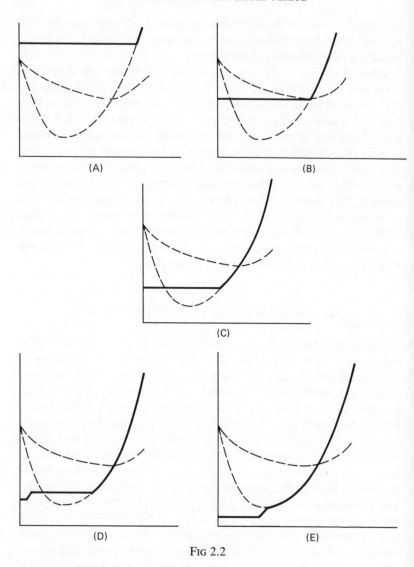

(A)

(B)

(C)

(D)

(E)

FIG 2.2

to allow the reduced overdraft to expand. The traditions of British banking make it difficult for a bank to force a firm to cease producing, even though the bank knows that such a policy would be conceived not only in its own interests but also in those of the firm, not to mention the industry. But once such a firm has ceased producing it would be against all the best traditions to enable it to start again. The result of all this is that, unless a mill wants to adopt a policy which approaches that of permanent close-down in severity, it is forced to go on producing, to the embarrassment of itself, its competitors – and its bank.

These factors need not cause any substantial modification to our conclusions as to the level of output when price is greater than prime cost; it is when production, if carried on at all, must be attended by a prime loss that they become significant. They set up a preference for a small output as opposed to no output at all; they are not likely to add substantially to the advantages of a larger output compared with those of a smaller output.

The level of output, when production is carried on at a prime loss, depends on the relation between the loss and the output. This is

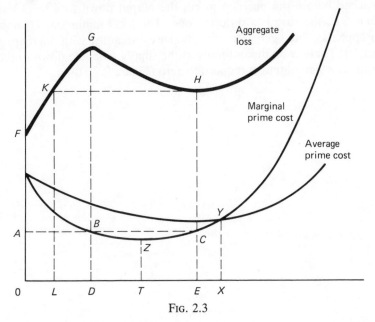

FIG. 2.3

denoted by the uppermost curve in Figure 2.3, in which the ordinate represents aggregate loss for a certain price, the abscissa output: OF is therefore the fixed cost. The other two curves are the prime cost curves, transferred from Figure 2.1. The price being supposed equal to OA, there are two values of the output, OD and OE, at which the marginal prime cost is equal to the price. At the first the loss DG

is a maximum; at the second the loss *EH*, while it is greater than the fixed cost *OF*, is a local minimum. Unless it is decided to adopt a small level of output less than *OL*, the level at which the loss is a minimum is *OE*, determined by the equality of marginal prime cost and price. The supply curve therefore continues to coincide with the marginal prime cost curve below the critical point.

For still lower values of the price, the loss when the output is *OE* may become so great that it is decided to reduce it by cutting the output down either to zero (as in Figure 2.2C) or to a level below *OL*. The latter case is represented in Figure 2.2D; increased losses due to still lower prices are supposed to induce a reduction of the output, until finally a point is reached at which it is discontinuously reduced to zero.

If, however, the minimum, *Z*, on the marginal prime cost curve is reached before the decision to cut the output down to a level less than *OL*, the case is a different one. The local minimum, *H*, now disappears: the aggregate loss increases steadily with increasing output. There is no discontinuity in the supply schedule down to the point at which output is reduced to zero (Figure 2.2E).

CHAPTER 3
THE EFFECTS OF A LOSS

I SCOPE OF THE CHAPTER

In this chapter will be considered various questions that arise when a firm's production is carried on at a loss. The treatment of these questions will be primarily directed towards a firm producing under conditions of perfect competition, which was the subject of the last chapter; and perfect competition will throughout be an implicit assumption. But it will easily be seen that most of the conclusions are applicable in a general sort of way even when competition is not perfect. The nature of their application is usually obvious and for the sake of simplicity in exposition it will not be specified. A single example will probably suffice. It will appear that under certain conditions the prime cost curves of a firm are raised and consequently, under conditions of perfect competition, its output is reduced. But just as surely, if in a different way, the same result follows when the market is imperfect.

II HOW A LOSS IS MET

A firm's loss is a loss to its individual owners just as surely as a profit represents a gain to them. This is made sufficiently obvious when, in the case of a private firm, the loss has to be met out of the owner's private pockets. The calling-up of uncalled capital by a joint-stock company is an equally blunt method of bringing the situation home to the owners. It has been resorted to in a considerable degree by the American section of the Lancashire cotton-spinning industry (but capital has in addition been called up to fill the gaps created by the withdrawal of short-term deposits). Outside Lancashire and the banking world uncalled liability is a rare phenomenon.

Most commonly a loss falls on those assets which are not actually employed in the processes of production. In good years prudent firms put by some of their harvest in the form of investments and surplus cash: these they can then draw on in the lean years, first on the interest and dividends that they yield and finally on the investments themselves. Liquid stocks of goods, which are held for speculative purposes rather than as a necessary adjunct of the productive process, are also available for meeting losses. If the loss persists for only a short period of time, it may not appear in the yearly balance sheet, being met out of the profits that accrue during the successful portion of the year.

In rare instances the banks may assist in meeting temporary losses, though in such cases the banker is more likely to be acting as the dupe than as the servant of the industrialist. Some years ago the losses of the cotton industry were being met in part by increased borrowing from the banks. But this practice has now ceased; the banks have continued to lend to the industry, but no faster than deposits have been withdrawn from it.

When all else fails, a firm may be forced to draw upon its own working capital thus restricting its own productive capacity. This and similar repercussions are dealt with in § 15.

III　IMPORTANCE OF THE LEVEL OF THE FIXED COST

§ 4　　Throughout this essay a question that will continually arise is the effect in the short period of the level of fixed costs on the output of an industry. It will assist the development of a somewhat complicated argument if it can be assumed for the moment that financial fixed cost is zero. Then it can safely be stated that a firm undergoes a loss only when there is some slight hope that it will in the future make a profit: otherwise it closes down permanently. In the longer period, as opposed to the short period, no firms suffer losses.[1]

§ 5　　Rather more questionable is the contention, which now follows, that the ability to meet a persistent loss is reduced by the passage of time. At first sight this appears obvious; none of the sources which have just been detailed (on at least one of which a firm must draw if

---

[1] But the era of the longer period may be slow in arriving when all the firms are fairly equal in size and financial strength. For there is then no *a priori* reason why one firm rather than another should close down, and each will try to hang on in the hope that sufficient of the others will give way.

it is making a loss) are inexhaustible, except the return from investments; and this is usually insufficient. But on the other hand it might be argued that incurring a loss is in investment. The owners of the firm, on whom the loss falls, are willing to sacrifice resources now in the speculative hope of a big return in the future. The attractiveness of the investment is capable of an objective measure, which should be independent of the amount of resources that happen to be available. The point of time at which resources run dry and the point of time at which investment in a losing concern ceases to be attractive are not logically connected. In other words, when the further operation of a firm becomes impossible through lack of means, it is always possible to find a buyer who will continue to lose money by running it; and bankruptcy is no cure for surplus capacity.

Individual instances can be produced to support this statement, but as a general proposition it is manifestly untrue. The amount of resources available for meeting losses *does* affect a firm's policy in incurring losses.[1] The reason is twofold. First there is a natural inertia which prevents the modification of a policy until other forces have become sufficiently strong to overcome it. Losses are not purposively weighed up against probable future profits, but are allowed to continue until they can be met no longer. This element of inertia is particularly strong in the management of joint-stock companies and is there reinforced by factors of the type mentioned in § 7 of the last chapter.

It presupposes too high a standard of business morality to suggest that directors and managers are likely to advise their shareholders to adopt a policy which will cut off their own means of livelihood. Joint-stock companies carry on until they can carry on no longer; a company which enters into liquidation sufficiently early to return part of their capital to its shareholders is a curiosity of the world of commerce. The second reason that can be put forward applies particularly to private businesses. It is based on the business man's innate belief that the organism to which he has devoted so much of his efforts and with which his own existence is so inextricably bound up must again flourish and prosper. It follows that any potential buyer of a firm will regard its future much less optimistically than its present owner, and is consequently far less likely to continue financing a policy which

---

[1] There is, for instance, a tendency for the more efficient coal mines to close down before the less efficient: the more efficient mines are the newer mines and the newer mines have less reserves, and therefore lose them more quickly, than the older mines.

finds its justification in mere speculative hope. If in addition the goodwill of the firm partly depends upon its connection with its present owner, this psychological factor is reinforced by a real one.

§ 6   It may therefore be concluded that the amount of fixed cost affects policy in three different ways:

(a) The amount of the fixed cost determines the amount of the loss, which is the difference between fixed cost and prime profit (or the sum of fixed cost and prime loss). The higher the fixed cost of a firm, the greater is its loss.

(b) Through its effect on losses in the past, fixed cost determines the ability to meet losses in the present. If a loss has been incurred for some time, the higher the fixed cost, the greater is the drain on a firm's resources.

(c) Again through its effect on the amount of the loss, the amount of fixed cost determines the change that will be necessary to convert a loss into a profit. The higher the fixed cost, the smaller and the more remote is the hope of a profit in the future; and the less likely is a policy which hinges upon such a hope.

IV   ALTERNATIVE POLICIES

§ 7   A firm which is confronted with a loss has the choice of the following alternative policies.

(i) If the price is greater than the minimum prime cost, XY (Figure 2.1), production may be carried on at such a level as to equalise marginal prime cost and price. The loss is then less than the fixed cost (by an amount equal to the prime profit).

(ii) If the price is less than the minimum prime cost, XY, the loss is a minimum, when the output is zero. The firm may be maintained as a going concern producing nothing. The loss is then equal to the fixed cost.

(iii) Production may be carried on at a prime loss in order to maintain connections, and so on; but the output may be such as to equate marginal prime cost and price. The loss is greater than the fixed cost (by an amount equal to the prime loss).

(iv) Production may be carried on for the same reasons as in (iii), but the output may not be perfectly determinate as it is in (iii) (when the price is given). As in (iii) the loss is greater than the prime cost.

(v) The firm may close down temporarily. The loss is equal to the shut-down cost (which is less than the fixed cost).

(vi) The firm may close down permanently.

As soon as a particular policy has been adopted, the output can depend on the fixed cost only under policy (iv). But the choice of policy depends upon the fixed cost in a somewhat complicated manner. It will however finally appear that fixed cost affects output only when it is unduly high, and that if it does affect the output at all the only effect it can produce, except again under policy (iv), is that of reducing it to zero (i.e. of promoting policies (ii), (v), or (vi). The introduction of financial fixed cost in the next section involves no modification to this important conclusion.

In the first place it is clear that policy (vi), that of closing down permanently, is favoured by a high level of fixed cost under all three heads (a), (b), and (c) of § 6.

The other policies are only adopted when there is some hope that prime profit will again, in the not too distant future, exceed fixed cost. Policy (v), that of closing down temporarily, involves the smallest loss, unless the difference between shut-down cost and fixed cost is less than the prime profit that would result from adopting policy (i). But, owing to the costs of reopening, this policy is only profitable when a firm is closed down for a considerable period of time. It is cheaper to maintain a cotton mill as a going concern at a cost of £10,000 per annum, or less (if price is greater than prime cost), than to close it down at a cost of £3,300 per annum and then, after a year or two, to spend £25,000 on reopening it. But a high level of fixed cost, while increasing, under heads (a) and (b), the desirability of such economy as a temporary close-down entails, lengthens, under head (c), the probable period of unprofitableness. Provided, then, that the hopes of the business man cling to a distant rather than to a near future, high fixed cost actively promotes the adoption of the policy (v) of closing down temporarily, as against policies (i) or (ii), (iii), (iv). But in general the business man, if he hopes at all, hopes for a speedy recovery. The cotton industry today provides an extreme example of such irrational aspiration. Some mills have, it is true, closed down (in the spring of 1929 seventy to eighty mills were closed in the American section alone), but not, in most cases, because the probable epoch of prosperity is relegated to a more remote future by their owners than by the rest of the spinners. A temporary close-down is regarded merely as a less drastic method of achieving economy than a permanent close-down when lack of resources makes economy a matter of imperative necessity. A high level of fixed cost, in the case of the cotton industry and indeed in the case of many other industries, frequently compels a close-down under head (b): it rarely increases the attractiveness of temporarily closing down – under head (c).

§ 10   We now turn to policies (iii) and (iv). The extra loss that they entail, over and above the loss (equal to the fixed cost) that policy (ii) entails, is independent of the fixed cost: it depends solely on the prime cost. If the price is only a little less than prime cost, this extra cost, besides being independent of the fixed cost, is small compared to the fixed cost. It is reasonable to suppose that in such a case the decisions involved in policies (iii) and (iv) are independent of the fixed cost. A high level of fixed cost may prevent the adoption of all three policies (ii), (iii), and (iv). But if policy (ii) is acceptable and the loss of the fixed cost is regarded with reasonable equanimity, the decision to adopt policy (iii) or (iv), and the level of the output if policy (iv) is adopted, depends on the small extra loss thereby involved, which is independent of the fixed cost, and not on the amount of the fixed cost, which has to be lost anyway.

If, however, the price is considerably less than the prime cost, the extra loss incurred by adopting policies (iii) or (iv) becomes comparable with the fixed cost itself. If the fixed cost is high, the ability to incur this considerable extra loss is less than if the fixed cost is low. In such a case high fixed cost may be said to have a depressing influence on output, either by preventing the adoption of policies (iii) and (iv) or by restraining the output if policy (iv) is adopted.

In point of fact it is a rare occurrence for a firm to follow policy (ii). If the fixed cost is to be lost anyhow for the sake of maintaining the organisation, it is worth while to lose a little more in order to maintain connections and to retain valuable workmen.

If the price is only a little less than prime cost, the amount of the output may be large and is independent of the fixed cost. It happens to be extremely convenient to run a cotton mill at half-time. The operatives can then draw a full wage one week and full dole the next week. If a mill has got to lose £10,000 a year even if its output is zero, it is worth its while to produce half its capacity output at a price, say, of $\frac{1}{8}d$ per lb below prime cost, thus losing only an additional £625 per annum (on medium counts).

But if the price is considerably less than the prime cost, production can still be carried on at a moderate additional loss provided the output is made sufficiently small. In this case, as has just been said, the level of output depends on the fixed cost.

V FINANCIAL FIXED COST

This mass of patches becomes yet more tangled when part of the fixed cost belongs to the category which we have designated financial. In general it may be said that financial fixed cost influences policy and output through its effect in draining away resources in the past (head (b)), rather than in increasing losses in the present (head (a)) or in decreasing the probability of profits in the future (head (c)). Cotton mills close down through lack of further means with which to meet losses. In bringing about this state of penury, financial fixed cost has played an equal proportional part with technical fixed cost.

But if the price is greater than the prime cost and if the maximum prime profit that could be secured by continuing production is greater than technical fixed cost (in other words, if the loss under policy (i) is less than the financial fixed cost), the position is a different one. Cleared of all or part of its financial fixed cost, the firm is a profitable one and can find a purchaser anxious to run it. The worst that can happen is that the bank and debenture holders lose part of their money and that the firm changes hands. But the existence of the financial fixed cost does not result in the closing-down of the firm (except, possibly, during an interim period of negotiation). Bankruptcy, in such a case, is no cure for surplus capacity. The orgies of 1920 have helped to aggravate the troubles of the cotton industry and to reduce its output, but they cannot be cited as the sole offence. If the contracting of high interest charges were the only thing that had happened to the industry, they would either produce no effect upon its output, or, in trying to produce an effect, would destroy themselves.

Nor is it possible to argue that high financial fixed cost promotes a permanent close-down by causing high losses in the present (head (a)) or by reducing, materially or completely, the probability that the firm will again earn a profit in the future (head (c)). The reason is that the bank and debenture-holders are always willing to cut down their claims sufficiently to induce the potential layer of another golden egg to give up its intention of committing suicide. It is true that the carcase would belong to them. But it is likely to be a scraggy one. And in any case, if the carcase in the hand is regarded by the bank and debenture-holders as more attractive than the golden egg in the bush, so would it in most cases be regarded by the owners of the firm if there were no financial fixed cost; and the firm would close down anyhow.

§ 14   In respect to a temporary close-down, financial fixed cost is unlikely to have any effect under head (a), since it appears equally in shut-down cost under the guise of financial shut-down cost. For the same reason it has no effect under head (c). Policy (i) becomes more profitable than policy (v) when the prime profit attainable is greater than the difference between fixed cost and shut-down cost, into both of which financial cost enters equally. From this it follows that financial fixed cost is not taken into account in the estimation of the period of time for which it is likely to be profitable to keep a firm closed down, and it does not therefore affect the decision to close down temporarily so far as head (c) is concerned.

VI REPERCUSSIONS ON PRODUCTIVE EFFICIENCY

§ 15   It now becomes necessary to qualify the argument with several complications. The first is sufficiently straightforward. A firm that is in a weak financial position may have difficulty in obtaining or continuing loans from its bank or in buying raw material and selling its product under those credit facilities on which it is accustomed to depend. The effect is much the same if the firm is meeting its losses by drawing on its working capital. (It is, of course, obvious that such a policy cannot be continued for long.) These factors may express themselves either by setting a definite limit to the possible output, or by raising the prime cost curves throughout their length, or by both manifestations. In any case fixed cost, both technical and financial, may be said, under such conditions, to exert a depressing influence on the level of output. This influence comes under all three heads (a), (b) and (c): it may be associated with the amount of the losses both of the past and of the present, and in addition, where the question arises of how far the firm can be trusted to repay loans, it may depend on the probable losses of the future.[1]

---

[1] The paradox of the cotton industry has already been noted (in § 7 of Chapter 2). Instead of the existence of pressure from the banks inducing the industry to reduce its output, the fear of such pressure encourages it to maintain its output.

Next it is essential to take into account the difficulty, already admitted in Chapter 1, §§ 3 and 4, that fixed cost may be altered within a period of time which, if not 'short' in the technical sense, is small enough to be awkward. Fixed cost was defined in relation to the effects of changes of output when a certain policy is in force. But there is nothing to prevent such a policy from being altered in the course of time. Such an alteration may be induced by two main types of causes.

(i) Economy may be *necessitated* by high losses, by the drain upon resources of past losses, and by the likelihood of the persistence of losses. Both technical and financial fixed cost here play equal parts under all three heads (a), (b) and (c).

(ii) A change of policy may be *desirable* when regard is paid to the conditions that obtain in the industry and to the likelihood that they will persist. A policy that is economic when the industry is prosperous may no longer be economic when the industry is depressed, not merely temporarily, but with the prospect of the depression continuing for some length of time.

Retrenchment is most rapid in its effects when it takes the form of a reduction of expenditure on staff and organisation. The result is an increase in prime cost; but nevertheless the organisation that is at the economic level when the output is normal is probably too big when the output is both less than normal and likely to continue less than normal. The reduction in organisation that is economically desirable depends only on the output, and on the increase in prime cost to which the reduction will give rise.[1] It can only depend on the existing level of fixed cost in so far as fixed cost affects output. But it was stated in § 8 and was demonstrated in the subsequent pages that, except when policy (iv) is adopted, if the fixed cost is exerting any effect at all on the output, then the output is zero. It follows that the *desirable* reduction of expenditure on organisation only depends on the fixed cost when it can have no effect on the output, because the output is already zero.

But in actual practice it may require the pinch of necessity to waken the business man to the realities of the moment. It is only when cause (i), the magnitude of his losses, compels retrenchment that he becomes sufficiently pessimistic for cause (ii) to have any

---

[1] If a reduction $\triangle F$ in aggregate fixed cost causes an increase in the average prime cost from c to $c + \triangle c$ and consequently a lowering of the average level of the probable output from u by $\triangle u$, there is a tendency for $\triangle F - u\triangle c - \triangle u\,(p - c)$ to be maximised, where p is the probable price.

force; and by that time cause (i) is all-powerful and may carry retrenchment further even than at a long-sighted view is desirable.

§ 19   The effect of the increase in prime cost that results from this form of economy is a reduction in output (except under policy (iv)). But in point of fact the increase in prime cost is not generally very large at the current level of output. It is only if output again expands that the productive organisation would be subjected to any serious strain. The prime cost curves are raised more at points corresponding to greater outputs.

§ 20   The other important direction in which fixed cost can be reduced is in that of expenditure on upkeep, repairs, and renewals of fixed capital. If the expected marginal net productivity of the capital is less than the rate of interest, it is profitable to allow it to decay to some extent. This is not however quite so simple a statement as it sounds, since the value of the marginal net productivity depends upon whether we are considering upkeep and repairs on the one hand or renewals on the other hand.

The simplest case is that of renewals. If the installation of a new machine is not profitable, because the marginal net productivity of the capital is less than the rate of interest, the substitution of an old machine by a new one is also, in general, unprofitable. Our firm of Chapter 1, § 12, with 200 machines, instead of replacing every machine as it reaches the age of 20, will either continue to run its machines beyond the age of 20 or allow its productive capacity to run down. Depreciation is no longer made good by renewals.

But because the renewal of a machine does not represent a profitable investment of capital, it does not necessarily follow that a big reduction in the expenditure on upkeep and repairs is desirable. The marginal net productivity of capital invested in a new machine is quite a different thing from the marginal net productivity of capital invested in the shape of upkeep and repairs. If a small reduction in such expenditure results in very rapid deterioration and if the machine adds something, or is expected in the near future to add something (even if not an adequate return to the capital invested in it) to aggregate profits (or subtracts something from aggregate losses), the marginal net productivity of this type of investment is high, and a substantial reduction is not justified. It still remains desirable that the capital should decay, but the processes of decay should not be assisted to more than a slight degree by economies which are small in relation to their degradatory powers. If, however, a large reduction in the expenditure on upkeep and repairs can be undertaken without a devastating acceleration of these processes of decay, such a reduction is likely to be a proper one.

When this type of retrenchment is undertaken in a purposive kind of way, three different objects may be in view.

(i) It may be considered desirable to reduce fixed cost at the expense of prime cost. This object is the same as that on account of which expenditure on organisation may be reduced; and the existing level of fixed cost is not relevant to the question, which depends entirely on the actual level of output and the resultant increase in prime cost; this has been explained in § 17.

Let us again take the firm with 200 machines and let us suppose that it is considering whether it is profitable to prolong the life of each machine from 20 to 25 years. The number of new machines bought each year would be reduced from ten to eight. If each machine costs £1,000 and if the whole of the cost of renewals enters into fixed cost (in other words, if the life of a machine does not depend on the extent to which it is used: this is a big assumption, unless obsolescence is the main cause of old age) – then the reduction in fixed cost would be £2,000.[1] If the increase in prime costs, resulting from the higher average age of the machines, is £2,400, the prolongation of the lives of the machines is not profitable. But suppose now that the output is reached, and is likely to remain reduced, to three-quarters of its former level.[2] Then the increase in prime cost is probably only three-quarters of £2,400, i.e. £1,800, which is less than the reduction in fixed cost of £2,000; so that the prolongation of the lives of the machines is profitable at the lower level of output.

(ii) If the profit that is being earned, and is likely to be earned, is not an adequate return to the fixed capital, the object in view may be to withdraw the capital by allowing the plant to decay until the whole concern closes down. The criterion of adequacy of the return to the fixed capital is whether the subtraction of normal interest and fixed depreciation from the profit leaves a sufficient return to the entrepreneur or, if there is no entrepreneur to be rewarded, whether it leaves anything at all; in other words, whether the overhead cost

---

[1] The amount of depreciation would be reduced by an equal sum, the cost of each machine being spread over 25 instead of 20 years. If the accounts were not to take into consideration the fact that depreciation is diminished, the reduction in fixed cost would not accrue to profits but would tend to lead *pro tanto* to a continual increase in cash and investments.

[2] It is assumed that all the machines continue to be operated, but each for fewer hours a year.

is covered. The value of the technical fixed cost is therefore one of the major elements on which the decision depends.

§ 23   But the financial fixed cost may again fail to exert an influence. Just as in § 13 above, the bank and debenture-holders will reduce their claims if it is the financial fixed cost that is inducing a firm to aim towards an eventual permanent close-down. Gradual debilitation on the part of the goose is just as repugnant to them as instant suicide. If, however, the bank and debenture holders fail to realise the gravity of the situation, the effect of financial fixed cost is obvious. Faced with the alternatives of small profits over a long course of years and large profits over a short course of years, a firm may choose the latter, and so allow its plant to depreciate at the expense of the bank and debenture-holders. This policy would avail the firm nothing if the full amount of the depreciation were taken into its accounts, since in that case distributable profits are not increased, and the compensating increase in cash and investments would accrue, not to the owners of the firm, but to the bank and debenture-holders upon liquidation. The policy is therefore only likely to be adopted, in consequence of the existence of financial fixed cost, in the direction of reducing the work of upkeep and repairs. Such a reduction affords a method of distributing profits out of capital. If, however, the amount of depreciation that appears in the accounts can be improperly reduced without effective from the creditors, a reduction of expenditure upon renewals provides similar attractions.

§ 24   (iii) If the output of a firm is less and is likely to continue less than its normal output, it usually possesses plant that is surplus to its requirements, the expense of maintaining which it could profitably forgo. The decision docs not depend on the fixed cost, unless it would bring with it a diminution in fixed cost additional to the diminution in expenditure on maintenance and renewal (for example, a reduction in rates). It follows that it is in any case independent of financial fixed cost. (But here again, as in the case of the reduction of expenditure upon organisation considered in § 17, if the output is partly dependent upon the level of fixed cost, the decision also depends on the fixed cost).

§ 25   But, as has already been indicated, the purposive, long-sighted view is rare, and the requirements of economic theory have to be satisfied as best they may by the compulsion of dire necessity, in the shape of cause (i) of § 16, rather than by the promptings of commercial intelligence, typified by cause (ii). The consequent importance of fixed cost is even more evident in this case than in that of expenditure upon organisation, because the conception of marginal net productivity of capital, or even its implications, are not such as to lend themselves to apprehension by the business man. Moreover, opposed to the attainment of object (ii), gradual decay culminating in permanent close-down, are all the factors that were enumerated in § 5. The result is that, provided a firm can make a profit at all, it is likely to continue in operation for a very much longer period of time than might have been expected. It is this somewhat irrational tendency which gives special point to the definition in Chapter 1, § 6, of the 'longer period', in which no firms make a loss but in which a profit, however small, is a sufficient criterion of continued existence.

When the type of economy that is now being considered is practised only on that part of the fixed plant which is in excess of requirements, the effects on prime cost and output are very much the same as those of a reduction of expenditure on organisation (see § 17). The effect is small at the current level of output, but might be very great if the output again expands. If, on the other hand, the plant that is actually in use has to suffer the ravages of economy, prime cost is increased even for the current level of output. The result is a reduction of output, with the usual exception in favour of policy (iv) of § 7.

In contrast to economies in respect of organisation, a reduction of expenditure on maintenance and renewals has but little immediate result. The effect becomes a progressively greater one, increasing either indefinitely (when object (ii) is in view) or up to a certain limit (as in the cases of objects (i) and (iii)).

The subject of maintenance and renewal has so far been treated as though the whole of the cost appeared in fixed cost. This is manifestly an unreal assumption. A large part of the cost is incurred as a direct consequence of production, and is an element in prime cost. It is to this prime cost portion of the cost of maintenance and renewal to which it is now necessary to turn.

The same inducements and compulsions operate towards a reduction of this prime cost portion as towards a reduction of the fixed cost portion, and the discussion need not be repeated. But there is one exception: object (i) of § 21 cannot often be the aim of a reduction of the prime cost portion of the cost of maintenance and renewal, because if such a reduction at the expense of an increase in the rest of the prime cost is profitable at a low level of output, it is likely to be equally profitable at a high level of output. But, of course, if the fixed cost portion is reduced with object (i) in view, the prime cost portion is probably reduced incidentally: the two are not technically separable.

§ 28   The distinction between the fixed cost portion and the prime cost portion becomes important in connection with the effects of a reduction on the output. A reduction of the fixed cost portion tends, as we have seen, to increase prime cost and to reduce output, the effect increasing with the passage of time. This effect is due to the increase in prime cost that follows on the reduction of expenditure on maintenance and renewal. But if this reduction is itself associated with a decrease of an element in prime cost, the net effect on prime cost may, for a time (and will, for a considerable time, if the whole reduction is in prime cost and none of it in fixed cost) be a decrease. Consequently output is in the first place increased, and only falls below its original level when the forces of decay have achieved substantial progress. Inasmuch as the necessity for reducing expenditure on maintenance and renewals may sometimes be ascribed to a high level of financial fixed cost, this result indicates a method by which unduly low prices (i.e. unduly high output) in an industry might be caused by the heavy burdens of financial fixed cost carried by some of the firms. The low price of cotton yarn is often explained as being partially due to the high interest charges that some of the mills have to meet; but I have been unable to obtain any evidence to indicate that these mills are neglecting the work of maintenance and are for this reason in a position to undercut their more fortunate competitors.

VII   THE EXCLUSION OF PRIME DEPRECIATION FROM PRIME COST

§ 29   But there is an easier and more attractive method of reducing prime cost. It was shown in § 14 of Chapter 1 that prime cost must include, not only the money expenses that stand for present sacrifices, but also the future sacrifice that is represented by the actual prime depreciation. There are, however, several reasons for believing that in a depressed industry firms discount these future sacrifices at a very high rate or disregard them entirely. The effect then is that the output of an individual firm is greater than would be the case if it included the full prime depreciation in its prime cost; and its plant therefore wears out more rapidly. Among the reasons are the following:

    (a) The closing down of the firm in the future may be visualised as a possibility. If the possibility is sufficiently great, the discounted value of the future sacrifice involved through wear and tear in the present is very small.

(b) It may be desirable to raise the average age of the plant or to put some of it out of commission. In this case, too, wear and tear is a sacrifice that can be temporarily excluded from prime cost.

(c) The necessity for increasing profits or reducing losses in the present may be so pressing that it completely overweighs the future loss that increased wear and tear entails. This is obviously true when a firm is working at a loss and is being hard pressed to meet it. But it is also true when a firm that has adequate resources is working at a loss or at a profit that is abnormally small. For even though it is not involved in financial difficulty it would usually welcome a reduction in its loss or an increase in its profit at the expense of an actuarially greater reduction of future profits.

(d) The discounted probable future value of the plant may be very small compared with its nominal value, on which depreciation is usually reckoned. For the nominal value tends to be set rather by the original cost than by the market value. So long as the firm is making a loss, the amount of the fixed depreciation is a matter for almost complete indifference,[1] and may just as well be related to the original cost as to the market value. But the amount of the prime depreciation is a factor that has an effect on policy, and should therefore be reckoned at its true value, which is frequently very small.

It can easily be seen that a high level of fixed cost, both technical and, to a lesser extent, financial, tends to secure the elimination of prime depreciation from prime cost, or a reduction of its amount, through the agency of all these reasons, except reason (b) (and reason (d) in respect of financial fixed cost). This indicates another explanation of the alleged fact that price-cutting in the cotton-spinning industry is due particularly to those mills that are saddled with high loan and debenture charges.[2]

I shall, however, adopt the view that all cotton mills can be assumed, in effect, to omit the element of prime depreciation when they are deciding on productive policy. On the basis of the nominal depreciation figures that are normally put down, the prime depreciation of a standard mill working full-time would be £2,250 per

---

[1] See Chapter 1, § 11.
[2] This possibility was suggested to me by Professor Sraffa.

annum.[1] This represents a contribution to prime cost of almost $\frac{1}{4}d$ a pound, which is substantial. But when we come to deal with actual figures, we shall omit entirely any such element. Conversely, there will be no counterbalancing item to subtract from fixed cost.

It must also be doubted whether in the coal industry in its present condition regard is paid to the fact that 'the special costs involved in maintaining the maximum output include a considerable allowance for depreciation of the capital value of the property.'[2] It is true that in the case of extractive industries 'the rendering of their characteristic service is only postponed and not irretrievably abandoned by restriction.'[3] But it is probable that in most mines to-day the financial position is so precarious and the prospects for the future so dubious that no account is taken of the possibility that the coal that is sold to-day at a low price could possibly be sold in the distant future at a somewhat higher price.

---

[1] See Chapter 1, § 14.

[2] D. H. Robertson, *A Study of Industrial Fluctuations*, London, P. S. King, 1915, p. 34.

[3] Ibid.

CHAPTER 4

SUPPLY SCHEDULE OF AN INDUSTRY UNDER PERFECT COMPETITION

I   THE AGGREGATE SUPPLY SCHEDULE

It is now quite apparent that if reference is made at all to the supply schedule of a firm, it must be made with considerable caution. It is not a definite thing; its shape depends both on past history and on future prospects, and its discontinuities are such as to prevent any semblance of reversibility. But, in a given set of circumstances, a supply schedule can be drawn for each firm in the industry. Then an aggregate supply schedule can be derived so as to indicate the effect on the industry's output of a change in the price of the product, occurring in the manner which is appropriate to the individual supply schedules.

If the supply schedules of the individual firms are independent of the output of the whole industry, the process is a simple one. It is necessary merely to add together all the individual outputs that correspond to each value of the price. Now the basis of the individual supply curve has been shown to be a complicated one, but through all the complications the truth of one important fact has persisted free of suspicion: an increase of price is never associated with a decrease in output. It follows that the supply curve of the industry is also a constantly rising one. An increase of demand cannot, in the short period, be associated with a lowering of price.

In practice the prime cost of an individual firm may often be slightly raised as a result of an increase in the output of the industry, for instance, owing to increased costs of raw material,[1] labour and

---

[1] If, as in the textile industries, it is the margin between the price of the product and the cost of the raw material that is adopted as the variable, the cost of the raw material is nearly completely eliminated.

transport. The effect of such external diseconomies is to cause the aggregate supply curve to rise more steeply.

II   A COMMON FALLACY

§ 2   Little need here be said of the common fallacy that a protective tariff on the product of a depressed industry may lead to a decrease in its price owing to the reduction in overhead cost per unit of output that results from an increase in the output. The fallacy takes its origin in the misconceptions that are so rife, even in the highest quarters, as to the significance of overhead costs. Meanwhile it is interesting, if not very surprising, to note that the fallacy has recently received the cachet of truthfulness at the hands of the Balfour Committee. In their Final Report (pp. 274 and 275) the Committee on Industry and Trade conclude that the effect of an import duty on prices depends on the outcome of the conflict between the direct effect, which is apparently to raise the price by the full amount of the tax, and 'the reduction of costs due to the wider spreading of overhead charges'.[1] When however the same belief, dressed up in rather more subtle clothes, is found to have crept into the pages of *Britain's Industrial Future*, we may well take pause to wonder whether our analysis is quite correct. The Liberal Industrial Enquiry suggest that the orders of the Central Electricity Board should be given out

> as a balance to secure constant work for the British factories, at something like full output, over a period of years. This means a reduction in the manufacturer's overhead charges, and will there-fore tend to put the British manufacturer into an improved position to compete in overseas markets against foreign competitors.[2]

§ 3   It is perfectly true that we have so far been confining our attention to a state of perfect competition and that the actual conditions of the real world may provide such views as these with a more substantial

---

[1] This inaccurate and misleading suggestion that there are two different forces at work is analogous to the insistence of the Colwyn Committee 'on the unfruitful distinction between the "incidence" of a tax and its "effects"'. (D. H. Robertson, 'The Colwyn Committee and the Income Tax', *Economic Journal*, December 1927, p. 574).

[2] *Britain's Industrial Future*, p. 310. This statement is consistent with the views expressed by the Liberal Enquiry on the effects of rates.

basis. When we come to widen the scope of our treatment, this possibility will be kept in sight; but all attempts to defend the view that an increase in demand may under certain circumstances cause a fall of price in the short run will end in failure.[1] Meanwhile it may be noticed that the Balfour Committee rely on 'the presence of active internal competition' to secure the neutralisation 'through decreasing overhead costs' of the rise in price caused by a tariff 'through restricting competition';[2] and that the enunciation of these and similar statements is never attended by any restrictions on their generality. It may be quite obvious that, if in a state of perfect competition it does not pay a single manufacturer to lower his price in order to increase his output, it will not pay him to do so after the demand for the product of the industry has increased. But it would appear to be even more obvious that a reduction in average cost per unit of output is likely to be attended by a reduction in price. The difficulty that, if this were so, prices would be highest when trade was not stagnant is one that is seldom faced, or even realised.

No reference has been made to external economies, which save the theoretical situation for long-period increasing returns. The reason is simply that it is very difficult to imagine the possibility of short-period external economies. If however they are in operation and if the cost of each individual firm depends simply on the output of the whole industry, the condition for increasing returns is that the sum of the period differential coefficients of the output of each firm with respect to the output of the industry should be greater than unity.[3]

---

[1] There is one possible exception. If an increase in demand and output is associated with a substantial decrease in the imperfection of the market, the price may fall. But such a fall, if it ever occurs, is altogether independent of the level, or indeed of the existence, of overhead cost.

[2] *Britain's Industrial Future*, p. 275.

[3] Let u_r be the output of the rth firm, U the output of the industry, and p the price of the product.

Then $U = \Sigma u_r = \Sigma f_r\,(p,\,U)$

$$\therefore \frac{dU}{dp} = \Sigma\,\frac{\partial u_r}{\partial p} + \frac{dU}{dp}\,\Sigma\,\frac{\partial u_r}{\partial U}$$

$$\therefore \frac{dU}{dp}\left(1 - \Sigma\,\frac{\partial u_r}{\partial U}\right) = \Sigma\,\frac{\partial u_r}{\partial p}$$

But $\dfrac{\partial u}{\partial p}$ is positive. Therefore $\dfrac{dU}{dp}$ is negative if $\Sigma\,\dfrac{\partial u}{\partial U} > 1$.

III DIAGRAMMATIC REPRESENTATION: PART PLAYED BY OVERHEAD COST

§ 5   If external economies and diseconomies can be neglected and the special assumption is made that the individual supply curves are of the character denoted in Figure 2.2B (so that the output is determined by the marginal prime cost down to the point at which the prime profit becomes zero), the interesting result is obtained that, S_1S_1'

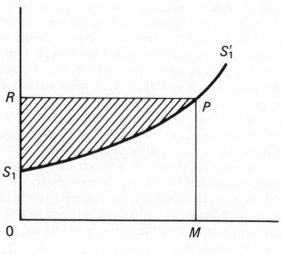

FIG. 4.1

(Figure 4.1) being the short-period supply curve of the industry, PM the price, and RP the output, the total contribution to overhead costs (i.e. the total prime profit) is given by the area RPS_1. This result is stated by Professor Pigou in the second edition of his *Economics of Welfare*.[1]

The proof is simple. Figure 4.2 represents the average and marginal prime cost curves of a single firm. When the price is PR and the profit OP, the prime profit is given by the area $CQRD$. But the area

[1] Appendix G, p. 755. The appendix is omitted from the third edition.

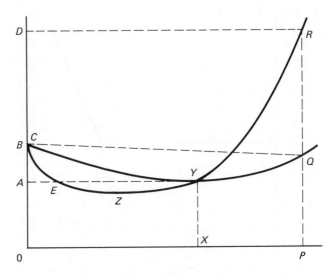

Fig. 4.2

$CQPO$ is equal to the area $BZYRPO$. Therefore the area $CQRD$ is equal to the area $BZYRD$.

But the area $BZYXO$ is equal to the area $AYXO$. Therefore the area BEA is equal to the area EZY. Therefore the area $BZYRD$ is equal to the area $AYRD$. Therefore the area $CQRD$ is equal to the area $AYRD$. Therefore the prime profit is given by the area $AYRD$.

Now the aggregate supply curve is derived from the individual supply curves of the type AYR (Figure 4.3) by a process of horizontal addition. It follows that the sum of the areas $AYRD$ is equal to the area RPS of Figure 4.1.

Thus RPS_1 represents the total prime profit and $OMPS_1$ the total prime cost. Professor Pigou deduces that 'S_1S_1' is steeper the more important is the relative part played by supplementary costs',[1] and that consequently 'with given demand variations, the extent of (the associated price variations) should be especially great in industries where the part played by supplementary costs . . . is large relatively to the part played by prime costs'.[2] If the curve S_1S_1' (Figure 4.1) rises at a uniform rate, Professor Pigou's conclusion follows at once.

[1] Pigou, *Economics of Welfare*, p. 755.
[2] Ibid, p. 344; 3rd edition, p. 377.

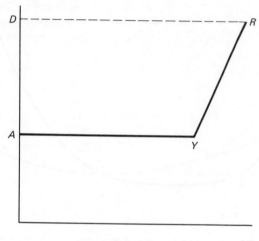

FIG. 4.3

But in practice when the output is large the curve often rises steeply quite independently of the relative importance of overhead costs. The reason is merely that the productive capacity is being fully utilised. (An extreme example is provided by the ⌐-shaped curve to be discussed in Chapter 5 (see § 24); the length of the vertical portion, not of course its steepness, depends on the overhead cost.) In such a case it is the fall in price due to an appropriately large fall in demand that depends on the relative part played by overhead costs rather than the price variation associated with an upward or small downward variation of demand.

IV   THE PREDOMINANCE OF PRIME COST IN GENERAL AND OF WAGES COST IN PARTICULAR

§ 6   The shape of the supply curve is related to the amount of the overhead cost in the manner that has just been discussed. But the interdependence is only a true one when both the overhead cost and the fixed plant and organisation of the industry are appropriate to one and the same position of long-period equilibrium. An alteration of overhead cost, or in particular of fixed cost, that is not reflected in, or is not the reflexion of, an alteration in fixed plant and organisation has only a secondary effect on the conditions of production in the short period. On the special assumptions made at the beginning of § 5, assumptions which represent the short period in its purest essence, there is no effect at all. The nature of the effect when these special assumptions are not fulfilled has already been discussed in Chapter 3 and will be alluded to again under the guise of the consequences of de-rating.

But, in any case, it is clear that in the short period prime cost is a major factor and fixed cost a very minor factor, so far as effects on output and price are concerned. 'The Economics of Prime Cost' would be a more appropriate title for a work on the short period than 'The Economics of Overhead Costs'.

But we can go even further in separating the factors that are available to operate on price and output in the short period. Prime cost consists very largely of the costs of wages and raw material. Now raw material is either imported, in which case its cost must be regarded as outside the sphere of national influences, or it is derived, directly or indirectly, from industries whose prime costs consist almost entirely of wages. It may, therefore, be concluded that on the side of supply the only factor that in the short period can have a substantial influence on the price and magnitude of the national output is the level of money wages. (On the side of demand there are, of course, such very important influences as the rates of credit creation, of investment, and of saving, tariffs, the rate of exchange, and the repercussions of an alteration in the level of unemployment.)

This conclusion is an important one, even if it is fairly obvious. Professor Clay's criticism of Professor's Pigou's article on 'Wage Policy and Unemployment'[1] on the ground that 'wages are not the only element in the costs of industries suffering from unemployment that has risen disproportionately,[2] may be irrelevant for other reasons – I imagine it is somewhat irrelevant because Professor Pigou is considering, not so much the effect of wages costs on prices, but the effect of the cost of labour on the amount of labour that employers are willing to employ – but it is mainly irrelevant because the categories of cost cited by Professor Clay are all part of fixed cost; and therefore a reduction in their amount will have but little effect on the price in the short period. And for depressed industries the short period is very long.

A similar point arises in connection with the payment by Germany

[1] *Economic Journal*, September 1927, pp. 355–68.
[2] *Economic Journal*, March 1928, p. 2

of reparations. Mr Keynes has pointed out that 'the solution of the Transfer Problem requires a reduction of German gold-costs of production compared with elsewhere'.[1] Apart from the possibility of an increase of relative efficiency, 'the rate of interest in Germany must be lower than elsewhere, or the gold-rates of efficiency-wages must be reduced compared with elsewhere'. Since the rate of interest is likely to remain high, Mr Keynes confines his treatment to the possibility and effects of a reduction of money-wages. But the rate of interest only enters into prime cost in the shape of the cost of working capital, which is relatively unimportant. Unless, therefore, we are considering the possibility of the erection of new fixed plant in Germany's exporting industries and are, therefore, wandering outside the bounds of the short period, the rate of interest is not a relevant factor; and this is a further reason for concentrating on money wages. Moreover, it is wages only in the strict sense of the term, excluding salaries and directors' fees, which enter into the problem. To secure a permanent reduction in costs of production and prices within a reasonably short space of time, it is necessary to operate on the wages paid to manual workers. The reduction of real wages is greater initially than it is later on, when the money remunerations of the other factors of production have also fallen.

§ 8   Changes in efficiency have to be treated in a similar manner. In so far as they involve changes in prime costs, they have the same effect on prices and on profits as a corresponding change in wage-rates. But if they are confined to fixed costs, the whole of the saving that is involved accrues, in the short period, to profits. 'Supposing the efficiency of production was greatly improved,' suggested Sir Herbert Samuel to the Permanent Under-Secretary for Mines,[2] 'the advantage of that might go in one of three ways. It might go in more profits to the employer, or it might go in lower prices to the consumer, or it might go to the worker either in the form of more wages or in the form of greater leisure.' On some such basis as we have outlined, it would have been feasible to go some distance beyond this agnostic statement of alternative possibilities.

---

[1] J. M. Keynes, *Economic Journal*, March 1929, p. 4.
[2] Minutes of Evidence of Royal Commission, p. 18.

CHAPTER 5

SHAPE OF THE PRIME COST CURVES

I GENERAL FEATURES

A short survey will now be attempted of the factors that determine the shape of the prime cost curves. It is in the first place clear that prime cost of production commonly includes certain elements of an overhead nature which are excluded from fixed cost by the rigidity of our definition. They are overhead in the sense that they are rather inflexible, but they are not fixed in the sense that they are part of the cost of producing nothing.[1] Expenditure on fuel, lighting, repairs and renewals, and salaries would often increase very rapidly as the output is raised from zero to a small level; beyond this point it would increase much more slowly. The effect of these quasi-fixed elements on the average prime cost curve is similar to that of fixed cost on the average total cost curve: the curve falls as the output increases.

An example may be quoted from the imaginary figures supplied by Professor J. M. Clark for a motor-car factory.[2] Professor Clark does not, of course, draw our distinction between prime cost and fixed cost; but his figures for the cost of production at 0 per cent of capacity denote the fixed cost, and these may be subtracted from his figures for the costs at other levels of output in order to obtain the aggregate prime cost at these levels. In this way it appears that the average prime cost per car in respect to 'office, sales, etc.' is $1,206 at 60 per cent of capacity and only $933 at 80 per cent.

But as output expands, a point will be reached at which its production by means of the available plant and organisation will meet with increasing resistances of various kinds. The cost curves now begin to rise with increasing output: first, the marginal prime cost curve (which is the short-period marginal total cost curve); at a higher

---

[1] The distinction here drawn between the words 'overhead' (used in its everyday sense) and 'fixed' is not to be confused with that of Chapter 1, where a special meaning is arbitrarily assigned to the word 'overhead'.

[2] *Studies in the Economics of Overhead Costs*, 1923, p. 185.

level of output the average prime cost curve, and finally, the average total cost curve.

II MEANS OF VARYING OUTPUT

§ 3   More precise investigation depends on the technical aspects of a variation of output, which may occur in several different ways:

    (i) The amount of machinery in actual use may be altered.
    (ii) The intensity at which the machinery is used may be altered in respect to
        (a) the speed at which it is driven,
        (b) the efforts exerted by the workers,
        (c) the number of workers employed on each machine.
    (iii) The number of hours worked per shift may be altered.
    (iv) The number of shifts per day may be altered.
    (v) The number of days on which work is done per week (or per month) may be altered.

The possibility, vogue, and consequences of these methods will now be examined.

§ 4   (i) If part of the machinery is more efficient than the rest, it may obviously be advantageous to confine production as far as possible to the more efficient elements. As output increases, more and more inefficient machinery has to be utilised, and the cost curves eventually rise.

The more uniform the machinery, the less is the counteraction of this factor on the effect of the quasi-fixed elements of cost; the curves reach their minima at higher levels of output and rise less steeply after these levels have been attained.

§ 5   It will shortly appear that in practice the choice of a method by which output may be varied often resolves into a decision between the relative advantages of methods (i) and (v). The effective length of the working day is to be regarded as given, and the question is whether to work part of the machinery every day or all of the machinery only some days. The answer depends simply on whether the cost of production (prime or total) is less under the one method or under the other.

The decisive factor must usually be those quasi-fixed elements in the cost of production to which reference has just been made. If their amount, measured over an appreciable period of time, were independent of the method adopted, they would play no part in securing the adoption of a particular method, any more than does fixed cost itself. But it is obvious that they are greater under method (i), and in many cases substantially greater. On every day that production is carried on at all it is necessary to employ foremen and key-men, and the central power plant has to be run; but the expenditure for these purposes varies less rapidly than does the daily output. It may therefore be economical to force the maximum output from each of the fewest working days possible.

Whether it is so or not depends upon the economies to be derived by confining production to the more efficient portions of the plant. The matter is best illustrated by a diagram representing the prime

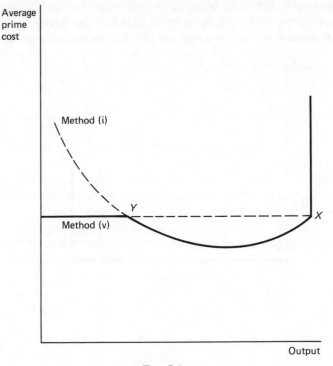

FIG. 5.1

cost curves under the two methods (Figure 5.1) When all the machinery is in use under method (i) the position is precisely the same as when the maximum number of days is being worked under method (v). At this point X the two curves meet: it is the point of capacity output. Now it will be shown below that under method (v) the prime cost is appreciably constant, while it has been seen that under method (i) it falls to a minimum. It follows that method (v) is the more economical for low levels of output, but above the point Y, at which the two curves cross, method (i) becomes the more economical. The full line in Figure 5.1 represents the actual average prime cost curve. This result is in agreement with the empirical fact that complete stoppage (for a day or more at a time) is resorted to by factories only when output is substantially below capacity output. From what has already been said it is clear that the greater the importance of quasi-fixed cost and the more uniform the machinery, the greater is the output at which the two curves cross; and, consequently, the wider is the range over which method (v) prevails. Where the machinery is completely uniform, the prime cost curve under method (i) may be expected to fall continuously, as in Figure

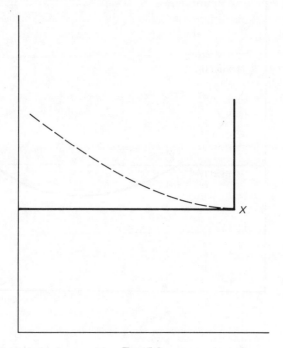

Fig. 5.2

5.2 and method (v) is the more economical for all levels of output.

In point of fact there are many industries in which uniformity, inside the separate productive units, is fairly complete. Thus the spindles in most cotton-spinning mills, at any rate those employed on standard counts, were mostly installed at the time each mill was built, and additions have been few. It is, therefore, natural to find that in cotton-spinning short-time working proceeds almost entirely by way of method (v). It would appear that in some wool-spinning mills there is a greater variety of plant and in point of fact the method of confining production to a portion of the plant is often adopted in Bradford; but it is usually combined with the reverse of method (ii)(c), for reasons which are discussed below.[1]

The extreme opposite of uniformity might well be expected in coal-mining. Most coal-mines consist of a number of seams that vary considerably in ease of working. The notion that a temporary reduction of output is effected by ceasing work in the more difficult seams and that price is determined in the short period by the prime cost of working the 'marginal seam' is a peculiarly inviting one. But in point of fact coal-mines are not conducted in this kind of way. Like cotton mills they work to a standard basis on some days and cease work entirely on other days.[2] One reason is doubtless that the quasi-fixed elements of prime cost, the cost of running the shaft and surface workings, are particularly heavy. But in addition there is in operation a peculiar factor, dependent on the physical nature of coal-mining. 'When long wall is the system of working there is a serious

[1] Of the cotton industry the Balfour Committee write (*Survey of Textile Industries*, p. 30): 'No marked change seems to have taken place in the efficiency of the machinery . . . Mills have in many cases been unable to replace their equipment on account of the high costs and the economic depression in the industry.' On the other hand in the wool textile industry (ibid, p. 203), 'during the war a certain amount of new machinery had to be installed . . . After the war a large amount of machinery . . . was renewed.'

A further factor, where method (i) is in sole operation (without the reverse of (ii)(c)), is the fact that piece-work is apparently not so general in the wool industry as in the cotton industry (ibid, p. 188). The implications of this factor are discussed below.

It is possible that the difference between the cotton and the silk industries can be explained in the same way. The figures given by Professor Chapman (*Unemployment in Lancashire*, p. 51), quoted by Professor Pigou (*Economics of Welfare*, 3rd edition, p. 522), indicate that short time is relatively much less prominent in the silk industry.

In the same way the greater diversity of machinery in the weaving section of the cotton industry may explain the fact that, while the spinning section employs method (v), the weaving section employs a combination of method (i) with the opposite of method (ii)(c) (see § 13).

[2] This 'standard basis' is however a far more flexible thing, over quite short periods, in coal-mining than it is in manufacturing industries.

risk that the roof may fall in and the working faces be closed up if any portion of the pit is left unworked for more than a few days.'[1] If, then, it is desired to maintain the productive capacity of the mine, method (v) provides a considerably less costly means of doing so than method (i); for method (v) involves total idleness for, at the most, a few days a time.[2]

§ 6   Precisely the opposite tendency is at work when economies in respect to upkeep, repairs, and renewals, such as were considered in Chapter 3, §§ 20 to 25, are desired or enforced. Method (i) then provides a means of practising these economies on plant that is at present in excess of requirements, and the efficiency of production at the current level need not be prejudiced.

§ 7   But additional reasons for the prevalence of method (i) in certain trades must be sought elsewhere. The method is favoured particularly in those industries where production depends on specific orders from customers, and where the orders have to be executed in a reasonably short space of time. Such industries are those of printing and of various branches of engineering. When the period in the productive process occupied by a given type of plant is very long, the adoption of method (i), in respect at any rate to this type of plant, becomes essential. Such is the case in heavy engineering, an extreme example being afforded by shipbuilding.

§ 8   Professor Pigou has pointed out a further factor that operates a favour of method (i).[3] Not only does this method provide a means of concentrating on the more efficient plant, but it can be applied so as to eliminate the less efficient workmen. The advantage that can be gained is greater where a uniform time-rate is in operation than where piece-wages are paid. Professor Pigou draws attention to the fact that the industries in which the method of dismissal rules supreme – building, engineering and shipbuilding – are those in which time-wages predominate.[4] We may now sum up and suggest five reasons why these and similar industries rely so largely on method (i):

(a)   The plant possessed by individual firms varies in efficiency.

---

[1] *Economist*, History Supplement of 1896, p. 20: quoted by D. H. Robertson in his *Industrial Fluctuations*.

[2] Another factor that operates in respect to seasonal fluctuations is mentioned below in the second footnote to § 9.

[3] Pigou, *Economics of Welfare*, 3rd edition, p. 520.

[4] Ibid, p. 521.

(b) The workers employed by individual firms vary in efficiency, but they all have to be paid the same time-wages.

(c) The quasi-fixed elements of prime cost are comparatively low.

(d) Output depends on orders, which must be promptly executed.

(e) Long portions of the period of production are occupied by separate units of plant.

In theory the application of method (i) does not necessitate the permanent dismissal of a portion of the labour force. Through a system of rotation the available work could be divided among the whole body of workers. But 'the rotation method is troublesome to arrange and involves a good deal of organisation and collaboration with the work-people', and 'broadly speaking, the inconvenience of this method has not permitted it to be adopted at all widely'.[1] Method (v) attains automatically the end which under method (i) involves great difficulty. It therefore offers advantages in all those cases where individual firms desire to maintain a lien on some of their workers, or where, under the stimulus of philanthropy or trade-union pressure, employers prefer an equitable distribution of the burden of unemployment.[2]

(ii) (a) In many cases the speed of machinery depends mainly on technical factors, and is not susceptible to economic influences. Even if the speed is variable, it is usually economical to drive machinery at the maximum rate which is technically and humanly possible. In spinning and weaving the speed 'is limited by liability to breakage of the yarn or warp when these are subjected to undue strain', and 'skill and assiduity on the part of the operatives certainly count for much in securing that the output approaches the maximum standard of quantity and quality'.[3] A reduction in speed is likely to be the most economical method of reducing output only if piece-wages are being paid. But even then it is only to be preferred if the proportional reduction in the prime portion of the aggregate cost of fuel, maintenance, and repairs and renewals is greater than the proportional reduction in output. In general it is less; and the method will not be considered further.

[1] Ibid, pp. 521 and 522.

[2] Ibid, pp. 519 and 520. Professor Pigou mentions a suggestion that the reason for the adoption of the short-time method to meet seasonal fluctuations in the coal-mining industry is because 'an employer . . . will like to keep in touch with more men than he needs at the moment, so as to make sure that enough will be available later on', when the busy season again sets in.

[3] Balfour Committee, *Survey of Textile Industries*, p. 30.

§ 11   (ii) (b) Except when flexible schemes of bonus payments are in operation, it is difficult for an employer to induce any advantageous alteration in the intensity of the efforts exerted by his workers. It is true that the piece-rate at which the individual's output is an optimum (not necessarily a maximum) from the point of view of the employer depends on the economic circumstances of the industry. But in practice piece-rates are not determined in this manner.

§ 12   (ii) (c) In many cases the ratio of the number of men employed to the number of machines in operation is capable of continuous variation, the speed of the machines being, if necessary, appropriately adjusted. The theory of marginal net productivity provides the criterion for determining the optimum output, which falls with the price so long as time-wages are paid; and the same holds true where piece-wages are paid if the piece-rates are altered in proportion to the average output per man. The method is only applicable within certain limits: a point is eventually, often very speedily, reached at which the continued operation of all the plant with a reduced labour force becomes uneconomical, if not physically impossible. Over the range in which it is applicable the method results in a tendency for the prime cost curve to rise with increase of output.[1]

§ 13   When, however, a fixed scale of piece-rates is in operation, the result is rather different. As the number of workers and the output are reduced, the wages bill, instead of diminishing in proportion to the number of workers, diminishes only in proportion to the output. It follows that the marginal prime cost of labour is constant, being equal to the piece-rate. Unless, therefore, one of the other elements of prime cost increases faster than the output, which is unlikely, the marginal prime cost does not increase with the output. There is, consequently, no point of equilibrium. An increase of output by this method, (ii)(c), is always profitable. No matter how small the resultant increase in output may be, it is always worthwhile to employ an extra man, because earnings per head are sufficiently reduced to prevent the wages bill from increasing faster than the output.

The solution of this paradox must be that in practice a fixed scale

---

[1] Contrasting the short-time method, Professor Pigou writes that 'one or other of the rival plans is favoured when much expensive machinery is employed and it is practicable, by spreading labour more sparsely, to keep the whole of this going with a reduced staff' (Pigou, *Economics of Welfare*, p. 518). The effect of the cost of the machinery on the choice of plan is not self-evident. Neither fixed cost nor overhead cost (which includes interest on and depreciation of fixed capital) can very well enter into the merits of the various methods.

of piece-rates is not feasible. If two operatives are working on a spinning mule, it would be profitable to add a third if the earnings of the three operatives could be computed on the same basis as that on which the earnings of the two are computed. The result would be that these two would find their earnings decreased by rather less than a third. To this, it may be imagined, they would be unwilling to consent; private objection or trade-union resistance would secure a modification of the standard piece-rate.[1]

We are now prepared to offer a tentative explanation of the paradox that in the weaving section of the cotton industry a reduction of output is secured, not by reducing 'the number of workers employed on each machine', but by a 'reduction in the number of machines per worker';[2] 'the number of looms tended by the individual operative weavers [is reduced]'.[3] The precise opposite of method (ii)(c) is combined with method (i). The advantages of method (i) have already been suggested. The reason for its combination with method (ii)(c) reversed must surely lie in the partial removal at times of depression of the barrier that we have just seen stands in the way of an indefinite increase in the number of workers per machine in a piece-work industry. The weaving operatives presumably recognise that the reduction in daily earnings that results when more operatives are put on to a machine is equivalent to the reduction in the number of working days that would result from the adoption of method (v); and they appear to be willing to sacrifice the assistance from the Unemployment Fund for which method (v) would qualify them.

It has already been mentioned that the same method is general in the wool industry. 'Weavers wait in their turn for warps and menders for pieces, spinners mind fewer spindles . . . two loom weavers with one loom standing, three-side worsted-frame tenters with only two sides working, etc.'[4]

(iii) In many industries overtime provides the recognised means of expanding output above the normal level. Special rates of wages have to be paid,[5] and efficiency is likely to be reduced by fatigue. The result is that the prime cost curves almost certainly rise with increase

---

[1] Balfour Committee, *Survey of Textile Industries*, p. 32.

[2] Ibid, p. 40.

[3] Thus the cotton-weavers have recently applied 'for a payment of 7s 6d a week for each loom stopped when they are kept at work on less than the normal number of looms'. *The Times*, November 2, 1929.

[4] G. H. Wood, *Journal of the Royal Statistical Society*, vol. 90, pt. 2, 1927, p. 276.

[5] Amounting, usually, to a quarter or a half more than the normal rates.

of output, and the optimum output is quite simply determinable on the ordinary marginal principle.

§ 15   But it is not possible to assume that prime cost can in general be *reduced* by *reducing* output below the normal level. The effect of a shorter working day in stimulating efficiency still remains (it is, of course, more important when time-wages are paid) but with the hours of work that now rule the effect may be imagined to be a small one. On the other hand, a reduction of the length of the working day is not accompanied by any reduction in piece- or hourly wage-rates, corresponding to the big increases that have to be paid for overtime. The most that can be assumed, and it is a good deal, is that hourly- and piece-rates remain unchanged. Any reduction in average and marginal prime costs then depends on increased efficiency. Against this has to be set the increase in average prime cost that results from the quasi-fixed element of prime cost. Unless this falls in proportion to the output, it tends to cause an increase of average prime cost when the daily output is reduced. In practice the fall in the quasi-fixed element would be small in relation to the reduction of output, because foremen and key-men have to be paid daily wages and the cost of starting and stopping machinery (including, for instance, the cost of setting furnaces going and, in the case of coal-mining, of haulage) are quite considerable. For this reason method (iii) may be regarded as an uneconomic method of reducing output. In fact it is indisputable that, at the normal hourly and piece wage-rates, it would usually be profitable for an *individual* firm to extend its *daily* hours beyond the limit set by the law or the trade union, even at a time of trade depression.

§ 16   But in point of fact the case is an even stronger one. An attempt to reduce the length of the working day would usually be met by a determined resistance on the part of the trade union in the defence of daily earnings. Hourly- and piece-rates would have to be increased in proportion to the reduction in hours. (This is the difficulty that is confronting the government to-day in their attempt to fulfil their pledge to restore the seven-hour day to the coal-miners).

Actually, indeed, it is an *increase* in the length of the working day for which employers clamour at a time of depression. It is difficult to believe that the reason is that they desire to increase their output,[1]

----

[1] But no other object can have been in view when the cotton-spinners and manufacturers in January 1928 made their demand for a 55-hour week. They appear to have laid more stress on this demand than on the demand for reduced wage-rates with which it was coupled. The futility of asking for an increase in the length of the

except in so far as such an increase would be accompanied by a reduction in the quasi-fixed elements of prime cost. It provides a means of reducing wage costs without encroaching on daily earnings. It was with this object that the miners' day was lengthened in 1926: piece-rates were reduced in proportion.

When, however, this method, (iii), is merely an alternative to method (v), insistence on a compensatory increase in piece-rates is not so likely. The loss to the worker through working fewer hours a day will be compensated by the gain through working more days a week; that is to say, provided there is no extra loss in respect of unemployment benefits. This appears to be the position in Bradford. By a special arrangement with the Unemployment Fund half-days can be worked by the worsted spinners and benefits drawn just as if work ceased entirely every second week. Nevertheless the operatives prefer to work a full week and then to stop a full week. But the masters prefer the half-day method, and this, I am told, is in fairly general operation. The reason is by no means clear. But it may be bound up with the smallness of that portion of the quasi-fixed element of prime cost which does not fall in proportion to the daily output: foremen and key-men can be paid a half-day's wage like everyone else, so that the wastefulness of working only half a day is not very great, particularly when consideration is paid to the importance of being able to meet the requirements of customers without delay.

A further factor, that should be considered, has been indicated by Professor Pigou. In most cases 'an appreciable advantage can be gained by cutting down the most expensive *hours* of work, those, for example, that involve extra charges for lighting and heating'.[1]

---

working day when most firms are working short-time is well brought out by B. Bowker (*Lancashire under the Hammer*, 1923, p. 95). The action of the masters has never, so far as I know been satisfactorily accounted for. Mr Bowker (ibid, p. 96) suggests three tentative explanations:

(i) In their 'bewildered state of mind' they were 'captivated by a nice-sounding phrase.'
(ii) A few employers were working full-time and desired to increase their output further.
(iii) The employers wanted to be in a position to place an obstacle in the way of the ratification of the Washington Hours Convention, which they realised was fairly imminent, by pointing out how it would penalise an already hard-pressed industry.

However, the demand for a reduction of wage-rates which has precipitated the present strike (July 1929) is not coupled with any reference to hours. This is in favour of Mr Bowker's first, and most plausible, explanation; one and a half years' reflexion has sufficed to show that an increase in an industry's capacity is of little avail if the industry is working far below it.

[1] Pigou, *Economics of Welfare*, p. 518.

§ 19   (iv) Restrictions of various kinds often operate against the working of more than one shift a day. In the first place there is a legal restriction on the employment of women and young persons at immoderately early or late hours. This restriction is decisive in industries, like the textile industries, in which women constitute an essential element. But it may be noted that 'the Secretary of State, upon joint application from the employer and the majority of work-people concerned, may make orders' which would enable two shifts to be worked.[1]

In many industries the trade unions take up a definite stand against multiple shifts. In the engineering industry 'an agreement was arrived at in 1920 under which employers were free to introduce a two or three-shift system, but little has been done in this direction, and the employers contend that the system as provided for in the agreement is not economic'.[2] In coal-mining the position varies according to the locality. Two shifts

> have been worked for generations in Durham and Northumberland, and are usual in South Yorkshire. In Scotland their use is limited by the extensive employment of machinery. In South Wales there is a fixed policy of opposition on the part of the men . . . In other districts, though there is no formal opposition by the men, the single shift system is almost general, except in some of the larger mines.[3]

§ 20   In other industries again multiple shifts are not merely possible but essential. These are the industries in which continuous work is technically necessary, as in some branches of the metal industries. But precisely the reason that makes this field such an important one for multiple shifts prevents method (iv) from being applied to it. Multiple shifts are worked because they must be worked, and the number of shifts a day cannot be reduced.

§ 21   The effect on the prime cost of working an extra shift in the course of a day is a little complex. The quasi-fixed element is likely to be reduced; the costs of foremen, fuel, and so on, probably increase in a smaller proportion than the output. And other economies may be derived as a result of the more continuous production. Thus in coal-

---

[1] Balfour Committe: *Survey of Textile Industries*, p. 31.
[2] Balfour Committee: *Survey of Metal Industries*, p. 153.
[3] *Report of Commission on Coal Industry* (1925) pp. 176 and 177.

mining 'the quicker advance of the face generally makes for better roof conditions and so for safety, as well as allowing a saving in timber'.[1] On the other hand, in night work lie well-known sources of inefficiency.

If, as seems likely, the net effect is a decrease of prime cost, method (iv) is not an economical method of reducing output. Any firm that can do so will work a multiple shift and employ method (v) or some even better method of producing an output less than its capacity level.

But like an increase of hours, the introduction of a double shift, not its abolition, is what conditions of depression are sometimes stated to demand. At first sight, the strenuous advocacy by the Samuel Commission of the policy of multiple shifts is inconsistent with their refusal to sanction longer hours. But, while criticism can perhaps be passed on the method of the Commission's advocacy, it is perfectly true that an increase of hours only fails to achieve an increase in unemployment if there follows a proportional increase of output (and a sufficient reduction of price); on the other hand the introduction of multiple shifts can at the very worst only cause a redistribution of the existing volume of unemployment.

(v) It has already been indicated that a very common method of reducing output, notably in cotton-spinning and coal-mining, is to close down the whole plant on some days and to work the whole plant for a full shift on other days.

In coal-mining it is important to curtail the period of idleness for the reason specified in § 5, and the method adopted is usually to work, say, three or four or five days each week. In cotton-spinning, on the other hand, the period of idleness is so far as possible concentrated into a week (either an actual week or the latter part of one week and the beginning of the next week), so as to enable the operatives to claim unemployment benefit.

The cost involved during the period of idleness is the fixed cost, or, as it is often called, the 'stopped cost'. We have seen that the cost of maintaining a coal-mine in good condition begins to increase after a few days owing to the difficulty of preventing falls. But for such short periods of idleness as occur in practice the fixed cost can probably be assumed to be constant.

In the case of a cotton mill, on the other hand, which may be stopped for several weeks, it might be expected that certain economies

---

[1] *Report of Royal Commission on Coal Industry*, p. 176.

can be achieved in a prolonged stoppage that are not attainable in a stoppage lasting only a day or two. I am informed, however, that this is not the case, and that the stopped cost of a standard mill is at the rate of £9,500 per annum whatever the length of the period. This figure for the technical fixed cost consists of the following items:

Salaries	£4,500	per annum
Directors' fees	500	
Rates	1,400	
Schedule A	600	
Insurance	1,00	
Coal, gas and electricity	1,000	
Fees, stationery, etc.	500	
	£9,500	

These figures are taken from a return which applies to a standard mill of 100,000 spindles working on 42's weft.[1] But actually they are substantially the same for all standard mule mills of 100,000 spindles working on weft and twist and for all standard ring mills of 60,000 spindles.[2] (In actual practice most mills consist of a mixture of different types of spindles. The idea of a standard mill working exclusively on a single count is a convenient fiction of which we shall make much use. For the present certain difficulties that are set up by this fiction must be overlooked.)

§ 24   The difference between the total cost of a full working day and the fixed cost per day is the prime cost per day. Here too it appears that the prime cost per day is independent of the length of the period over which production is daily carried on without the interruption of a period of idleness. There are no economies due to continuous production (when only one shift is worked each day). Now the output due to a day's work is fixed in amount, being the normal daily output. It follows then that the average prime cost, which is the quotient of the prime cost per day divided by the daily output, is independent of the output; and consequently that the marginal prime cost is equal to this constant average prime cost.

[1] Cotton Yarn Association, July 28, 1927.
[2] This is indicated by the Association's standard costs statistics of December 6, 1927.

When the maximum possible number of days is being worked each week, output cannot be increased further. The output is now equal to what may be called the capacity output. At this point the prime cost curves, which have hitherto been a horizontal straight line, move up vertically.

The result is thus obtained that the prime cost curve (marginal or average) has the shape of a laterally inverted letter L. It will in future be described as an ⌐-shaped curve.

III COLLAPSE OF ASSUMPTION OF PERFECT COMPETITION

The essential feature of such a curve is that it does not begin to rise until the point of capacity output is reached. As a determinant of output it loses most of the significance which we have hitherto attached to the marginal prime cost curve. If the price is greater than the average prime cost (denoted by the horizontal part of the curve), we should expect that under conditions of perfect competition, the output would be equal to the capacity output. For, so long as the output is less than the maximum, an increased output would be associated with a proportionately increased prime profit and could be procured by an infinitesimal reduction of price. If this were so we should find that the only firms that work below capacity are the inefficient firms whose prime costs are greater than the price; which are therefore losing more than their fixed costs and would lose less if they were to produce less or nothing at all. But it happens to be a fact that short-time working is not confined to these firms, which produce merely in order to keep up their connections or for one of the other reasons specified in Chapter 2, § 7. Both in cotton-spinning and in coal-mining, short-time is practised to a significant extent by firms which are losing very much less than their fixed costs. And it is not possible, it seems, to fall back upon such limitations to output as were set out in Chapter 3, § 15.

It is on this Scylla that the assumptions of perfect competition come to grief and precipitate us into the Charybdis, I am afraid, of subsequent chapters: no *via media* is open. It is somewhat remarkable that the first cloud of suspicion to creep over the horizon of perfect competition should appear in the shape of the facts of the cotton-spinning industry. If competition is not perfect in cotton-spinning, it might well be asked where perfection is to be found. Mills are large in number and small in size. The sturdy individualism of the spinner is sufficiently notorious. And 'dispersed in hundreds of small units, he finds himself flanked with a phalanx of merchants at either end whose chief interest is to buy cheap and sell dear'.[1] But it will presently become clear that the degree of imperfection required to explain the position of a depressed industry may be very small – so small as to be inappreciable under normal circumstances.

§ 27   Honesty demands a certain admission: even in the case of a cotton mill there appears to be a slight rise in the prime cost curve. It is due to the fact that when a mill is working only half-time there is not enough work fully to occupy the permanent staff, whose salaries form part of fixed cost. One or two of the permanent staff are thus set free to do work which would ordinarily be performed by wage-earners, and the prime cost is correspondingly reduced. The rise in the prime cost is, however, far too small to solve our problem. Its amount can be deduced from the following figures, showing the annual loss involved by various degrees of working for three different values of the margin by a standard mill of 100,000 spindles spinning 42's weft and 38's twist.[2]

	Full time working	*50% working*	*Temporarily stopped*
(a)	Nil	£4,350	£9,550
(b)	£10,000	£9,350	£9,550
(c)	£20,000	£14,350	£9,550

Let u be the annual output, p_F the average prime cost for full-time working, p_H for 50 per cent working. Then from any row of figures it follows that:

$$(9550 + \tfrac{1}{2}u\, p_H) - \tfrac{1}{2}(9550 + u\, p_F) = 4350$$

$$\therefore P_F - P_H = \frac{850}{u}$$

But the output per spindle per week is about half a pound,[3] and the total annual output is therefore 2,500,000 lbs. Hence the difference between the two prime costs in pence per pound is $\dfrac{850 \times 240}{2,500,000} = 0.08$ approximately.

---

[1] *The Times*; leading article: March 11, 1929.
[2] Cotton Yarn Assocation, December 22, 1927.
[3] Cotton Yarn Association, December 6, 1927.

It is then only when the margin lies within a range of less than a tenth of a penny and very close to prime cost that this factor is operative.

Case (b), for which figures are given in the above table, was obviously selected so as to lie inside this range. 50 per cent working is more profitable than either full-time working or stopping. It was asserted that 'the present prices for American yarns shew that the second example represents the position to-day' (the end of 1927) and the circular was admittedly intended to prove the advantages of curtailed output. But other evidence shows that the loss at the end of 1927 of such a standard mill as we are considering was at the rate of £7,000 per annum rather than £10,000.[1] The force of example (b) is then lost – the margin is too much above prime cost – and we are thrown back to the fundamental difficulty of the ⌐-shaped prime cost curve.

IV THE MARGINAL DOCTRINE IN THE SHORT PERIOD

It is quite true that the doctrine of the equality of marginal prime cost and price, of whose merits we are now becoming a little critical, is seldom enunciated, still more seldom in a definite form. But this can scarcely be through any realisation of the difficulties. Either the doctrine is not appreciated at all or, if it is regarded as a truism that does not require enunciation, the difficulties are neither apprehended nor faced.

The doctrine is, of course, implicit in the pages of Marshall, who recognises, too, the necessity for qualification; but his qualifications do not, I think, extend very much further than 'the fear of spoiling the market'. Marshall's 'fear of spoiling the market', however, covers a wider range of inhibitions than are generally attributed to the term. His most important connotation is that to which the term is usually confined in modern practice, 'the fear of incurring the resentment of other producers'.[2] But in addition there is the 'fear of temporarily spoiling a man's special market':[3] 'each man fears to spoil his chance

---

[1] Cotton Yarn Association, December 22, 1927.
[2] *Principles*, p. 374.
[3] Ibid, p. 849.

of getting a better price later on from his own customers'.[1] It is clear from these quotations that the effects of imperfection in the market, with which Marshall qualifies the short-period marginal doctrine, are regarded as transient in character, possibly bound up with stocks rather than with rates of flow. Marshall recognised that the market is never perfect. But it may perhaps be suggested, and it will be suggested in § 2 of Chapter 7, that he was inclined to minimise the relevance of deviations from perfection.

At the hands of Professor Pigou both doctrine and qualifications receive explicit treatment. 'The curve representing the marginal prime expenses of successive quantities of output', which 'will, after a point, be greater, the larger is the output', 'is the short-period supply curve of the commodity'.[2] 'There are three influences, which, inactive in good times, tend in bad times to make business men restrict their output below the short-period norm.' These are the 'objection to "spoiling the market"', the tendency to price materials at cost, and the fear of frightening away buyers by lowering prices; and finally there is the question of convenience. But Professor Pigou does not, I think, include the influence, operative in good times as well as in bad, to which, rightly or wrongly, the position of predominance is being devoted in this essay; I mean the imperfection of the market. (Such predominance has at least the advantage that, while the influences cited by Professor Pigou are intangible by nature and spasmodic in effect, imperfection of the market lends itself to somewhat more rigorous treatment.)

Professor J. M. Clark, in his *Economics of Overhead Costs*, continually refers to the tendency of 'differential cost' to be equal to price. He does not, however, make use of the term 'marginal prime cost', but appears to recognise that differential cost (in the short period) is often about equal to prime cost. Thus 'in such a case one might simply take for granted, within proper limits, that direct operating expenses are a measure of differential cost'.[3] Throughout the course of Professor Clark's book there are constantly looming up influences of the sort that prevent the equality of differential cost and price. Among these imperfection of the market plays a peculiarly hazy role. While on page 195 Clark alludes to it by implication rather than specification, but omits it entirely from the category on page

---

[1] Ibid, p. 374.
[2] *Industrial Fluctuations*, 2nd edition, p. 185.
[3] *Industrial Fluctuations*, p. 210: similarly on p. 245.

435, and it is not, I think, till page 441 that it receives adequate recognition.

To Professor J. H. Jones is due the credit of introducing references to a short-period theory of value into discussions about specific industries. Such are the accepted standards of these discussions that his references inevitably have the air of intruders from another planet. No mention is made of the imperfection of the market, although Professor Jones is dealing with the two industries, cotton-spinning and coal-mining, in which we have just found it impossible to maintain that competition is perfect. But Professor Jones's statements are capable of an interpretation to which no exception can be taken. In one place 'differential costs being defined as the difference between the cost of producing and the cost of not producing',[1] in other words as our average prime cost, Professor Jones criticises the views of Professor Daniels and Mr Jewkes on the effect of overhead costs in the cotton industry upon price: 'the aim of a firm is to secure the largest possible margin between the total revenue from sales and the differential costs incurred in producing'.[2] With reference to the coal industry Professor Jones writes elsewhere of 'differential cost of production' (without defining the term at all) as 'the true determinant of prices over a short period'.[3] In both these quotations the way is left open for the operation of the imperfection of the market and similar factors, though their necessity is not indicated.

[1] In at least one passage Professor Clark, somewhat inconsistently, refers to 'the differential cost of producing (goods) rather than not producing them.' *Economics of Overhead Costs*, p. 244.

[2] *Journal of Royal Statistical Society*; vol. 91, pt. 4, 1928, p. 201.

[3] *Economic Journal*, June 1929, p. 163. Professor Jones goes on to say that the 'differential cost of production' 'is so much below prime cost'. It is to be presumed that by prime cost is meant the cost of labour, raw materials, etc., which may exceed what we call prime cost (because appreciable amounts are spent on these items in maintaining an idle mine).

CHAPTER 6

FURTHER CONSIDERATION OF A STATE OF PERFECT COMPETITION

I JUSTIFICATION OF THIS CHAPTER

§ 1 Before going on to the modifications involved when the market is imperfect, it would be as well to follow out a little further the consequences of perfect competition. The results that follow differ to a greater or less extent from the facts of reality, but they will be useful as the basis of the next chapters.

Broad indication rather than accurate precision will be the aim of this chapter. The results are modified rather than upset by the complications that are neglected.

II AN IDEAL CASE: PRICES IN A DEPRESSED INDUSTRY

§ 2 We begin by considering an industry that consists of firms whose prime cost curves are all of the ⌐-shape and whose prime costs are all equal. The firms are not necessarily of the same size.

If the possibility of closing down is ruled out and if each firm reduces its output to zero as soon as the price is slightly less than the prime cost, the supply curve of each firm coincides with its prime cost curves; and the supply curve of the industry is of the ⌐ shape. So long as the demand curve cuts the vertical portion of this supply curve, the price exceeds prime cost. If the industry is in long-period equilibrium, the excess of the price over the prime cost is equal to the overhead cost per unit of output. As the demand curve falls, the price falls but the output remains at its capacity level. This continues until the demand curve cuts the horizontal portion of the supply curve. The price is then equal to the prime cost. The price now remains equal to the prime cost and the output decreases as the demand falls off further.[1] The fall in price from the time when the industry was earning normal profits is equal to the average overhead cost. This is great not only in industries where fixed cost is great, but also in industries which employ large amounts of fixed capital in proportion to their output.

So long as the price exceeds prime cost, a firm that is short of orders undercuts its competitors in an attempt to work full-time. The process of undercutting continues in a cumulative way until either the price is driven down to prime cost, when output falls off, or the demand responds to the fall in price sufficiently to permit the whole industry to work full-time. If the demand is rather inelastic, as it usually is, the drop in price due to a small falling off in demand is very great, and it takes but little to send prices hurtling down to prime cost. 'Given an inelastic demand and an inelastic supply, it follows that a minor change in demand or supply produces a disproportionate effect upon price.[2]

The tendency for prices to fall to the neighbourhood of prime cost in a depression is very well known. But it is often spoken of as being the consequence of some peculiarly violent form of competition that is not operative when adequate profits are being earned. Moreover a distinction is seldom drawn between this state of alleged economic hysteria and the state of real warfare described by Professor Pigou as 'designed to secure future gains by driving a rival from the field or exacting favourable terms of agreement from him.'[3] In point of fact the catastrophic consequences of surplus capacity, while differing in their magnitude and in the speed with which they are attained from less deadly economic changes, are the work of the forces of perfectly

---

[1] We should naturally suppose that the decrease of output comes about through some firms reducing their output to zero while others continues to produce at their capacity levels. But since the loss, which is equal to the fixed cost, is independent of the output when the price is equal to the prime cost, we might suppose that firms produce at intermediate levels of output.

[2] J. H. Jones, 'The Coal Industry', *Economic Journal*, June 1929, p. 158.

[3] *Economics of Welfare*, 3rd edition, p. 269. Professor Pigou proposes to overcome the confusion by confining the term 'cut-throat competition' to this kind of price warfare. 'Cut-throat competition proper occurs only when the sale price of any quantity of commodity stands below the short-period supply price of that quantity.' The use of the term in any other sense is highly misleading, but is quite common. Thus Professor J. M. Clark, in his *Economics of Overhead Costs*, uses the term 'cut-throat competition' almost consistently to specify the type of competition that results in a substantial fall of price at a time of depression.

normal competition. It may be objected that the attempts of some firms to steal away orders from others are more aggressive acts than are the expansion of existing firms and the entry of new ones, which result in the attainment of long-period equilibrium. But such acts of expansion and entry are only perpetrated in conjunction with precisely the same process of stealing away orders by cutting prices as is responsible for the often distressing nature of short-period equilibrium.

§ 5   One of the depressed industries that conforms most closely to the assumptions that have been made is that of cotton-spinning. This industry also has the advantage of providing us with several different brands on which to test our conclusions. The deviations between prime costs and margins are a matter for future discussion; for our present purpose it is sufficient to show that these deviations are small. We make use of a return showing,[1] on the basis of the margins being quoted at the end of 1927, the hypothetical loss per pound of a standard mill working full-time on various counts. Since this is calculated 'before any interest or depreciation is charged', it can be compared with the amount of the technical fixed cost per pound of capacity output. If the average loss, so calculated, is less than the average fixed cost, the margin is above prime cost; if it is greater, the margin is below prime cost.

The same result can also be portrayed more directly by comparing the hypothetical weekly loss of a mill working full-time with the amount of the technical fixed cost. The margin is above or below prime cost according as this hypothetical weekly loss is less than or greater than the fixed cost.

We have seen that the fixed cost (technical) of a standard mill is £9,500 per annum: that is to say, £180 a week.[2] The figures of production per spindle per week in the following table are taken from another return.[3] This is multiplied by the number of spindles and the result is divided into £180 to obtain the average fixed cost per pound of output of a mill working full-time.

The weekly loss can be seen to lie about £180 in a rough sort of way and the prime profit or loss is, for most counts, very small.

---

[1] Cotton Yarn Association, December 29, 1927.
[2] Chapter 5, § 23.
[3] Cotton Yarn Association, December 6, 1927.

TABLE 6.1

Count	Weekly loss on full-time working	No. of spindles	Weekly production per spindle	Loss per pound	Fixed cost per pound	Prime profit per pound
Weft						
16's	£255	100,000	1.42 lbs	0.43d	0.31d	−0.12d
32's	217	100,000	0.66	0.79	0.67	−0.12
42's	139	100,000	0.49	0.68	0.90	+0.22
54's	56	100,000	0.36	0.38	1.22	+0.84
Twist						
16's	115	100,000	1.46	0.19	0.30	+0.11
32's	175	100,000	0.68	0.62	0.64	+0.02
38's	155	100,000	0.56	0.67	0.78	+0.11
44's	202	100,000	0.45	1.09	0.97	−0.12
Ring						
20's	256	60,000	1.90	0.54	0.38	−0.16
38's	294	60,000	0.84	1.41	0.88	−0.53
44's	198	60,000	0.66	1.21	1.11	−0.10

III WAGE DISPUTES IN THIS IDEAL CASE

When the price of the product is equal to the average prime cost, the loss of each firm is equal to its total fixed cost and is independent both of the level of prime cost and of the output.[1] That is to say, so

[1] I am indebted to Mr Shove for an important criticism of this statement. Prime cost includes interest on working capital (see Chapter 1, § 8), and, consequently, the loss is equal to the fixed cost only if it is reckoned after the payment of interest on working capital. Now working capital is usually obtained either by borrowing or by withdrawing money from some other investment. If the rate of interest which the business man includes in his prime cost is the same as the rate that he has to pay on loans or the rate which he could earn in alternative investments, then the interest that he obtains on his working capital is just equal to the interest that he has to pay or forgo. It is then true that his net loss is independent of his output when the price is equal to his prime cost.

But actually, as Mr Shove has indicated to me, the former rate of interest is likely to be the higher one. The reason is that the rate of interest includes the remuneration of risk-bearing, and that investment in working capital is usually more risky than both the alternative investments that are suitable for this kind of purpose and the lending of money to a business man to enable him to invest in working capital. It then follows that when the price is equal to prime cost the net loss diminishes as the output increases. The decreased loss corresponds precisely to the increased risk that the business man is running on account of his increased output. An increase in his output enables him to increase the amount of risk-bearing that he is putting forward, and to draw a corresponding reward.

But even when the business man takes proper account of this factor, its numerical importance must be very small. In the first place, interest on working capital is often

long as the output of the industry remains below the capacity output, changes in demand and such changes in prime cost as affect the whole industry equally should be matters of indifference to the *employers*. On the other hand, by reason of their effect on employment, they should be matters of keen interest to the workers. So long as the output is less than the capacity output, neither a tariff nor a reduction in wages, although it increases employment, has any effect on profits.

We are in this way brought face to face with the clear-cut caricature of a conflict that, with outlines somewhat blurred, will be considered at a later stage. A demand for a wage reduction invariably proceeds from the employers and is as invariably resisted by the workers.[1] Yet in a depressed industry that conforms to our assumptions, the employers can derive a gain from a reduction in wages only either if wages constitute an element in fixed cost (as they do to some extent in coal-mining) or if the reduction is sufficient to raise the output of the industry to its capacity level. Otherwise the reduction is reflected in an equivalent reduction in price and the loss remains equal to the fixed cost. Leaving aside the consumer, we see that the only party that derives an advantage from the reduction in wages is the wage-earner – in the form of increased employment. When the demand is inelastic, this advantage is small – in fact unless the elasticity is greater than unity it does not compensate for the reduction in wages. And conversely, apart from the reduction in employment, the only party that suffers from an increase in wages is the consumer. When the demand is inelastic, therefore, we should expect a cooperative exploitation of the consumers by the workers, with the employers standing aside in a position of neutrality. It is due to the employers' self-interest, working along individualist channels, that the consumers derive so great an advantage when an industry is depressed: it would be the self-interest of the workers, acting corporately, that would deprive them of that advantage.

§ 7   On the other hand, when the industry is producing up to its full capacity, the level of wages has no effect on the price in the short

---

itself a very slight element in prime cost (we shall neglect it entirely when we come to deal with figures for cotton-spinning). Second, the element due to risk-bearing is very much smaller for investment in working capital than for investment in fixed capital. In both cases the risk may be supposed to be one of price fluctuation. But, while in the case of fixed capital it is necessary to consider the possible fluctuation over a term of years, in the case of working capital the period is quite a short one. Finally, it is possible in some industries to place the risk on the shoulders of the speculator.

[1] To a lesser degree this, and to a greater degree most of what follows, applies equally well to the question of a tariff.

period. While in a depressed industry the price is determined entirely by the level of prime cost, in an industry that is using all its fixed plant it is dependent purely on the conditions of demand. An increase in wages falls wholly on profits and the employers have every incentive to resist it.

We now have to explain why in point of fact wages do not rise when an industry becomes depressed and why employers exercise a greater pressure for a reduction of wages at times of depression than at times of prosperity.

It is of course assumed that when employers clamour for a reduction of wages or resist demands for an increase the imagined effect of a change on their profits or losses is the force that actuates them. But an overt confession of their desire to make more money, or to lose less, would be an offence against good taste; and their natural instincts have to be cloaked under polite references to the necessity for increasing output. We are thus faced with the paradox that, while an increase of output is precisely the effect – the sole effect – that we can admit, we still have to explain the employers' attitude, which is *officially* based on the necessity for increasing output.

The following arguments suggest themselves:

(1) Our assumptions are at first sight so extreme as to be absurd. But their absurdity is surely not sufficient to account for the apparent absurdity of the conclusions to which they lead. A state of perfect competition among firms working under ⌐-shaped supply schedules, with the price at which the supply becomes perfectly elastic the same for each firm (the firms need not even be equal in size), may be improbable, but there is nothing essentially ridiculous about it. While we shall find that more real assumptions lead to the conclusion that the losses in a depressed industry are to some, usually small, extent dependent on the level of wages, it is still necessary to find an answer to cover the ideal case that has been postulated.

(2) The answer that is to be suggested will cover too those more practical cases where an answer does not appear so necessary. For even in those cases, where a reduction in wages can be shown to be to the advantage of the employer, the actual advantage is often extraordinarily small in relation to the stress that is laid on it.

The attitude of the ordinary employer on a question of a change in wages suggests that he is not at all clear in his own mind as to the difference between the effects of a change that is confined to his own firm and the effects of a change that is adopted throughout an industry. He knows very well that if he paid his workers less he would benefit to a degree that is substantial and calculable. But he sometimes forgets, or fails to realise, that if all the employers in a depressed industry were to pay their workers less, the price would fall and the benefit would become small and hypothetical. The same parochial kind of confusion between the individual unit and the aggregate whole is apparent in the views of the late Mr Walter Leaf as to the impossibility of 'credit creation'.[1] The late Chairman of the Westminster Bank knew from his own experience that it was difficult for a single bank, acting by itself, to cause an expansion of deposits and on this rule, that does not apply perfectly even to a single bank, he appears to have based his sweeping generalisation. The business man has the excuse that under normal conditions his view that a reduction in wages is not reflected in a reduction in price (at any rate, not in the short period), is borne out by theoretical reasoning. It is unreasonable to expect him to realise that in an industry which is not employing its fixed plant to the full the position is an entirely different one.

§ 11   Experts do little or nothing to assist him towards a better realisation of the situation. It is true that there is a general tendency for writers on the dispute in the cotton industry (August 1929) to admit that a reduction of prices would follow a reduction of wages. But the reasons that are alleged are special ones, bound up with those peculiarly desperate conditions in Lancashire which afford a breeding ground for violent forms of competition unknown in other industries. Thus in the opinion of a *Times* leader-writer: "Until the finances of the over-capitalised mills have been thoroughly and drastically reorganised there scarcely seems any prospect of the spinners, in the American section at any rate, being able to retain the *benefits which might be expected from a lowering of wage costs*. In the present state of unorganised competition prices would probably fall almost immediately to a level no more remunerative than before."[2] Over-capitalisation is a red herring indeed.

§ 12   As is to be expected, it is the more enlightened business man who lends little or no support to a proposal for reducing wages. This may sometimes be the effect of a correlation between intellectual enlightenment and emotional charity. But it is more likely to be the result of a realisation of the small benefit that would accrue. Thus

---

[1] *Banking*, p. 102.
[2] *The Times*, July 22, 1929. The italics are mine. A report in the same edition of *The Times* mentions that some forward contracts contained a "fall" clause, to allow for the possibility of a reduction in wages.

Mr C. P. Markham, who started as an office boy and is now connected with mines, most of them comparatively successful, which produce one twenty-sixth part of the country's output, told the Samuel Commission that he was prepared to carry on at the previous level of wages. He recognised that 'the whole of the subsidy', which was equivalent to a reduction of wages, had 'simply come off the price of coal'.[1]

Mr Markham's mines are not affiliated to the Mining Association. This body, always zealous in the cause of lower wages and longer hours, represents the ordinary mine-owner and presumably puts forward his views. At any rate no better illustration of the working of the ordinary business man's mind could be supplied than by the arguments that have been advanced by the Mining Association. They presented a very elaborate table to the Samuel Commission,[2] in which they worked out the effect on costs of production in the various districts of the introduction of an eight-hour day (coupled with an equivalent decrease in piece-rates) and of economies in other directions. The table then proceeds to show the further reduction in wages that would be necessary to bring costs down to a certain level of prices.[3] But the level of prices is regarded as completely independent of the level of costs. This fond belief appeared to be shared by members of the Royal Commission themselves. At any rate in their Report they based their recommendation of a reduction in wages on the same tacit assumption.[4]

And the same assumption has run through all the recent discussions on the effect of a return to a seven-hour day. Costs, it is said, would rise by two shillings a ton, or whatever the figure may be. That there is a presumption that prices would rise correspondingly is not realised, or if it is realised the fact is concealed. The editorial imprimatur is affixed to Sir F. Mills's announcement that, as a result of the increase in costs of two shillings a ton, 'our own group, with its five million tons of output, would be half a million pounds a year worse off, and it is obvious that it would be a financial impossibility for us to carry on'.[5] Sir F. Mills appears delightfully unaware that he had just stated that the 'reduction [in costs of two shillings a ton resulting from the

---

[1] Minutes of Evidence of Royal Commission on Coal Industry (1925).
[2] Minutes of Evidence, p. 935.
[3] This was fixed, rather arbitrarily, at 40 per cent above the mean level of the years 1909–13.
[4] Report, pp. 228, 293 and 294.
[5] General Meeting of the Ebbw Vale Company, June 24, 1929.

introduction of the eight-hour day] has enabled us to regain by slow degrees some of our lost markets', and had presumably intended to imply that the introduction of the eight-hour day resulted in a reduction of prices.

§ 14   But the Mining Association appear to have felt uneasy and proposed an explanation for their assumption that the price of coal was fixed. 'The Association have had in mind that the price obtainable for British coal, whether for export or for inland consumption, is ultimately determined by world conditions.'[1] Sir Herbert Samuel, while apparently willing to accept their conclusion that prices would not be altered by a change in wages, refused to accept as a reason their plea that prices were unalterable. A long duel ensued between Sir Herbert on the one hand and Mr Evan Williams and Mr W. A. Lee, representatives of the Mining Association, on the other hand. 'If we say that prices are determined by the Germans why should not the Germans say that prices are determined by us?' was in effect the argument of Sir Herbert. And Mr Williams emerged lamely from the corner into which he had been driven with this curious answer: 'We have to take such prices as our competitors are willing to take, and if their costs of production are substantially lower than ours it must follow that they can take prices substantially lower than ours.' The absurdity of this argument will be made clear later on.[2]

Meanwhile it is sufficient to note that the argument of the Mining Association is one that is often present in the mind of the business man. 'It is not the competition between the collieries in this country which fixes the prices for export. Export prices are fixed by the price at which foreign producers of coal are willing to sell in the export markets.'[3] So that if fifty British coal-owners and five German coal-owners sell coal in Hamburg, the price quoted is quite independent of anything the British may feel or do. The foreign demand is regarded as perfectly elastic. Sir Herbert Samuel's suggestion that a rise in price of two shillings a ton would entail the sacrifice of merely some 5 per cent was regarded as ridiculous: 'We lose large contracts very frequently on $1\frac{1}{2}d$ or $3d$ a ton', was the reply. In the same way it is quite usual to explain the low level of the prices of cotton, steel, and other commodities in the international trade in which Great Britain plays a big part. It is not recognised as being due to the

---

[1] Minutes of Evidence, p. 935, or Report, p. 289.
[2] See § 32.
[3] Mining Association, Proof, Minutes of Evidence, p. 933.

normal play of competition between British producers acting on a situation where the aggregate demand (home and foreign) has fallen. If it cannot be explained as being caused by a peculiarly nasty form of competition at home it is ascribed to competition from foreign manufacturers enjoying cheaper facilities for production. And the price is determined by conditions abroad.

(3) Seldom is any attempt made to distinguish between the profitableness of an industry and its output (in relation to its normal output). It is reasoned, quite correctly, that a reduction of wages leads to an increase of output; but the false deduction is drawn that this means increased prosperity (from the point of view of the employer). It is true, as will be shown, that if the market is imperfect an increase of output does go hand-in-hand with some increase in profits (or, more often, a decrease in losses). But the confusion of thought that results in a failure to distinguish between effects on output and effects on profits is independent of any assumptions as to the nature of the market and would persist under the ideal conditions that are at present being specified.

This confusion extends very far, even into the political sphere. The Labour Party looks with horror upon any industry that is incurring losses to the capitalist class. Its members would support schemes of international control which, while reducing these losses, could only increase unemployment. The principle of derating, which primarily increases profits, is virtually accepted by them. And Mr Ramsay MacDonald attacks the coal subsidy because it resulted in lower prices – and so in less unemployment! 'If [the coal industry] is assisted, as in 1925, the assistance is wasted by international competition.'[1]

(4) Having evaluated the benefit that would accrue from a reduction of wages or from the maintenance of the present level of wages in the face of the workers' opposition, the employers have to measure it against the cost of forcing a reduction or of resisting the demand for an increase. The weapon, actual or potential, is the strike or the lock-out.

The cost of maintaining a firm in a condition in which it may be ready to produce as soon as the strike comes to an end is likely to be the fixed cost. The loss which a strike involves is therefore the prime profit that would otherwise be earned. But if our ideal industry is producing less than its capacity output, its prime profit is zero. A strike therefore costs it nothing: it loses the same amount anyway.

---

[1] House of Commons, July 2, 1929.

But that is not all. When the strike comes to an end, provided it has lasted a reasonable time, the industry will very probably be enabled for a certain period to work full-time and earn a prime profit.[1] In this way the same kind of benefit is attained as could be attained by a scheme of organised restriction of output, with the significant advantage that the blackleg is a less formidable obstacle. An attempt to induce the cotton industry to stop its mills in alternate weeks would be an abject failure. But a stoppage of several weeks, with the manifest purpose of reducing wages, is a huge success.

§ 17   It is however generally recognised that an export trade may suffer considerable harm of a persistent kind through loss of goodwill. It is said that during the coal strike of 1926 foreigners discovered for the first time that the pre-eminence of British coal was partly imaginary. Moreover strikes undermine confidence in the certainty of future delivery and, under the conditions of famine-like scarcity which they set up, foreign sellers can extort contracts extending for long periods into the future.

§ 18   (5) The last paragraph presupposes that there is some expectation of a return of prosperity, when profits will again be secured. And of course it is this expectation which prevents firms from going out of business in sufficient numbers to reduce the capacity of the industry to its actual output: if there were no such expectation there would be no problem of surplus capacity.

Its repercussion on the envisaged period of prosperity provides us at last with a really rational basis for the employers' insistence on a reduction of wages – at any rate in an export industry. Such a reduction leads to an increase in the output of the home industry and to a decrease in the output of its competitors abroad. The losses of the home industry are not reduced, unless its output now attains the capacity level; but if some of the foreign competitors have been enjoying cheaper facilities for production (for instance, lower wages) their profits may be reduced (or their losses increased). This in turn may react on the process of capital investment abroad. The result of the reduction in wages may therefore be that in the future foreign competition will be less severe than it otherwise would be. If then prosperity returns, the industry will be enabled to earn bigger profits.

This consideration should be of particular importance in industries,

---

[1] In Professor Pigou's phraseology, the net cost of a strike to the employers is then negative.

like those of cotton and coal, whose troubles, now at least, are due more to gradual expansion of productive capacity in other parts of the world which enjoy better facilities for production, than to a contraction in the aggregate world demand.

But the business man who is actuated by this motive has a corporate sense and a telescopic faculty which are rare in the coal and cotton industries.

(6) Again, when and if the industry is fully employed, it will be to the advantage of the employers to have wages as low as possible. By forcing a reduction or refusing an increase at a time when a strike costs the employers but little and when the resistance of the workers is already undermined by unemployment, the employers prepare the way for the advantage which a low wage level will secure to them at a time of subsequent prosperity.

IV   THE EFFECT OF FLUCTUATIONS IN THE IDEAL CASE

Before we leave this highly ideal industry with its ⌐-shaped supply schedule, it would be interesting to make use of it to obtain some indication of the effect of a fluctuating demand on the size of an industry. It may be noted that the assumption of the ⌐-shape is particularly appropriate in dealing with fluctuations of a somewhat short period, though long in relation to the period of production, about a fixed central position; for then the difficulties due both to closing down, temporarily or permanently, and to long-period changes are devoid of significance.

It will be supposed in the first place that the demand curve moves in a perfectly regular manner, for instance in simple harmonic motion, about its central position.[1] The industry is imagined to be of such a fixed size that normal profits are earned over the period of fluctuation.

So long as the amplitude of oscillation is insufficient to cause the demand curve to cut the horizontal portion of the supply curve, the output is always the same and the price oscillates in a regular manner. The size of the industry is the same as it would be if the demand remained constant at its mean level.

---

[1] If the horizontal motion of the demand curve is symmetrical about its central position, the vertical motion is not symmetrical unless the demand curve is a straight line. The curve can be assumed to be straight over the necessary range.

If however the amplitude is so large that in the course of a fluctuation the price falls to prime cost and the output is reduced, the fall of price is limited while there is no such limitation on its rise. For an industry of a given size the average profits are greater, the wider are the fluctuations of demand. And the actual size of the industry is greater than it would be if the demand curve remained fixed at its mean position. Such a position is the more likely to occur, and in a more intense degree, the greater are the fluctuations and the smaller is overhead cost in relation to the vertical amplitude of oscillation of the demand curve.

§ 22   So long as the fluctuations follow a well-determined course, it is natural to assume, as has just been done, that the size of an industry is adjusted so as to earn normal profits in the long run. The position may be an entirely different one when the fluctuations are haphazard and unexpected. As a result of lack of foresight and misguided optimism, there is a tendency for capital to flow into an industry at a time of boom to an extent that would only be appropriate if the conditions of demand were normal or subnormal.

The boom can, however, only react on the size of the industry if it lasts sufficiently long for appreciable expansion to occur. At the same time the depression must not be so protracted that the industry has time to contract. In other words the boom must last longer and the slump shorter than the short period. There is nothing incompatible in this. It is the shorter of Mr Robertson's two ends that obtrudes into the boom,[1] the longer one into the slump.

It is a well-known fact that in many industries the level of profits, averaged over a term of years, is abnormally low, and it is generally recognised that the deficiency is to be attributed to a fluctuating demand. Thus the late Sir Charles Macara ascertained that over a period of thirty years before the War the average return to the share capital of 100 cotton-spinning companies was $5\frac{1}{3}$ per cent (to the share and loan capital it was about $4\frac{1}{2}$ per cent).[2] The average return in coal-mining before the War has been estimated by Sir Josiah Stamp at the 'extraordinarily low' level of rather under 9 per cent.[3]

§ 23   The perniciousness of this effect would be very much greater if it were not for the accident to which allusion was made in the Introduction – the accident that we are living in a world of progress.

---

[1] See Chapter 1.
[2] Report of the Proceedings of the Provisional Emergency Cotton Committee, vol. III, p. 150.
[3] Report of Samuel Commission, p. 217.

A slump that is large relatively to an upward-moving trend may be small, in point both of magnitude and duration, relatively to the previous boom. The same degree of fluctuation in a more static state, such as the post-war period compared with the pre-war period, will result in a far more vicious presentation of the problem of surplus capacity. 'Methods which were well adapted to continually expanding business are ill adapted to stationary or declining industries . . . Combination in the business world . . . is the order of the day.'[1]

It appears then that if fluctuations are regular and fully discounted, the industry is larger (assuming that the price is driven down to prime cost in the course of a fluctuation) than would be the case if there were no fluctuations. If the fluctuations are not fully discounted, the industry is still larger and profits are subnormal.

It remains to consider the case of an industry in which fluctuations are potential rather than actual. A small slump in an inelastic demand will, as has been shown, send prices hurtling down to prime cost. In a 'static' state, as opposed to one of continuous expansion, such a small slump is by no means improbable. It would at first sight appear that the risk of such an occurrence will have to be covered by abnormal profits. 'People will not continue indefinitely to invest in industries whose profits are wiped out by cutthroat underbidding.'[2] This first impression is doubtless correct but it must be based on a more substantial foundation. For it is reasonable to suppose that a rise in the demand is as likely as a fall; and the price increases by as much through a rise in the demand as it decreases through an equal fall – or by more if the decrease is carried right down to prime cost. Here again the difference between the two ends of the short period is of great importance. When demand rises, the short period is at an end; capital flows in and the price falls again or fails altogether to rise. But when demand falls, capital cannot immediately, or indeed for some time, leave the industry; and the price remains depressed. Moreover the chance of a loss is not compensated for by an actuarially equal chance of a profit. It follows that where demand is likely to alter more capriciously than in the general run of industries, profits are abnormally high and the industry is smaller than it would be if there were no such expectation.

---

[1] J. M. Keynes on 'Liberalism and Industry' in *Liberal Points of View*.
[2] Taussig, *Principles of Economics*, vol. II, New York, Macmillan, p. 458.

V A LESS IDEAL CASE: PRIME COSTS NOT ALL EQUAL

§ 26   We now proceed to certain qualifications that must be applied to some of the argument of this chapter when the prime costs of the firms are not all equal. We still assume that the individual prime cost curves are of the ⅃-shape and that the prime cost curves represent the individual supply schedules (so that firms reduce their output to zero when their prime cost exceeds the price).[1]

§ 27   The shape of the supply schedule depends on the distribution of prime cost and on the correlation between the prime cost and the size of the individual firm. Each factor is best dealt with separately.

§ 28   First, therefore, let it be assumed that there is a uniform distribution of prime cost between the extreme limits Y_1 and Y_2; let there be a firm for every unit range of prime cost. Let $x = f(y)$ be the relation between the capacity output and the prime cost of the individual firms. Then the supply curve of the industry is given by:

$$x = \int_{Y_1}^{y} a f(y) \, dy, \text{ up to the point } y = Y_2$$

$$\therefore \frac{dx}{dy} = a f(y)$$

It follows that if there is a negative correlation between size and prime cost, the supply curve is concave upwards; if the correlation is positive, the supply curve is convex upwards.

§ 29   Next we suppose all the firms to have the same capacity output X. Let the distribution of prime cost be given by the law $n = F(y)$, where n is the number of firms per unit range of prime cost in the neighbourhood of the prime cost y. Then the supply curve of the industry is given by:

[1] The broadening of our assumptions paradoxically necessitates a further departure from reality. When the price is equal to its prime cost, the loss of a firm is the same whatever may be its output. But if the prime costs are all equal, the price is equal to the prime cost of every firm whenever the industry's output is below normal, and it is immaterial whether it is assumed that some firms produce their capacity outputs while others produce nothing or that all the firms work short-time (see footnote to Chapter 6, § 2).

$$x = \int_0^y X\, F(y)\, dy$$

$$\therefore\ \frac{dx}{dy} = X\, F(y)$$

$$\text{and}\ \frac{d^2x}{dy^2} = X\, F'(y)$$

It follows that the point of inflexion on the supply curve (shown

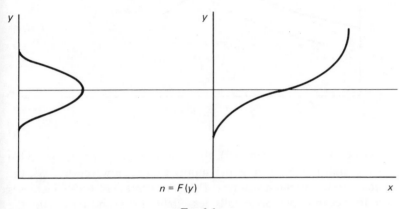

$$n = F(y)$$

FIG 6.1

on the right of Figure 6.1) lies on the value of the prime cost at which the firms are most closely concentrated (i.e. the mode of the distribution curve shown on the left.[1]

The effect of a lowering of prime costs on profits is best examined by the method of § 5 of Chapter 4. If the demand curve cuts the

---

[1] Precisely the same result is true of the longer period when total cost is substituted for prime cost. This is interesting in view of the results obtained by a group of American investigators. These indicate a tendency for the price to approximate to the 'bulk line cost', the point of inflexion on the cost curve when the curve 'breaks' away from the high values of cost. (See Taussig, *Quarterly Journal of Economics*, February 1919, p. 205 and Simpson, *Quarterly Journal of Economics*, February 1921, p. 264.) These American investigations require closer study. But, after a superficial view, the suggestion may be risked that they make use of cost curves that are relevant to the longer period and apply them to the short period.

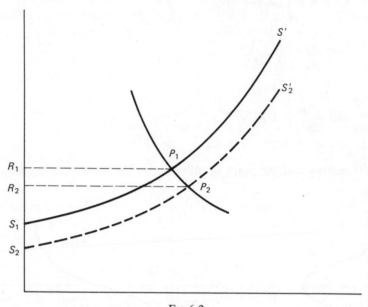

FIG 6.2

supply curve at P_1 (Figure 6.2), the aggregate prime profits are given by the area $R_1P_1S_1$. If now the supply curve is lowered to S_2S_2', the prime profits are increased to $R_2P_2S_2$. A decrease of wages increases profits because the price falls less than the prime cost. But the increase is small if the demand is rather inelastic or if the supply is rather elastic. The demand is often inelastic, and in a depressed industry the supply is usually elastic because the majority of the firms are comprised within a small range of prime cost (so that $F(y)$, in § 29 above, is very large in this range and therefore $\dfrac{dy}{dx}$ very small). Thus in the case of the spinning of American cotton – doubtless an extreme case – all but a small number of mills are said to have prime costs differing by no more than $\frac{1}{4}d$ per pound of output.

The rigour of the argument of Section III of this chapter must therefore be abated. But its necessity remains, because it is seldom recognised that the employers in a depressed industry can only gain from a reduction of wages, within the scope of the present bounds of our assumptions, in so far as there are inefficient firms which have hitherto been producing nothing and will now be enabled to produce.

Again on the basis of our present assumptions (outside which popular discussion on these matters seldom explicitly roams), cotton-mill and coal-mine owners can only benefit from lower wage-rates if at the same time the process of the survival of the fittest, to which they attach such hopes, is substantially impeded; if the reduction is insufficient to bring the inefficient units into the field of production, prices ought to fall by an equivalent amount. For reasons why they will not do so it is necessary to search elsewhere, along paths of whose existence the owners display no knowledge.

If now we proceed a stage further and admit the possibility of firms producing at a prime loss with the object of maintaining their connections, and for other reasons specified in § 7 of Chapter 2, the benefits of a reduction of wages in a depressed industry become yet a little more apparent. In such a state all firms with prime costs below the price work at their capacity level, while some of the others work short-time. A given rise in the price then results in a smaller increase of output than would be the case if all firms with prime costs greater than the price were producing nothing; for while the same firms are lifted from the prime loss to the prime profit category, the increase in their output is less. In other words the supply is less elastic. The fall in price due to a reduction of wages is less and the increase in profits or the reduction in losses, in the shape of an increase in prime profits, is greater; in addition there is a decrease of prime losses.

Finally we may revert to the argument so often heard (it was referred to in § 14 above) that the prices charged by the staple British exporting industries are set by manufacturers abroad whose costs of production are less. The exponents of this doctrine, for instance Mr Evan Williams of the Mining Association, make no such qualifications as would render it unfair to test it on the assumption of a home industry with a ⅃-shaped supply curve in competition with foreign firms each with individual ⅃-shaped supply curves. It is clear, moreover, that the world market is tacitly supposed to be perfect. Then if the home industry is producing less than its capacity output, the world price is equal to the British prime cost. All foreign firms whose prime costs are less than the British prime cost produce their capacity outputs. If no foreign firms have prime costs greater than the British prime cost, the foreign output cannot increase or diminish.[1]

---

[1] This, of course, is in the short period. The possibility of repercussions on the process of capital investment abroad was dealt with in § 18. They are only likely to be rapid when some of the foreign firms enjoy prime costs so much lower than the British level that they are earning normal profits. A rise in the world price may then

The foreign supply is perfectly inelastic, and therefore the foreign demand for British exports is not perfectly elastic even if they play but a small part in the world market. In fact instead of the price being fixed by our competitors whose 'costs of production are substantially lower than ours', as Mr Evan Williams suggested,[1] the price is actually equal to our own prime cost.

§ 33   Of course, it is obvious that in many industries foreign firms with lower prime costs than ours nevertheless produce less than their capacity outputs. In fact, it is just as necessary, or perhaps more necessary, to assume that the world market is imperfect as to make this saving assumption for the home market, and reasons for such imperfection are far more obvious. The fact that foreign competition is effective along a narrow fringe – in the case of coal the fringe is mainly geographical, in other cases it may be partly psychological – rather than over the whole area is a point on which Sir Herbert Samuel seized but which he was unable to bring within the apprehension of the representatives of the Mining Association.

---

be speedily prevented by an expansion of these firms. In other words, if the British prime cost rises, British exports will cease. This argument cannot be applied to exclude the possibility of a fall in the world price, unless the process of expansion abroad is going on in any case and would be retarded as soon as the price attempted to fall.

[1] See § 14.

CHAPTER 7

IMPERFECTION OF THE MARKET

I INTRODUCTORY

A large portion of this essay is concerned with the question of short-time working, a phenomenon of which the recent history of this country's staple industries supplies depressing but good illustrations. Much expert writing has been devoted to those depressed industries and Royal Commissions and Government Committees have enquired into them. But having accounted for the falling-off in demand the expert finds little more to interest him. If output must decrease, short-time is surely the obvious result; except indeed in so far as productive units are closed down. The principles of symmetry are then taken to indicate that such short-time as is necessary will, in the absence of reasons to the contrary, be divided equally among the various firms. There is generally a complete failure to recognise that the existence of short-time must often be incompatible with a state of perfect competition. Indeed the slump in prices is often itself ascribed to the prevalence of a peculiar and violent kind of competition, brought on by severe depression and despair (apparently quite different from, and much keener than, that kind of competition on which economists rely to secure the tendencies towards normal long-period equilibrium). The crucial question should usually be why prices are not even lower: the expert attempts to explain why they are not higher.

Having failed to receive satisfaction from the expert, the economist may be excused for turning to the business man, who is after all responsible for things as they are as opposed to things as they should be according to the economist's deductions. To ask the business man why he is working short-time requires considerable daring. Such a question coming from an economist is only too likely to confirm the business man in his opinion of economic theory. His answer may be delivered with every sign of contempt and yet its very obviousness probably conceals the clue to the puzzle. A firm works short-time, as every schoolboy might imagine, because it does not receive sufficient orders to keep it fully occupied. Behind this answer lies the implication that an increase in output could only be secured by such a reduction in price as would be unprofitable, assuming that it would not be prevented by any of the factors to be considered in later chapters. 'Business men, who regard themselves as being subject to competitive conditions, would consider absurd the assertion that the limit to their production is to be found in the internal conditions of production in their firms, which do not permit of the production of a greater quantity without an increase in cost.'[1] In other words, though conditions of polypoly may prevail, the market is not perfect. A finite increase in output (or rather in sales) cannot be secured by an infinitesimal reduction in price.

§ 2   Marshall makes it quite evident that the market is never perfect. 'Though monopoly and free competition are ideally wide apart, yet in practice they shade into one another by imperceptible degrees . . . there is an element of monopoly in nearly all competitive businesses.'[2] Stress, too, is laid by Marshall on the part played by imperfection in the market in preventing the indefinite expansion of firms that operate under conditions of individual decreasing cost.[3] But the impression one receives on reading the *Principles* is, I think, that imperfection of the market is one of many economic frictions whose 'peculiar features [should be left] to be analysed separately in special discussions, and . . . our normal illustration [should be taken] from a case in which the individual is only one of many who have efficient, if indirect, access to the market.'[4] Again:

> we cannot . . . regard the conditions of supply by an individual producer as typical of those which govern the general supply in the market. We must take account of the fact that very few firms have a long-continued life of active progress, and of the fact that the relations between the individual producer and this special market differ in important respects from those between the whole body of producers and the general market.[5]

The traditional treatment may be summed up in the words of Professor Sraffa:

---

[1] Sraffa, *Economic Journal*, December 1926, p. 534.
[2] *Industry and Trade*, p. 397.
[3] For instance, in his *Principles*, pp. 286 and 458.
[4] *Principles*, p. 849.
[5] Ibid, p. 459.

We are thus led to believe that when production is in the hands of a large number of concerns entirely independent of one another as regards control, the conclusions proper to competition may be applied even if the market in which the goods are exchanged is not absolutely perfect, for its imperfections are in general constituted by frictions which may simply retard or slightly modify the effects of the active forces of competition, but which the latter ultimately succeed in substantially overcoming. This view appears to be fundamentally inadmissable. Many of the obstacles which break up that unity of the market which is the essential condition of competition are not of the nature of 'frictions', but are themselves active forces which produce permanent and even cumulative effects. They are frequently, moreover, endowed with sufficient stability to enable them to be made the subject of analysis based on statical assumptions.[1]

A somewhat similar criticism of the traditional view was expressed by Professor H. L. Moore at a very much earlier date. He asks:

What is the nature of the limitation of the applicability of propositions deduced under the hypothesis of perfect competition? The almost invariable answer to this last question is that the imperfection of competition is simply a form of friction, producing for the most part, a negligible variation from the standards that prevail in a régime of perfect competition.[2]

The credit for introducing the conception of imperfection in the market into the corpus of the classical theory of value is largely due to Professor Sraffa.[3] The idea has recently received further application at the hands of Professor Hotelling.[4] Professor Sraffa in his article is mainly concerned with the long period, and with the dilemma of increasing returns.

It is clear, however, that his methods are of even greater significance in the case of the short period, and it is with their application to the short period that we are mainly concerned. It may, however, be suggested in passing that imperfection of the market must in some

---

[1] Sraffa, *Economic Journal*, December 1926, p. 542.
[2] *Quarterly Journal of Economics*, February 1906, p. 211.
[3] *Economic Journal*, December 1926.
[4] *Economic Journal*, March 1929.

cases itself be regarded as a short-period phenomenon, but that like other short-period factors it has long-period repercussions.

II EFFECTS IN THE SHORT PERIOD

§ 3   The modifications that are introduced into the theory of short-period polypoly when imperfection is ascribed to the market are sufficiently obvious in a general sort of way. Price and marginal prime cost are no longer necessarily equal. Rather is the product of output and the difference between price and average prime cost a maximum: output is determined by the ordinary principles of monopoly applied to the individual demand curve and the average prime cost curve.

The result is that the output of an industry is less, and the price is greater, than would be the case if the market were more perfect. Moreover profits are greater. Professor Hotelling gives the impression that he regards that element of profits which is due to the imperfection of the market as being something quite additional to the profits that enter into ordinary long-period cost of production. He refers to 'the existence of incomes not properly belonging to any of the categories usually discussed'.[1] But of course abnormal profits are not possible in the long-period so long as there is free entry into an industry.[2] Imperfection of the market operates on price and output in the long period through its effect on the number and size of the firms comprising the industry. It is true, as Professor Sraffa points out,[3] that the entry of new firms is likely to be difficult or impossible into an industry whose market is very imperfect. But the abnormal profits that result should be ascribed to their direct cause; they are in every way comparable to those earned in a polypolistic industry where the market is perfect but where the entry of new firms is restricted in one way or another.

The essence of imperfection lies not in the fact that it promotes abnormal profits, but in the fact that a reduction of the amount of imperfection causes – in the short run at any rate – a fall in price and in profits.[4]

[1] *Economic Journal*, March 1929, p. 41.
[2] But, as Professor Sraffa has pointed out to me, the effect of imperfection over the whole, or an appreciable part, of the field of industry is to raise the level of normal profits; because entrepreneurs constitute a limited class.
[3] *Economic Journal*, December 1926, p. 549.
[4] This statement involves the conflict with Professor Sraffa which is discussed in § 15, etc., below.

The short-period effects of a slight degree of imperfection in the market can easily be seen to be very small so long as an industry is working under fairly normal conditions. This statement means that an alteration of the degree of imperfection would have but little immediate reaction on such an industry. It does not mean that imperfection is unimportant in the determination of the number and size of the firms in an industry, and so of the long-period price.

If the marginal prime cost curve is rising very steeply, as it is likely to be doing for a firm working under normal full-time conditions; if the individual demand curve cuts it at a point well above the average prime cost curve, as is the case under normal conditions for an industry in which overhead costs are a large part of total costs; and if the individual demand curve is highly elastic, as when imperfection in the market is slight; then the values of the price (and output) determined by maximising the monopoly revenue are not much higher (and lower) than those determined by the intersection of the demand and marginal prime cost curves. In the special case of ⌐-shaped prime cost curves the difference is likely, as will be shown later, to vanish altogether.[1]

It is however just when the theory of perfect competition appears to break down, namely during a period of slump, that a slight degree of imperfection may have very far-reaching effects. Short-time working is no longer the mystery that it was before.[2] Moreover, as will shortly appear, the closer price is to average prime cost, the greater is the significance of a given degree of imperfection.

In those cases where the degree of imperfection is fairly substantial it is possible to explain why competition is not more cataclysmic in its effect upon price that is actually observed to be the case. A substantial improvement in the perfection of the market, while of little consequence to a prosperous industry, would often be devastating in its effects on a depressed industry. It is in such a case that it is possible to ascribe the fullest significance to the general import of Professor Hotelling's dictum: 'These particular merchants would do well, instead of organising improvement clubs and booster associations to better the roads, to make transportation as difficult as possible.[3]

---

[1] See Chapter 8, § 3.
[2] See Chapter 5, § 25.
[3] *Economic Journal*, March 1929.

III SPECIALITIES AND STANDARDISATION

§ 5   This beneficial influence of imperfection of the market in restraining competition from exerting its full effect in times of depression has an interesting bearing on the modern tendency of manufacturers to concentrate on specialities, or alternatively to try to imbue their goods with some of the psychological attributes of specialities. To quote an American writer, Mr Spurgeon Bell, 'Merchants and manufacturers, especially those whose fixed expenses are large, prefer specialities.'[1] In the same article Mr Bell mentions that when Dodge Bros desired to set up in competition with Mr Ford they designed their model, not as a direct rival to a particular Ford model, but so as to fill a price gap that had been left open. In the same way Mr Bell accounts for the continually shifting varieties of dresses and shoes.

This tendency is in direct opposition to the one enunciated by Professor Hotelling, who shows that the expectation of profit of a firm about to set up in an industry increases as the position it chooses, in regard both to site and to the quality and variety of its product, approaches nearer to that of some firm already settled down in the industry (the argument depends upon the assumption that the aggregate demand is fairly inelastic). 'Methodist and Presbyterian churches are too much alike; cider is too homogeneous.'[2] It is clear that actual practice represents a compromise between the tendencies propounded by Professor Hotelling and Mr Bell. When the conditions of demand in relation to supply are likely to be fairly stable, the former may be expected to preponderate; when the possibility of an occasional slump has to be reckoned with, the latter tendency is more likely to be decisive.

§ 6   Neither of these two arguments takes into account the substantial economies, both of production and of consumption, that result from the standardisation of the products of certain types of industries. Such standardisation appears to constitute an important element of the somewhat mysterious processes covered by the word 'rationalisation'.

---

[1] *Quarterly Journal of Economics*, May 1918, p. 507. Presumably what is meant is that there is a greater preference for specialities in *those industries* where overhead costs are high, not by those manufacturers in *a given industry* whose overhead costs are higher than those of their competitors. It is the general level of overhead costs in the industry, not the particular level in an individual firm, that determines the seriousness of a slump.

[2] *Economic Journal*, March 1929, p. 57.

One of the main features of rationalisation is said to be that its progress in an industry depends on a considerable degree of cooperation between the separate firms. Now it would be reasonable to imagine that this cooperation is required in order to raise prices sufficiently to facilitate and justify the investment of new capital in improved methods of production. But that rationalisation is a cloak for any form of monopolistic action is strenuously denied by many of its apostles. If this denial is accepted, it becomes necessary to discover why cooperation is essential to effect those improvements in production which the word rationalisation represents. It is not easy to see why most of them should be at all dependent on cooperation; but the one outstanding exception is standardisation. This type of improvement can clearly be introduced only by some form of cooperative effort (failing the intervention of an outside party, such as the government). In this respect rationalisation must weigh down the scales heavily against imperfection of the market. It may be true that the process, while demanding cooperation, involves no element of monopoly. It is equally true that its completion may, by perfecting the market, produce a state of affairs in which some degree of monopolistic combination is the only alternative to suicide.

IV   SIMPLIFYING ASSUMPTIONS

A more detailed examination of the subject of these chapters necessitates a more precise examination of the conditions that are being assumed. Imperfection of the market is essentially complex, both in itself and in its effects; so far as possible the complications will be eliminated from our treatment at the stage to which it has so far advanced.

A producer who desires to increase his output is generally confronted with two alternatives, which are not mutually exclusive. He can reduce his price or he can increase his selling and advertising expenses. To avoid complication it will be assumed that the former alternative is the only one that arises. Selling and advertising expenses are to be regarded as completely determined, being unambiguously dependent on the output. I understand from Professor Sraffa that when these expenses are *de facto*, if not *de jure*, a necessary adjunct to the process of production, both qualitatively and quantitatively, he would not regard them as marketing expenses at all. We are entitled therefore, on our special assumption, to disregard his objection that the inclusion of *marketing* expenses in costs of production renders the expression 'cost of production' 'dependent upon elements quite extraneous to the conditions under which the production of a given undertaking takes place'.[1] And at the same time, of course, it is possible to regard the individual demand curve as a definite independent entity, since we get round Professor Sraffa's plea that changes in marketing expenses should be conceived as shifting the demand curve.[2]

§ 9   One further simplifying assumption is necessary. It is to be supposed that the whole output of any firm is disposed of at a uniform price. It is clear that imperfection in the market provides a basis for discrimination. But this is a complication that must be deferred.

V   PREFERENCE AND TRANSPORT IMPERFECTION

§ 10   Imperfection in any market is due to two groups of causes, entirely different in their constitution but, subject to certain reservations, very similar in their effects. It may be caused by an absence of indifference among buyers between the products of different firms; or it may reside in the fact that greater freight charges have to be incurred on each additional unit of output if the circle of a firm's customers is widened. These two classes of imperfection will be referred to as 'preference imperfection' and 'transport imperfection'.

§ 11   It is at once obvious that transport imperfection cannot be the sole factor operating in restraint of a firm's output if part of it is being sent to the same point as the products of a large number of other firms. For then an infinitesimal reduction of price will result in a finite diversion of the flow at this point from the outputs of the other firms to the output of this firm. This restriction covers a multitude of possibilities. It covers in the first place the case where the particular firm is situated close to a large number of competing firms. It covers also the case where the particular firm supplies even a single consumer living in the midst of a body of consumers who buy from a large number of competing firms. But it also covers the case where part of the output of the particular firm passes through the same port or

---

[1] *Economic Journal*, December 1926, p. 544.

[2] Ibid, p. 543. Having urged these points, Professor Sraffa seems to base the further development of his article on the same implicit assumption as is here postulated; or, what comes to much the same thing, on the assumption that there are no selling and advertising expenses at all.

other centre of distribution as the products of a large number of competing firms.[1] Thus it is only possible for transport imperfection to exist by itself when no part of a firm's output is being sold under polypolistic conditions. This is likely to be the case for communities of such a nature that transport costs are heavy and producers are sparsely scattered among a widely distributed body of consumers.

But it does not follow that transport imperfection need be considered only in dealing with this rather special type of commodity. For as soon as preference imperfection is introduced, polypoly no longer exists in its simplest form; the transport imperfection may be provided with a basis. The reason can easily be seen. A reduction in its price increases the output of a firm in two ways. The first way is due to a diversion away from firms with which it was already before the reduction in price in effective competition; while the second way is due to a territorial expansion of the market within which it is possible for it to sell its product. Now if preference imperfection is very small, the magnitude of the first effect is very large compared with that of the second. But if there is a moderate degree of preference imperfection, the two effects may be comparable in magnitude. In fact a curious situation is possible in which the transport imperfection is greater than the preference imperfection, on whose presence its own existence depends.

It might also appear that preference imperfection is in part dependent upon the existence of transport imperfection. This is particularly the case when it is due to ignorance or apathy on the part of buyers rather than to their division into separate clienteles. For then the amount of preference imperfection depends not only on the nature of the market but on its size. When the owner of a coal-mine reduces his price, the effect on his output depends not only on the probability that the reduction can be brought home to any particular potential customer but also on the number of such potential customers in existence. Now if the cost of transporting coal

---

[1] This statement requires some qualification. It depends on the assumption that the difference between the cost of transport from C to D and from C to B (via X) is equal to that from A to D (via X) and from A to B. This is obviously not necessarily the case if the cost of handling at X depends on the route (as, for instance, if AB is a canal and CD a railway).

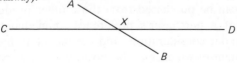

were inappreciable, the whole world would be open to him, and a small reduction in price might be attended with a large increase in demand. But, owing to the cost of transport, the radius of his circle of operations is limited and the number of new customers he is likely to obtain is smaller. In such a case if there were no transport imperfection (because there were no transport costs), there would be no preference imperfection. We have already seen that if there is no preference imperfection, there is likely to be no transport imperfection. Actual imperfection must often depend on the coexistence, in undefinable proportions, of both preference and transport imperfection.

But the symmetry of this argument is unduly forced. It is true that transport imperfection can only exist in the presence of preference imperfection. But, in the particular case just alluded to, the factor that directly determines the existence of preference imperfection is not transport imperfection, but the cost of transport, which itself determines transport imperfection. Moreover it is, so to speak, the marginal cost of transport on which transport imperfection depends while the size of the market, and so preference imperfection in our particular case, is determined by the average cost of transport.

VI   THE SIMPLEST KIND OF PREFERENCE IMPERFECTION

§ 14   The causes that underlie preference imperfection are many and varied. It will be convenient at this stage to assume the state of affairs that is most amenable to theoretical treatment. In this state preference imperfection, both in origin and in consequences, is entirely analogous with transport imperfection. Indeed Professor Hotelling bases his general conclusions on a mathematical study of the effects of transport imperfection in a particular case of duopoly. It is clear, too, that Professor Sraffa's treatment is based on the same underlying assumptions:

> Two elements enter into the composition of such demand prices [constituting the individual demand schedule] – the price at which the goods can be purchased from those other producers who, in the order of a purchaser's preference, immediately follow the producer under consideration, and the monetary measure of the value (a quantity which may be positive or negative) which the

purchaser puts on his preference for the products of the firm in question.[1]

In the case of pure transport imperfection the monetary measure of a purchaser's preference between the products of two prices is the difference of the costs of transport. It is assumed that preference imperfection can be represented by the same kind of stereotyped system of preferences as is set up by transport charges. The preferences may depend on something real or on something imaginary; but they are assumed to be stable. They may vary from one purchaser to another, just as do those preferences that are caused by the costs of transport. But for any given customer they are assumed to be constant within the period we are considering. Not only are they assumed to remain constant when everything else remains constant, but they are assumed to remain constant during and after changes in the other factors (in particular in the prices and outputs of the separate firms). It follows then that, when the price of each separate firm has been fixed, the individual demand schedule and the output of every firm is perfectly determinate. If now the price charged by a single firm is raised, its output will decrease and the outputs of the other firms will alter (they will almost certainly increase). But if the price is once again restored to its former level, the output of this and of every other firm will be the same as it was before the change. It is for the present assumed that a purchaser's system of preferences is not altered after he has been induced, by price alterations, to change his custom from one firm to another; his relative preference for the product of the former firm does not decrease and that for the product of the latter firm, of which he now becomes a customer, does not increase.

This is the short period. The possibility of long-period variations is not however ruled out. Indeed it appears reasonable to suppose that there generally exists among the whole body of purchasers a bias towards a preference for the old-established firms.

VII PROFESSOR SRAFFA ON THE PRICE ATTAINED IN AN IMPERFECT MARKET

If the price charged by one or more firms is increased, the demand

---

[1] Sraffa, *Economic Journal*, December 1926, p. 547.

curves of the other firms are raised. In general, the effect of raising the demand curve of a firm that is maximising its profits is to induce it to raise its own price in its turn.[1] This again makes it profitable for other firms to raise their prices. Upon this cumulative snowball effect Professor Sraffa bases his assertion that for an industry consisting of firms which are all similar and similarly situated the final position of equilibrium is the same as would be arrived at if the whole industry were controlled by a single monopolist.[2] Provided only that the market is in some degree imperfect, however minutely, the magnitude of the imperfection is, according to this proposition, irrelevant.

If Professor Sraffa's assertion is well-founded, it lands us in perhaps a greater difficulty than that from which the imperfection of the market has rescued us. Professor Sraffa is discussing the long period, but his arguments apply with equal or greater force to the short period. And though the complete case is that in which the firms are all similar, the general tendency towards maximum monopoly profits must be fairly effective in those ordinary cases in which individual variations are not very great. It would then follow that in any industry, provided the market is in the slightest degree imperfect, combination could exert but little influence in increasing profits in the short period. Still less could any uniform scheme of restriction of output increase the profits of all the firms. A completely *laissez-faire* policy would thus be completely justified. But this is altogether opposed to experience. Few would deny that our depressed industries benefit from those schemes of cooperative restriction that have been successful and that the others would benefit if their schemes had been successful. Moreover the idea that the state of equilibrium is

---

[1] It is on the assumption that the slope of the individual demand curve remains unchanged that we obtain Professor Sraffa's conclusion that the 'alternative', i.e. a position in which raising a firm's demand curve causes it to lower its price, 'involves great elasticity in the demand for the products of an individual business and rapidly diminishing costs for it'. (*Economic Journal*, December 1926, p. 547.) In fact, if A is the angle of slope of the individual demand curve and B that of the average cost curve (assumed to be positive in the case of decreasing costs), it involves the assumption that $\tan A$ is less than $2\tan B$. It therefore becomes quite impossible if costs are constant or increasing.

But, of course, the slope of the individual demand curve may alter. It will be seen in Section I of Chapter 9 that in what is called case A, the slope becomes a little greater when the demand curve is raised; and a fall in price is then still more unlikely. But when, in case B, the aggregate demand is more inelastic than the aggregate supply, the slope becomes less as the curve is raised; and then a fall in price is somewhat more likely to result.

[2] Sraffa, *Economic Journal*, December 1926, p. 549.

independent of the degree of imperfection in the market is opposed to common sense.

6   Professor Hotelling worked out mathematically a special case (in which demand is perfectly inelastic) of the effect of transport imperfection on duopoly. His conclusion would be that both the excess of the price over prime cost[1] – production is in effect assumed to take place under conditions of constant prime cost[2] – and the magnitude of the prime profit[3] are proportional to the cost of transport per unit distance. (For this unit cost of transport it would be necessary in the case of preference imperfection to substitute the rate of change of the money measures of individual preferences as we proceed through the market.) This is in direct contradiction to Professor Sraffa's theory, but Professor Hotelling failed to note the conflict.

7   The flaw in Professor Sraffa's reasoning is easily detected by taking the case of perfectly inelastic demand. In this case he would expect the process of *tâtonnement* to continue indefinitely until the price becomes infinite, as it would be under a monopolistic régime. On the same principle Achilles would never pass the Tortoise. It is true that each time a firm raises its price it induces the other firms to raise their prices. But the successive rises become smaller and smaller, and though they may be infinite in number their sum is not infinity.

VIII ASSUMPTIONS UNDERLYING THE INDIVIDUAL DEMAND CURVE

8   We are, however, advancing ahead of our assumptions. The ground is more broken than a first view would suggest, and a more detailed plan of approach is desirable. The mathematical bludgeon is being kept in reserve to strike the final blow at Professor Sraffa's conclusions;[4] but before it can be brought into play, it is necessary to grapple with a difficulty that is fundamental, not only to the present issue, but to the whole theory of economic equilibrium – at any rate in an imperfect market. It is a difficulty that has, I think, been overlooked by Professor Hotelling and by Professor Sraffa himself.

[1] *Economic Journal*, March 1929, p. 46.
[2] Ibid, p. 51.
[3] *Economic Journal*, March 1929, p. 50. Professor Hotelling does not of course make use of the term prime profit, nor of the term prime cost.
[4] I may, perhaps, be allowed to say that Professor Sraffa has admitted, subject to a possible reservation, the force of my objection to his argument.

Indeed, it is slurred over by most economic writers. I failed to face the difficulty in an earlier draft of this dissertation, and it is Professor Pigou who pointed out to me its essential importance and the necessity for grappling with it. It is a difficulty that constitutes the logical basis – though this is seldom recognised – of a controversy which originated in 1838, when Cournot published his *Principes Mathématiques*, and which is apparently still raging.

§ 19   Cournot, as is well-known, examined the case of two sellers competing in a perfect market.[1] Differentiating the profit of each with regard to his output, while regarding the output of the other as a constant, and equating the two differential coefficients to zero, Cournot came to the conclusion that there was a point of stable equilibrium: the equilibrium price was below the monopoly price but above the marginal cost of production. Against this conclusion Bertrand, forty-five years later, advanced an '*objection péremptoire*'. '*La baisse*', he wrote, '*n*' *aurait pas de limite; quel que soit en effet le prix commun adopté, si l'un des concurrents abaisse seul le sien, il attire à lui . . . la totalité de la vente.*'[2] The view that 'Cournot's conclusion has been shown to be erroneous by Bertrand'[3] has been current ever since. Cournot's conclusion is attributed to a *singulière inadvertance*':[4] 'only by the use of the quantities as independent variables instead of the prices is the fallacy concealed.'[5] Bertrand's verdict deserves to be quoted in full:

> *Si les formules de Cournot masquent ce résultat évident, c'est que, par une singulière inadvertance, il y introduit, sous le nom de D et D', les quantités vendues par les deux concurrents, et que, les traitant des variables indépendantes, il suppose que, l'une venant à changer par la volonté de l'un des propriétaires, l'autre pourra rester constante. Le contraire est de toute évidence.*[6]

The price must inevitably be forced down – such has been the common view – until, in the simplest case of constant returns, it reaches the limit provided by the cost of production.

§ 20   It is only quite recently that Wicksell pointed out, in one of his

---

[1] Cournot, *Principes Mathématiques*, p. 88.
[2] Bertrand, *Journal des Savants*, 1883, p. 503.
[3] Edgeworth, *Collected Papers*, vol. I, p. 117.
[4] Bertrand, *Journal des Savants*.
[5] Hotelling, *Economic Journal*, March 1929, p. 43.
[6] Bertrand, *Journal des Savants*.

last contributions to economic thought, that so far from being inevitable, the conclusion which was first set out by Bertrand and has since been upheld by Edgeworth and almost every economist – Professor Amoroso being a notable exception – depended on a very definite assumption; and that, in fact, if a different, but kindred, assumption is made, then Cournot's conclusion is correct and Bertrand's criticism fails. Of the two assumptions, Wicksell, indeed, preferred the second one, and he consequently upheld the cause of Cournot. This predilection we shall shortly have cause to criticise. But, for the moment, the important point is that there are two different assumptions (neither of which, we shall suggest later, can be regarded as altogether tenable.)

Their nature, is, in fact, quite obvious. Cournot's conclusion depends on the supposition that each seller, in trying to maximise his profits, imagines that the other will maintain his output unchanged.[1] On the other hand, the Bertrand–Edgeworth criticism and solution is justified, and only justified, if each imagines that the other will maintain his price unchanged.[2]

Whether Cournot was actually conscious of the underlying assumption on which his treatment depends is more doubtful. It is true that he states quite definitely that *'le propriétaire (1) ne peut pas influer directement sur la fixation de D_2: tout ce qu'il peut faire, c'est, lorsque D_2 est fixé par le propriétaire (2), de choisir pour D_1 la valeur qui lui convient le mieux.'*[3] But it seems more probable that this statement represents the assertion of an apparent inevitability than of an assumption which has still to be justified. Perhaps, after all, it was merely as a matter of convenience that Cournot used 'the quantities as independent variables instead of the prices'; for *'il*

---

[1] *'in der Annahme, dasz des andere sein Angebot nicht ändern werde,'* Wicksell, *Archiv für Sozialwissenschaft*, 1927, vol. 58, p. 270.

[2] *'dasz des andere [seinen Preis] beibehalten werde'* – Wicksell, *Archiv für Sozialwissenschaft*, 1927, vol. 58, p. 272. It is distinctly unfortunate that, in introducing to English readers 'one of the last of the many services Knut Wicksell has rendered to science' (Schumpeter, *Economic Journal*, September 1928, p. 369) Professor Schumpeter should have done so in a manner that renders Wicksell's argument, not only unintelligible, but ridiculous. After reproducing Wicksell's method of arriving at Cournot's result, with a very vague and half-hearted reference to the assumption on which it is based, Professor Schumpeter makes the amazing statement that 'it cannot be objected that neither of the two competitors is justified to assume, in deciding on how to adjust his output, that the other will stick to *his*. For no such assumption is really involved' (*Economic Journal*, September 1928, p. 370). It is difficult to conceive a more complete misunderstanding of the nature of Wicksell's argument, in the attempted interpretation of which this sentence constitutes an important element.

[3] Cournot, *Principes Mathématiques*, p. 89.

nous sera commode', he wrote, *'d'employer ici la notation inverse
p = f(D)'*.[1]

§ 22   In any case, the point to notice is that it has been usual for
economists to adopt the point of view of Bertrand and Edgeworth
without giving any indication that a different point of view is, at least,
a possibility that has to be reckoned with. Thus Professor Hotelling
declares quite categorically that 'each competitor adjusts his price so
that, with the existing value of the other price, his own profit will be
a maximum';[2] and it is clear that Professor Sraffa has the same
assumption tacitly in mind. But at least one mathematical economist
allows the assumption of the Cournot case – that it is the output of
the rest of the industry that is supposed to remain constant when a
single firm alters its price – to creep into his analysis. It creeps in,
however, quite unnoticed and the writer does not so much as pause
a moment, before differentiating, to point out that an assumption
has been made.[3] The necessity for basing the treatment of these
questions in further data must have been clear to Pareto when he
wrote, to quote from his French translator: *'L'économie pure . . . a
répondu tout ce qu'elle pouvait nous dire. C'est à l'observation des
faits de nous apprendre le reste.'*[4] But this necessity has since been
forgotten.

This matters less than at first appears. Provided the market is
perfect, Cournot's position of equilibrium moves nearer and nearer
to that of Bertrand and Edgeworth as the number of sellers increases.[5]
But if the market is not perfect, the distinction is fundamental even
in the case of polypoly. An individual demand curve can be drawn
for each seller to indicate what he imagines to be the relation between
his price and his output, and the position of equilibrium depends on
the slopes of these individual demand curves. These in their turn
depend on the particular assumptions that are in the minds of the
individuals when they draw up their demand curves. We have so far
set out, but have not discussed, two possible assumptions.

§ 23   Before we proceed any further, a slight digression may, perhaps,
be permitted to discuss the kind of indeterminateness that has been
shown to exist by Edgeworth in the case of duopoly, and, by

---

[1] Ibid, p. 89.
[2] Hotelling, *Economic Journal*, March 1929, p. 46.
[3] I refer to an article by C. F. Roos on 'The Mathematical Theory of Competition',
American Journal of Mathematics, vol. 47, 1925, p. 163.
[4] *Manuel d'Economie Politique*, p. 601.
[5] See Cournot, *Principes Mathématiques*, p. 101.

inference (to a steadily decreasing extent) in the case of monopolistic competition (or oligopoly). The indeterminateness is usually supposed to be a necessary consequence of Edgeworth's analysis. It is in this respect that Professor Schumpeter takes up the cause of Cournot and 'with reluctance contradicts the great shade of Edgeworth'.[1] 'Edgeworth . . . in an elaborate critique' writes Professor Pigou, 'maintains that the quantity is indeterminate. This latter view is now accepted by mathematical economists.'[2] Professor Pigou elucidates the matter thus:

> The quantity [of resources] employed by each – depends on his judgement of the policy which the other will pursue, and this judgement may be anything, according to the mood of each and his expectation of success from a policy of bluff. As in a game of chess, each player's move is related to his reading of the psychology of his opponent and his guess as to that opponent's reply.'[3]

Now, undoubtedly, indeterminateness can arise in the manner described by Professor Pigou. But Edgeworth, so far as I have been able to discover, clings throughout to the supposition that one man, when he changes his price, *assumes that the other man will keep his price unchanged*. Indeterminateness then arises when, and only to the extent to which, the individual producers are subject to diminishing returns. In 'the case in which the cost follows the law of diminishing returns' wrote Edgeworth, 'there will be an indeterminate tract through which the index of value will oscillate, or rather will vibrate irregularly for an indefinite length of time.'[4]

The reason is that when A's output is so great as to equate his marginal cost to the price that he is charging, B is able, since A's output cannot increase if his price does not change, to raise his price above A's price. If A's price is below a certain 'critical price', it pays B to raise his price, but if A's price is above this 'critical price', it pays B slightly to undercut A's price. And vice versa.

At first sight, then, this 'critical price' is a point of stable equilibrium. For, as soon as A falls below it, B rises above it. Then A will rise to a price which is just under B's. But A is now above the 'critical price'.

[1] Schumpeter, *Economic Journal*, September 1928, p. 367.
[2] *Economics of Welfare*, 3rd edition, p. 267.
[3] Pigou, *Economics of Welfare*, p. 268.
[4] *Collected Papers*, vol. I, London, Macmillan, 1925, p. 118.

It therefore pays B to undercut A; and so we revert to the 'critical price'.

But Professor Sraffa has pointed out to me that this view is a false one. It is only correct if changes of price cannot, for some reason or other, be undertaken discontinuously. If discontinuous changes are feasible, then as soon as A's price falls below the 'critical price', B raises his price to a finite level above the 'critical price' (say to the 'upper price'). A then raises his price to a level that is just under this 'upper price'.[1] B now undercuts A, and A in his turn undercuts B, and so on, until the 'critical price' is reached once more. Either A or B now makes a discontinuous jump up to the 'upper price', and the whole process starts all over again. The range of oscillation is between the 'critical price' and the 'upper price'. The upward part of the movement is discontinuous and instantaneous, while the downward part is a continuous process of alternate and mutual price-cutting.[2]

The oscillations will continue for ever. But this is only on the assumption that each seller, when he alters his price, fondly imagines that the other will maintain his price at the former level. Such a delusion is unlikely to persist for very long, and the indeterminateness will then be of the type referred to by Professor Pigou rather than of the type considered by Edgeworth.

§ 24   It is time, now, to try to gain a somewhat more realistic view of the nature of the assumptions that are in the mind of the business man when he maximises his profits. The question is not what actually happens when a firm alters its price but what the owner of the firm imagines is likely to happen. So far we have considered two possible cases. We shall describe as the first case that in which the conclusions of Bertrand and Edgeworth are justified: each firm imagines that if it alters its price, the prices charged by all the other firms will remain unaltered. The second case is Cournot's case: the outputs of the other firms are imagined to be constant. And, finally, we group under a third case all the complex possibilities that emerge when the business man realises that neither the outputs nor the prices of his competitors will remain constant if he alters his own price.

---

[1] In the simple case discussed by Edgeworth on p. 118 of vol. I of his *Collected Papers*, the 'upper price' is equal to the monopoly revenue price. This can easily be proved, though I do not think that Edgeworth really supplies a proof.

[2] For Edgeworth's account, see his *Collected Papers*, vol. I, pp. 118–20 and *Economic Journal*, September 1922, pp. 403–5. I venture to suggest that by means of the above conception of a 'critical price', which is, I think, implicit in Edgeworth's treatment, the solution can be obtained in a more satisfactory shape.

The first case is the one that is commonly discussed. Certain reasons can be advanced in its favour. In the first place, there are many industries in which firms fix their prices over long periods of time and alter them, at rare intervals, only in response to very appreciable impulses: smaller impulses fail to overcome the prevailing frictions. In such an industry a business man is entitled to believe that a small change in his own price will fail to react on the prices charged by his competitors.

But even when prices are fairly responsive, there will be a certain time lag between the inauguration of a change by a single firm and the completion of its repercussions on the other firms. The policy of a firm then depends on the extent of the time lag and the relation between its desire for immediate profits and its desire for profits in the more distant future. Thus Professor Hotelling, after describing how, in his type of duopoly, equilibrium may be attained on the basis of our third case (described in the last subsection) goes on to say:

> Let one of these business men, say B, find himself suddenly, in need of cash. Immediately at hand he will have a resource. Let him lower his price a little, increasing his sales. His profits will be larger until A decides to stop sacrificing his business and lowers his price to the point of maximum profit.[1]

But it is clear that great importance cannot be attached to this factor: it is probably overemphasised by Professor Hotelling.

Third, there is the most important reason of all. When a firm has a large number of competitors, the repercussion on each of them of a change in its own price will be small. The aggregate effect of a large number of such small repercussions may, indeed, be substantial. But that is a subtlety that is likely to elude the ordinary business man. He may realise that if he alters his own price, the prices charged by his competitors will alter. They will, however, alter only by small amounts; and the business man may well imagine that these small changes can be neglected.

But it is the method of trial and error that must in many cases determine the business man's conception of his individual demand curve. Full allowance would then appear to be made for the repercussions on other firms, and the case would conform to the type that we are describing as the third.

[1] Hotelling, *Economic Journal*, March 1929, p. 48.

This is true provided that a sufficient time interval is allowed to elapse: the rest of the industry must be given an opportunity of adjusting itself to the new conditions. But actually such economic experiments are rarely carried out over the period of time that is essential. Patience is usually lacking, and external factors are constantly changing. A demand curve that is based on experiment is, therefore, unlikely to adhere completely to the conditions of our third case. Whether it is closer to the first case or to the second case depends on the nature of the industry. If prices constitute the inflexible element, then the views of Bertrand and Edgeworth – and the assumption of the first case – are to some extent justified. But in many industries it is the level of output that fails to adjust itself rapidly: particularly is this the case when the period of production is long. The assumption on which Cournot's conclusions are based (i.e. the assumption of the second case), though it appears very ridiculous at first sight, then receives a certain degree of support. This suggestion I owe to Professor Sraffa.

§ 27   But it is on a different foundation that Wicksell based his support of Cournot. He did not discuss the absurdity of the Cournot assumption. It was the absurdity of the other assumption – the Bertrand–Edgeworth assumption of our second case – that decided his attitude. *'Dann wäre es ja sinnlos'*, he wrote, *'wenn der eine Monopolist seinen Preis in der Erwartung herabsetzte, dasz der andere den seinen beibehalten werde.'*[1] But this is not an argument in favour of the second case as against the first: it is rather an argument in favour of the third and against both the first and second cases.

§ 28   If the market is quite perfect, it is somewhat difficult to visualise the third case. The difficulty is due to the element of discontinuity that is inherent in complete perfection: if a single firm raises its price slightly, its output drops to zero. Thus, to take first the case of duopoly, it is true that if *A* raises his price, *B* will find it advantageous to raise his. But *A* will not for that reason find himself any better off: *B* will make sure that his price remains below *A*'s, and *A*'s output will still remain at a zero level. (We are supposing that the price is so high that diminishing returns, if present, are irrelevant.) If there is any solution at all, it is that of Professor Schumpeter: 'They cannot very well fail to realise their situation. But then it follows that they will hit upon, and adhere to, the price which maximises monopoly revenue for both taken together (as, whatever the price is, they

---

[1] Wicksell, *Archiv für Sozialwissenschaft*, 1927, vol. 58, p. 272.

would, in the absence of any preference of consumers for either of them, have to share equally what monopoly revenue there is.'[1]

But it is not easy to follow Professor Schumpeter in his assertion that his 'limiting instance . . . that of Duopoly, . . . can be easily generalised'. For suppose there are three sellers, A, B and C. If A raises his price above the price charged by B and C, it no longer remains true that B and C, acting individually, will raise their prices at all. For if B (or C) were to start raising his price, he would lose the whole of his output to C (or B).

This argument indicates an interesting conclusion. Suppose there are any number of sellers (more than two) all charging for the moment a certain price which happens, for some reason or other, to be in excess of the cost of production. (For the sake of simplicity, constant returns may be assumed.) Then a single firm may well be aware that if it were to lower its price in an attempt to increase its output, each of the other firms would be forced in self-defence to lower its price by an equal amount; so that it would actually be worse off than it is now. For this reason the price may be prevented from moving downwards. If, on the other hand, a single firm decides to raise its price, its output will drop to zero; but there will be nothing to induce the other firms – there are, if must be remembered, at least two other firms – to raise their prices. There is no reason, therefore, why the price should move upwards. But if the price can move neither downwards nor upwards, it must remain where it is. The equilibrium price is any and every price; and the price is where it is for no other reason than that it happens to be so.

Conversations with business men lead me to think that this conclusion – absurd though it may appear – has some bearing in practice. It applies more particularly in those industries where policy determines the price that a firm shall charge rather than the level of its output, where the price is fixed for fairly long periods at a time, where custom or convenience dictate that a change of price shall be substantial in amount, and where the number of firms is not too large. (And, of course, if we are dealing with the long period, the entry of new competitors into the industry must not be possible.)

But it is important to note that while there can be equilibrium in any position, the equilibrium is unstable for changes in a downward direction. If one single firm *does* decide to make a small cut in its price, the other firms will respond by making a slightly larger cut.

[1] *Economic Journal*, September 1928, p. 370.

Each firm will attempt to get its cuts in before its competitors can make their cuts; and the price will plunge headlong down to the marginal cost of production. And, in fact, when we come – as we now shortly shall – to work out the third case by means of mathematics, we shall find that in a perfect market the position of equilibrium is the same as for the first case – the price is equal to the marginal cost of production – and the same as the limiting position in the second case when the number of firms is very great.

§ 29   It is, therefore, when the market is imperfect that the third case becomes important. If we start from the position of equilibrium of the first case, it still pays a single producer to raise his price if he takes into account the fact – it usually is a fact, but there are exceptions – that, by doing so, he will be inducing his competitors to raise their prices (though by not so much). Therefore the equilibrium price of the third case is almost invariably above that of the first case.

Conversely, if we start from the position of equilibrium of the second case, it pays a single producer to *lower* his price provided it is a fact, which he takes into account, that, by doing so, he will be inducing his competitors to *decrease* their outputs. It follows that the equilibrium price of the third case is usually below that of the second case.

We shall, therefore, have disproved Professor Sraffa's assertion, apart from exceptions of an extreme type, when we have proved that the equilibrium price in the *second* case is less than the monopoly price. But it will be more satisfactory, and more interesting, to deal with each case separately.

§ 30   This is the more necessary because one is tempted at first to imagine that the conditions of our third case may lead to the same position of equilibrium as would be attained in the case of monopoly. This is the conclusion to which Professor Hotelling at any rate gives the appearance of arriving in his consideration of duopoly.[1] In the particular case that he is investigating he is, indeed, correct. But the reason is that he is assuming the aggregate demand to be perfectly inelastic: when the elasticity of demand is zero, the equilibrium prices in the second case, and in the third case, as in the case of monopoly, are all infinite (though they are not really equal).

In fact, Professor Hotelling's treatment of this matter is unsatisfactory largely because he is imbued – as I look at it – with the feeling that there is something analogous between those conditions that are

---

[1] *Economic Journal*, March 1929, p. 48.

typified by our third case and the conditions that are necessary in an industry consisting of more than one firm, for the maintenance of a monopoly price. Professor Hotelling describes how the price is raised above the 'equilibrium position E' as soon as A realises that if he raises his price, B will respond by raising his price. The process, as described by Professor Hotelling, operates quite independently of any assumption as to an understanding between the two competitors. But, while he admits that there need be no 'formal agreement', Professor Hotelling insists on the necessity for 'something of a tacit understanding'. And finally he comes to the conclusion that the position that is attained is an essentially unstable one. For 'the difficulties of maintaining a price-fixing agreement have often have been remarked. Not only may the short-sighted cupidity of one party send the whole system crashing through price-cutting; the very fear of a price cut will bring on a cut.'[1] And, 'always there is an insecurity at any point other than the point E which represents equilibrium' (the equilibrium of our first case). This view seems quite unwarranted. There is a position of equilibrium in our third case which is altogether independent of understandings and 'quasi-monopolistic schemes'. Moreover, unlike the peculiar kind of equilibrium in a perfect market that was discussed in § 28 (which is the type of equilibrium that Professor Hotelling appears to have in mind), it is completely stable. We can go even further, and suggest that Professor Hotelling's 'equilibrium point E', which he regards as the only position of true equilibrium, is not really likely to be a position of equilibrium at all. It is only a position of equilibrium if A makes the rather absurd assumption that a change in his price will not react on the price charged by B, and if B makes the same assumption about A. To the extent that A and B make more reasonable assumptions about one another, the price is higher than the price at the point E. But the equilibrium then has just the same kind of stability as has the equilibrium at the point E when our assumptions are the somewhat peculiar ones of our first case; if a slight movement is set up away from the original position, forces come into operation that impel a return.

I feel that at this point I ought to insert some reference to an article on duopoly by Dr Chamberlin which has just appeared,[2] and which I read only after I had completed the whole of my treatment of the

---

[1] *Economic Journal*, March 1929, p. 49.
[2] E. H. Chamberlin, *Quarterly Journal of Economics*, November 1929, p. 63.

subject – both the preceding portions and the mathematical section that brings this chapter to a close. It was then too late to make any alterations or additions to my manuscript, which was already in the hands of the typist, and, indeed, my perusal of the forty pages which Dr Chamberlin devotes to the subject has necessarily been so cursory that it is only with considerable diffidence that I refer to his article at all.

It may be said at once that, while in some respects Dr Chamberlin's treatment reveals a similarity that is almost curious to the treatment that has occupied the preceding pages, on at least one fundamental issue there is complete disagreement.

The distinction, which was above ascribed to Wicksell,[1] between Cournot's assumption and Bertrand's assumption is forcibly upheld. 'No presumption in favour of either the one or the other seems to be created by the general hypothesis that each seeks to maximise his profit.'[2] But both assumptions are unsatisfactory. 'When a move by one seller evidently forces the other to make a counter-move, he is very stupidly refusing to look further than his nose if he proceeds on the assumption that it will not'.[3] Thus Dr Chamberlin is forced, just as we were forced some pages back, to regard what I have called the third case as the really important one. And Dr Chamberlin supports the view which was expressed in the last subsection that there is no connection whatever between the assumptions of this third case and the existence of any sort of a 'tacit understanding': 'for the first seller to recognise the fact that his rival's policy is not a given datum, but is determined in part by his own, cannot be construed as a negation of independence.'[4]

Dr Chamberlin's conclusions as to the position of equilibrium in this third case are, however, very different from the conclusions at which we arrived in §§ 28–30, 'although the sellers are entirely independent', writes Dr Chamberlin, 'the equilibrium result is the same as though there were a monopolistic agreement between them'.[5] This is in a perfect market – Dr Chamberlin assumes throughout that the market is perfect – so that as we near the termination of this

[1] Dr Chamberlin's work, on which he has been engaged for a long time, owes nothing to Wicksell's recent article (see Schumpeter, *Economic Journal*, September 1928, p. 370).

[2] Chamberlin, *Quarterly Journal of Economics*, November 1929, p. 72.

[3] Ibid, p. 83.

[4] Ibid, p. 65.

[5] *Quarterly Journal of Economics*, November 1929, p. 85.

discursus, which originated in § 15 with Professor Sraffa's assertion that in an imperfect market – no matter how small the imperfection – the price is equal to the monopoly price, we are suddenly confronted with an even more extreme statement of the same theorem: it is now said to hold even when the market is perfect.

'There is no gradual descent', states Dr Chamberlin, 'to a purely competitive price with increase of numbers . . . The break comes when the individual's influence upon the price becomes so small that he neglects it.'[1] And again: 'If [numbers] are very large, [any one seller] can be certain that his incursions will be such a negligible factor to each other seller that no one will "follow suit" (i.e. cut *because* he did); and therefore everyone will cut.'[2] The extraordinary nature of this discontinuous 'break' as the number of sellers becomes large, which shows such a strong relationship to the discontinuity envisaged by Professor Sraffa as the imperfection of the market becomes vanishingly small, provides an *a priori* case for suspecting the conclusions on which it is based.

So long as Dr Chamberlin confines himself to the case of duopoly, there is little to be said. His conclusion then arises out of the same kind of reasoning as Professor Schumpeter's, which we quoted at the beginning of § 28. But it is difficult to justify his extension, in which Professor Schumpeter would perhaps join him, of the conclusion that may be true of duopoly to the case where the number of sellers is greater than two. The nature of the difficulty was set out in § 28 and need not be repeated here. I cannot see that Dr Chamberlin does anything to overcome it. His arguments are in support of the peculiar type of equilibrium that was described in § 28, the type that is possible at any price at or below the monopoly point. But he does little more than merely assert that the only position of equilibrium is at the monopoly point: 'since the result of a cut by anyone is inevitably to decrease his own profits, no one will cut, and, although the sellers are entirely independent, the equilibrium result is the same as though there were a monopolistic agreement between them'.[3] Dr Chamberlin fully accounts for his assertion that the price will not fall. But it does not seem to me that he adequately explains why the price will rise to the monopoly point, if it does not already happen to be there. 'No one will cut from the monopoly figure because he would force others

[1] Ibid, p. 84.
[2] Ibid, p. 89.
[3] *Quarterly Journal of Economics*, November 1929, p. 85.

to follow him, and thereby work his own undoing.'[1] But how is the monopoly figure attained in the first place?

It necessarily follows that Dr Chamberlin does not regard this type of equilibrium as unstable, as we have been led to regard it. It is, therefore, important to stress the conclusion of § 28 that, when the market is perfect, the only stable position of equilibrium which can be based on the assumption of our third case is at the point where the price is equal to the marginal cost of production, which is also the position of equilibrium in our first case. It is only when the market is imperfect that there is a stable position of equilibrium in the third case which differs both from the position of equilibrium in the first case and from the point where the price is equal to the marginal cost of production.

Dr Chamberlin's treatment of Edgeworth's type of indeterminateness also appears unsatisfactory. Only a passing glance was devoted above to Edgeworth's oscillations; it is, therefore, scarcely possible to enter very fully into the nature of Dr Chamberlin's criticisms. They group themselves under four separate heads.

(a) 'There is oscillation in Edgeworth's solution' writes Dr Chamberlin, 'because the process is not, as in his general theory, that of contract, or competitive bidding.'[2] This may be true – if it is incompatible with contract bidding to raise one's price, it obviously is true – but the criticism seems to be largely verbal in nature.

(b) Dr Chamberlin appears to think that it is necessary for Edgeworth to assume that during the upward movement of price the 'markets are completely separated'[3] 'after the price has been carried to its lowest point by competition, the market is split into parts so that each seller becomes a monopolist dealing with a portion of the buyers in isolation'.[4] In other words, if half the buyers had red hair and half the buyers had black hair, Edgeworth would, according to Dr Chamberlin, have to suppose that one seller will serve only red-haired customers and that the other seller will serve only black-haired customers. But, in such a case, 'the price is stable at [the monopoly] point with no cause for a downward movement'.[5]

Actually Edgeworth's implicit assumption appears to be quite a different one. He supposes that the customers of each seller are

[1] *Quarterly Journal of Economics*, November 1929, p. 86.
[2] *Quarterly Journal of Economics*, November 1929, p. 76.
[3] Ibid, p. 76.
[4] Ibid, p. 77.
[5] *Quarterly Journal of Economics*, November 1929, p. 77.

chosen completely at random. Then, if B's price is higher than A's price, B has at his disposal the random group of those customers whom A is unable to serve. If B's price is only just a little above A's price, his output is the difference between A's and the aggregate demand at that price. As B raises his prices, the demand of the group of customers which A leaves over for him steadily falls. It would only become zero if B were to raise his price to the point at which the aggregate demand becomes equal to A's output. Moreover, if the aggregate demand curve is a straight line, it can easily be proved that B's demand curve is a straight line; and it follows that B's monopoly price is the same as the monopoly price for A and B combined (assuming constant costs up to the point of maximum output).

There is an apparent paradox which is worth noting. The higher A's price (i.e. the less by which it falls short of B's), the smaller is the number of customers left over for B, and therefore the *smaller* is B's output.

(c) Dr Chamberlin seems to find it difficult to suppose that the prices of two separate firms can differ more than infinitesimally in a perfect market.[1] He forgets that if the output of A is limited, the highest degree of perfection on the *side of the buyers* cannot prevent B from charging a higher price than A; and that it is in the very essence of Edgeworth's analysis that A keeps his price fixed until B has finished raising his price. To overcome his scruples, Dr Chamberlin makes a different kind of assumption. He supposes that as B raises his price, A follows suit, 'being carried along closely behind him by the competition of buyers, but always enjoying the slight differential which enables him to sell his entire output'.[2] Dr Chamberlin concludes that oscillation will still take place, but over a smaller range than Edgeworth indicated, and over a range that diminishes in extent as the number of sellers increases. But in § 23 we concluded that in such a case as this, when B does not raise his price discontinuously, there is stable equilibrium at the 'critical price'. Dr Chamberlin appears to overlook the fact that as soon as A's price has risen above the critical point, it pays B better to undercut A than to try to reach the monopoly price.

(d) Perhaps Dr Chamberlin's most important contribution to this phase of our subject is his exposure of the fact that Edgeworth's oscillations would continue with unabated amplitude however great

[1] *Quarterly Journal of Economics*, November 1929, p. 77.
[2] Ibid, p. 78.

the number of sellers.[1] This opinion is contrary to the general view; perhaps it is contrary to Edgeworth's own view, for, to employ Dr Chamberlin's quotation, 'his general theory is that "contract with more or less perfect competition is less or more indeterminate" (*Mathematical Psychics*, p. 20)';[2] and, in accordance with this view, I stated above, at the opening of § 23, that indeterminates existed 'to a steadily decreasing extent' in the case of monopolistic competition.

There is, however, something to be said in favour of this view, and it appears that Dr Chamberlin overlooks it. It is true that if all the firms in an industry are producing outputs which, at the price that exists, they will not exceed, then it pays a single firm to raise its price to the monopoly price (on the assumption that the demand curve is a straight line) – provided that none of the other firms raise their prices at all. But it does not seem to follow, as Dr Chamberlin thinks, that it would now pay 'the second and third and *all* of them to go back to $O P$' (the monopoly price).[3] For, as soon as, say, one or two firms raise their prices to just under the monopoly price, the output of the firm which first made the jump is reduced to zero; and price-cutting restores the *status quo* before the great majority of the firms have a chance of moving. The *amplitude* of the oscillations is unaltered, but they affect a gradually diminishing proportion of the industry as the number of sellers is increased.

But, in any case, it seems unfair to lay at the door of Edgeworth's *method* the fault of the *assumption* on which he is working. Dr Chamberlin agrees that the assumption of our first case is not a practical one. He must not, therefore, feel surprised if the conclusions for which it is responsible reveal no relationship to reality. As the number of sellers increases, the 'critical price' approaches closer to the competitive price. If the number of sellers is very great, it requires only a very small rise in price throughout the industry to make it unprofitable for a single firm to raise its price to the monopoly price.

It is, finally, interesting to observe that Dr Chamberlin endorses the distinction that I drew in § 23 between Edgeworth's type of indeterminateness and Professor Pigou's type. 'Although apparently based upon Edgeworth, Professor Pigou's explanation of indeterminateness is lacking in Edgeworth's statement of the problem, and introduces a factor not yet touched upon.'[4] Then follows identically

[1] *Quarterly Journal of Economics*, November 1929, p. 77.
[2] Ibid, p. 77.
[3] Ibid, p. 77.
[4] *Quarterly Journal of Economics*, November 1929, p. 82.

the same quotation from *The Economics of Welfare* as was set out above in § 23.

Let us investigate the position of equilibrium of n firms, identical and similarly situated.[1] Let the output of the industry be X; then in the position of equilibrium each firm has an output $x = \frac{X}{n}$. Let each firm, when the industry is in equilibrium, imagine that its individual demand curve is given by the equation $y = f(x)$. Then, if $y = F(X)$ represents the demand curve for the whole industry, the price is $F(X) = f(x)$. Let the average cost curve – average prime cost if we are dealing with the short period – be denoted by the equation $y = g(x)$.

Then the criterion of equilibrium is that $x[f(x) - g(x)]$ is a maximum. It follows that

$$x = \frac{f(x) - g(x)}{g'(x) - f'(x)}$$

i.e. that

$$\frac{X}{n} = x = \frac{F(X) - g(x)}{g'(x) + (-f'(x))} = \frac{F(X) - g\left(\frac{X}{n}\right)}{g'\left(\frac{X}{n}\right) + \left(-f'\left(\frac{X}{n}\right)\right)} \tag{7.1}$$

If the industry were in the hands of a single monopolist the output X_m would be determined by the condition that

$$X\left[F(X) - g\left(\frac{X}{n}\right)\right] \text{ is a maximum when } X = X_m.$$

It follows that

$$\frac{X_m}{n} = \frac{F(X_m) - g\left(\frac{X_m}{n}\right)}{g'\left(\frac{X_m}{n}\right) + n(-F'(X_m))} \tag{7.2}$$

Hence X is equal to X_m only if

---

[1] For the present it is sufficient to assume that the symmetry is of the circular variety.

$$n(- F'(X)) = - f'(x)$$
$$\text{i.e. to } \left(- f'\left(\frac{X}{n}\right)\right)$$

It will be shown immediately that, for each of the three types of individual demand curve, $n(- F'(X))$ is greater than $(- f'(x))$. From this it can be concluded that X is greater than X_m.[1] In other words, the output of an industry is greater, and therefore its price is less, under conditions of polypoly (or oligopoly) then it would be under a monopolistic régime.

This is true even when each business man is aware that a change in his price will lead to alterations in both the prices and the outputs of all the other firms – our third case – in which there was *a priori* some reason to expect that Professor Sraffa's conclusion might be justified. It should however be pointed out that, if the aggregate demand is perfectly inelastic, the price in both the second and third cases, as will appear shortly, is infinite,[2] just as it would be if there were a monopoly.

§ 33   Suppose now that in any position in which demand is equal to supply – not necessarily a position of equilibrium – the outputs of the individual firms are $x_1, x_2, \cdots x_n$ and that their prices are $y_1, y_2, \cdots y_n$. If the output of the industry is X, then $X = x_1 + x_2 + \cdots + x_n$. In equilibrium, since the firms are all similar and similarly

---

[1] Provided that the various curves are moderately linear over the range that is in question. A formal proof is, perhaps, desirable. Let $X_m = X + DX$. Then, if second differential coefficients can be neglected,

$$\frac{X + DX}{n} = \frac{\left[(F(X) - g\left(\frac{X}{n}\right)\right] - DX\left[(- F'(X)) + \frac{1}{n} g'\left(\frac{X}{n}\right)\right]}{\left[g'\left(\frac{X}{n}\right) + n(- F'(X))\right]}$$

This relation has to be compared with equation (7.1). From the fact that $n (- F'(X))$ is greater than $\left(- f'\left(\frac{X}{n}\right)\right)$ it follows that, if DX is positive, $\left[(- F'(X)) + \frac{1}{n} g'\left(\frac{X}{n}\right)\right]$ must be negative. Since second differential coefficients can be neglected, this would require $\left[g'\left(\frac{X_m}{n}\right) + n (- F'(X_m))\right]$ to be negative. But equation (7.2) shows that this is impossible. Therefore DX cannot be positive.

[2] This is the result hinted at by Professor Hotelling in his investigation of the third case for a special kind of duopoly (*Economic Journal*, March 1929, p. 48). His conclusion that 'thus without a formal agreement the rivals may succeed in making themselves virtually a monopoly' is liable to be applied quite illegitimately to cases where the demand is not perfectly inelastic.

situated, $x_1 = x_2 \cdots = x_n = \dfrac{X}{n} = x$, say; and $y_1 = y_2 = \cdots$
$y_n = y = F(X)$.

The demand for the product of any firm is a function of the price charged by the firm and of the prices charged by all the other firms. We may, therefore, write

$$y_1 = K(x_1, x_2, \cdots x_n) \tag{7.3}$$

In the same way,

$$y_1 = L(x_1, y_2, \cdots y_n) \tag{7.4}$$

Let us now start from a position in which

$$x_1 = x_2 = \cdots = x_n = x$$

and

$$y_1 = y_2 = \cdots = y_n = y$$

and let us suppose that each firm raises its price by δy and that in consequence the output of each firm increases by δx – this is all in accordance with our assumption of symmetry.

Then

$$\delta y = F'(X) \, n\delta x,$$

i.e.

$$\frac{\delta y}{\delta x} = n \, F'(X).$$

But, from (7.3),

$$\delta y = \left(\frac{\partial K}{\partial x_1} + \frac{\partial K}{\partial x_2} + \cdots + \frac{\partial K}{\partial x_n} \right) \delta x.$$

$$\therefore \left(-\frac{\partial K}{\partial x_1} \right) = n \, (-F'(X)) - \left[\left(-\frac{\partial K}{\partial x_2} \right) + \cdots + \left(-\frac{\partial K}{\partial x_n} \right) \right] \tag{7.5}$$

From (7.4)

$$\delta y = \frac{\partial L}{\partial x_1}\, \delta x + \left(\frac{\partial L}{\partial y_2} + \cdots + \frac{\partial L}{\partial y_n}\right)\delta y$$

$$\therefore \left(-\frac{\partial L}{\partial x_1}\right) = n\,(-F'(X))\left[1 - \left(\frac{\partial L}{\partial y_2} + \cdots + \frac{\partial L}{\partial y_n}\right)\right] \qquad (7.6)$$

§ 34   The road has now been opened to the consideration of our three different cases.

In the first case the demand curve, in accordance with which each individual firm maximises its profit, is drawn on the assumption that the *prices* of all the other firms remain constant. It follows at once that in this case

$$f'(x) = \frac{\partial L}{\partial x_1}$$

so, that from equation (7.6)

$$(-f'(x)) = n\,(-F'(X))\left[1 - \left(\frac{\partial L}{\partial y_2} + \cdots + \frac{\partial L}{\partial y_n}\right)\right] \qquad (7.7)$$

Now $\left[\dfrac{\partial L}{\partial y_2}\cdots\right]$ etc. are clearly positive. We therefore arrive at the result at which we are aiming – namely, that $n(-F'(X))$ is greater than $(-f'(x))$.

It is to be noted that when the aggregate demand is perfectly inelastic, i.e. when $(-F'(X)) = \infty$, the individual demand is not in this case perfectly inelastic, i.e. $(-f'(x)) < \infty$; and the equilibrium price is finite, not infinite. At first sight equation (7.7) would indicate that $(-f'(x))$ *is* infinite when $(-F'(X))$ is equal to infinity. But it has to be remembered that $\left(\dfrac{\partial L}{\partial y_2} + \cdots + \dfrac{\partial L}{\partial y_n}\right)$ is then equal to 1, as may be seen by putting δx equal to zero in the equation that immediately precedes equation (7.6).

To trace the nature of the change that is associated with a progressive decline to zero of the imperfection of the market, it will be convenient to express $\left(\dfrac{\partial L}{\partial y_2} + \cdots + \dfrac{\partial L}{\partial y_n}\right)$ in terms based on a simple conception. Let us suppose a change in which, by raising y_1

by δy_1, x_1 is kept constant while $y_2, \cdots y_n$ all increase by δy_n. Then equation (7.4) tells us that

$$\frac{\delta y_1}{\delta y_n} = \frac{\partial L}{\partial y_2} + \cdots + \frac{\partial L}{\partial y_n}$$

In general, it is obvious, δy_1 is less than δy_n (except when the demand is perfectly inelastic). But in a perfect market only one price can rule and then δy_1 must be equal to δy_n. As the market becomes more perfect, $\left[\left(\frac{\partial L}{\partial y_2} + \cdots + \frac{\partial L}{\partial y_n}\right)\right]$ approaches unity, $(-f'(x))$ approaches zero, and the price approaches the marginal cost, which is $(xg'(x) + g(x))$ (see equation (7.1)).

We turn now to the second case. The individual demand curve is drawn on the assumption that the *outputs* of all the other firms remain constant. In this case, therefore,

$$f'(x) = \frac{\partial K}{\partial x_1}$$

so that, from equation (7.5)

$$(-f'(x)) = n\,(-F'(X)) - \left[\left(-\frac{\partial K}{\partial x_2}\right) + \cdots + \left(-\frac{\partial K}{\partial x_n}\right)\right] \quad (7.8)$$

It is obvious that $\frac{\partial K}{\partial x_2}$, etc. are negative. Here again, then, $n(-F'(X))$ is greater than $(-f'(x))$.

But, by way of contrast, when the demand is perfectly inelastic, $(-f'(x))$ is in this case infinite, though it is still less than $n(-F'(X))$. The reason is obvious: $\frac{\partial K}{\partial x_1}$ is infinite, because if the outputs of all the other firms remain constant, one firm can change its output by a finite amount only if it changes its price by an infinite amount. The price is infinite in this case when the demand is perfectly inelastic, but it may still be said to be less than the monopoly price.

If the market is a perfect one, it is obvious that

$$\frac{\partial K}{\partial x_1} = \frac{\partial K}{\partial x_2} = \cdots = \frac{\partial K}{\partial x_n} = F'(X);$$

and it follows that

$$f'(x) = F'(X).$$

Equation (7.1) now becomes

$$y = \frac{d}{dx}(x\ g(x)) + \frac{X}{n}(-F'(X))$$

and as n increases, the price approaches the marginal cost.

§ 36   Finally, there is the third case, in which the individual firm takes into account the fact that if it alters its price and output, the other firms will alter both their prices and their outputs – so as to continue to maximise their profits. This case is far more complicated, and, for the sake of simplicity, we shall determine an upper limit to $(-f'(x))$ rather than its actual value.

For this purpose it will now be assumed, not only that the firms are similar and similarly situated, but that the relation between any two firms is identical for every possible pair.[1] If the statement that $(-f'(x))$ is less than $n(-F'(X))$ can be proved on the basis of this assumption, however small the number of firms, it will hold *a fortiori* in the more general case where the influence of some firms on a given firm is less than that of others. The assumption implies that

$$\frac{\partial K}{\partial x_2} = \frac{\partial K}{\partial x_3} = \cdots = \frac{\partial K}{\partial x_n} = \frac{\partial K}{\partial x_r}$$

and equation (7.5) becomes

$$\left(-\frac{\partial K}{\partial x_1}\right) = n(-F'(X)) - (n-1)\left(-\frac{\partial K}{\partial x_r}\right) \qquad (7.9)$$

We have to suppose that we start from the position of equilibrium,

[1] If the simpler kind of symmetry is called circular symmetry, this more perfect kind may be called equilateral-triangular or regular-tetrahedronal. It is obvious that for the simplest variety of transport imperfection it is impossible for more than three firms to satisfy the condition that we are postulating. By complicating the basis on which the costs of transport depend, the number can be increased. But in the case of preference imperfection there is no such limit. The reason is that the customers of any one firm are not bound to such a stereotyped order of preference for the products of the other firms as that to which they are bound in the case of transport imperfection by geographical relationships.

in which $x_1 = x_2 = \cdots = x_n = x$ and $y_1 = y_2 = \cdots = y_n = y$, and that y_1 increases by δy_1.

As a consequence, let x_1 increase by δx_1 and, in accordance with our assumption of perfect symmetry, let $x_2, x_3 \cdots x_n$ all increase by δx_r and $y_2, y_3, \ldots y_n$ by δy_r. Then, by equation (7.3)

$$\delta y_1 = \frac{\partial K}{\partial x_1} \delta x_1 + (n - 1) \frac{\partial K}{\partial x_n} \delta x_1$$

and

$$\delta y_r = \frac{\partial K}{\partial x_1} \delta x_r + \frac{\partial K}{\partial x_r} \delta x_1 + (n - 2) \frac{\partial K}{\partial x_r} \delta x_r$$

Consequently

$$\delta y_1 \frac{\partial K}{\partial x_r} - \delta x_r \frac{\partial K}{\partial x_1} = \delta y_r \left[(n - 1) \frac{\partial K}{\partial x_r} + \frac{\partial K}{\partial x_1} \right] \left[\frac{\partial K}{\partial x_r} - \frac{\partial K}{\partial x_1} \right]$$

$$= \delta x_r . n \, F'(X) \left[\frac{\partial K}{\partial x_r} - \frac{\partial K}{\partial x_1} \right] \qquad (7.10)$$

by equation (7.9).

δx_r and δy_r are determined by the manner in which the other firms maximise their profits after (y_1) has increased by (δy_1). The most extreme assumption that can be made, from the point of view of proving that under conditions of polypoly the equilibrium price is less than under conditions of monopoly, is that δy_n is the same as it would be if the $n - 1$ firms were to act in cooperation. If $(- f'(x))$ can be proved even then to be less than $n(- F'(X))$, it follows that it is actually still less; because δy_r is actually less than on the extreme assumption that the $n - 1$ firms behave as though they were acting in cooperation – and therefore δx_1 is greater.

Originally the profit (prime profit if we are dealing with the short period) of each of the $n - 1$ firms is

$$x[y - g(x)].$$

After the change it becomes $(x + \delta x_r) [y + \delta y_r - g(x + \delta x_r)]$. The increase in profit is

$$\delta x_r[y - g(x)] - x\, g'(x)] + x\delta y_r = x[\delta y_r - f'\,(x)\delta x_r],$$

by equation (7.1).

δy_r can be regarded as a variable dependent only on δx_r, when δy_1 is given. Since the increase in profit is then to be supposed to be a maximum, the differential coefficient of the last expression is zero; i.e.

$$\frac{d(\delta y_r)}{d(\delta x_r)} = f'(x).$$

But, from equation (7.10)

$$\frac{d(\delta y_r)}{d(\delta x_r)} = n\, F'(X)\left[1 - \frac{\partial K}{\partial y_r} \left/ \frac{\partial K}{\partial x_1}\right.\right]$$

Hence:

$$(-f'(x)) = n(-F'(X))\left[1 - \frac{\left(-\dfrac{\partial K}{\partial y_r}\right)}{\left(-\dfrac{\partial K}{\partial x_1}\right)}\right]$$

Now $\dfrac{\partial K}{\partial x_r}$ and $\dfrac{\partial K}{\partial x_1}$ are both negative, and, for obvious reasons, $\dfrac{\partial K}{\partial x_r}$ is numerically less than $\dfrac{\partial K}{\partial x_1}$. Here, then, as before, $(-f'(x))$ is less than $n(-F'(X))$ – even on the extreme assumptions that have been used as a basis for argument.

If the demand is perfectly inelastic, $\left(-\dfrac{\partial K}{\partial x_r}\right)$ and $\left(-\dfrac{\partial K}{\partial x_1}\right)$ are both infinite but $\dfrac{\partial K}{\partial x_r}$ is still numerically less than $\dfrac{\partial K}{\partial x_1}$. It follows that $(-f'(x))$ is infinite, because $(-F'(X))$ is infinite; and the price is infinite but less than the monopoly price, just as in the second case. It may be imagined that this result is independent of the extreme assumption that has been made.

If the market is perfect, $\dfrac{\partial K}{\partial x_1} = \dfrac{\partial K}{\partial x_r}$. Hence $(-f'(x)) = 0$; and the price is equal to the marginal cost. This is the same result as in the first case, and is the limiting result in the second case as n becomes very great.

CHAPTER 8

EQUILIBRIUM IN AN IMPERFECT MARKET

I EQUILIBRIUM OF A SINGLE FIRM

We shall now examine in greater detail the case where the prime cost curves can be assumed to be of the characteristic ⌐-shape and the individual demand curves can be assumed to be straight lines. In reality, we shall for the most part be assuming much less than this. It will be sufficient usually to assume that the demand curves are appreciably straight over the range of variation that is in question and that the average prime cost curves, while approximating to the ⌐-shape, are horizontal straight lines over this same range. The capacity output will often be useful as a datum level of reference rather than as a definite conception; other quantities will be measured in terms of it and its precise magnitude will not always be a matter of great significance.

Conditions of polypoly will be supposed to prevail. As was explained at the end of the last chapter, it will be possible to make use of individual demand curves without presupposing the nature of the assumptions upon which business men act. The nature of these assumptions affects the slopes of the individual demand curves and consequently it affects the position of final equilibrium; but it does not affect the general argument by means of which the position of equilibrium can be determined.

In the position of equilibrium, let OT (Figure 8.1) be the output of a single firm and TM the price. Let LMP be the tangent at M to the individual demand curve, and let SRP be the tangent at R to the average prime cost curve. Then, by hypothesis, SRP is parallel to the x axis.

By ordinary monopoly considerations, $RM \times SR$ is a maximum. It follows that $SR = RP$.[1]

---

[1] This result is frequently employed by Professor Pigou with respect to demand and cost curves that are assumed to be straight lines. It is, of course, equally applicable to

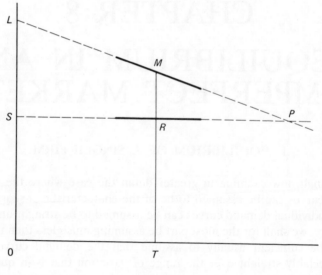

FIG 8.1

Let $\angle LPS = \theta$, so that $\tan \theta$ is the gradient of the individual demand curve, then

$$\tan \theta = \frac{RM}{RP}$$

$$= \frac{RM}{SR}$$

$$= \frac{\text{excess of the price over the prime cost}}{\text{the output}}$$

$$= \frac{p - r}{x}$$

where p is the price, r the average prime cost, and x the output. This relation:

---

the tangents to the demand and cost curves at the points which represent the state of affairs when the monopoly revenue is a maximum. But it is necessary to suppose that the curves follow the course of straight lines sufficiently exactly to prevent the difficulties that would ensue if there were several maxima to the monopoly revenue curve.

$p - r = x \tan \theta,$

is fundamental.

If f is the ratio of the output to the capacity output and q the product of the capacity output and $\tan \theta$, then the relation can be expressed in the form:

$$\text{excess of the price over the prime cost} = p - r = fq \qquad (8.1)$$

The function q, which would be equal to the gradient of the individual demand curve if the capacity output were the unit of output, is a measure of the imperfection of the market, and it is under this guise that the imperfection of the market will usually enter into our equations and into the discussions to which they will give rise. q will often be referred to as the 'annihilation coefficient'. The choice of this name is related to the fact that, in the case where the individual demand curve is a straight line through its length, q is the increase of price that would be necessary to reduce the firm's output by an amount equal to its capacity output. A more useful interpretation is that a firm that is working at 75 per cent of its capacity must reduce its price by $\frac{1}{4} q$ in order to work at its capacity level of output.[1]

If u is the capacity output, it follows from equation (8.1) that the prime profit is

$$f^2 q u \qquad (8.2)$$

II GENERAL CONCLUSIONS

It will be convenient for a moment to suppose that the prime cost curve is of the ⅃-shape throughout its length. Then, since f cannot be greater than unity, it is clear from equation (8.1) that, so long as the excess of price over prime cost is greater than q, the output is the capacity output. It follows that the price and output are determined by the point of intersection of the demand curve and the prime cost curve just as if the market were perfect.

---

[1] A graphical interpretation, which will be useful, is that q is the vertical distance between the points at which the individual demand curve cuts the y axis and the ordinate at the position of capacity output.

It was shown in Chapter 6, § 3, that under conditions of perfect competition a small slump in an elastic demand would send prices hurtling down to prime cost (if the prime costs of all the firms are fairly equal). It now appears that if the degree of imperfection is small there is no need to modify this view at all substantially. Prices are forced down, not it is true to prime cost, but to q above prime cost. In many industries q is very small. Thus I have been told that a mill spinning a medium count of American cotton would have to reduce its price by about $\frac{1}{4}d$ a pound to increase its output from 75 per cent of capacity to its capacity level. In other words q is about $1d$. The overhead cost on such a medium count is roughly $2\frac{1}{2}d$ per pound (the total cost, apart from raw material, being about $5\frac{1}{2}d$). If, therefore, the cotton industry were earning normal profits, the price could slump by about $1\frac{1}{2}d$ per pound as a result of a slump in demand before the imperfection of the market had the slightest effect.

In other industries q may be almost equal to the overhead cost. Thus it is not unreasonable to suppose that the manufacturer of a motor-car whose normal price is £600, half of which may be supposed to be prime cost, would have to reduce his price by something like £70 to increase his output by one quarter of his capacity output. In such an industry a small slump of demand from its normal position would exert but a very small effect on the output. (In the imaginary instance just quoted the price could fall from £600 only to £580 so long as the output remained close up to capacity.)

If q is greater than the overhead cost, it follows from equation (8.1) that even when the firm is earning normal profits it is working short time under the influence of the partial monopoly provided by the imperfection of the market. This somewhat surprising result can of course only occur when the whole industry is not in normal long-period equilibrium, even though it may be earning normal profits.

Reverting to the more usual case where q is fairly small, we have seen that, as the demand curve falls, output remains at its capacity level so long as the excess of price over prime cost is greater than q. However, as soon as it becomes less than q, output is reduced below its capacity level, and a direct proportionality is henceforth maintained between the output (or between f) and the excess of price over prime cost.[1] Imperfection of the market is now playing the role for which it

---

[1] Thus a reduction of output from full capacity to half capacity would be associated with a fall in price of $\frac{1}{2}q$. (It is assumed that the value of q for any one firm is fairly constant. This assumption is considered in the next chapter.)

was cast. It provides an explanation of the apparent paradox that firms work short-time although they are making a prime profit. And any degree of imperfection, no matter how small, is sufficient to account for any degree of short-time working. The smaller the imperfection, the closer is the price to prime cost; that is all.

III SUPPLY SCHEDULE OF A SINGLE FIRM AND OF AN INDUSTRY CONSISTING OF IDENTICAL FIRMS

We have just been considering, in a general sort of way, the conclusions that emerge from the equations of § 2. But, on the assumption that the annihilation coefficient, q, of a single firm is a constant, it is possible to differentiate expression (8.2) and to derive a value for the elasticity of supply of a single firm. And the results that are true of a single firm are equally true of an industry that consists of identical firms, external economies and diseconomies being neglected. The constancy of the annihilation coefficient will be examined in the next chapter; for the present it is assumed.

Then, q, is to be supposed constant for a particular firm. It follows at once from equation (8.1) that if a firm's prime cost remains constant and its output changes, as a result of a change of demand,

$$\text{change in the price} = \triangle p = q \triangle f \tag{8.3}$$

The change in price is, therefore, proportional to q and to the absolute change in output.

And

$$\frac{\triangle p}{\text{excess of the price over prime cost}} = \frac{\triangle f}{f},$$

or, in other words,

$$\frac{\text{proportional increase}}{\text{in output}} = \frac{\text{change in the price}}{\text{excess of the price over prime cost}} \tag{8.4}$$

This means that a 10 per cent increase in output is associated with a rise in the price of 10 per cent of its excess over prime cost.

From (8.4) it follows that the elasticity of supply of the single firm is equal to

$$\frac{\text{price}}{\text{excess of price over prime cost}} = \frac{p}{f q} \tag{8.5}$$

§ 5   From (8.2) the result is obtained that, when the output changes, the change in prime profit, and therefore in total profit, is

$$2fqu\triangle f. \tag{8.6}$$

It is here a matter of complete indifference whether the change in output is due to a change in demand or to a change in the prime cost. (It is, of course, being supposed that in every position the firm charges such a price as will maximise its prime profit.)

The proportional increase in prime profit is

$$\frac{2fqu\triangle f}{f^2qu} = \frac{2\triangle f}{f} \tag{8.7}$$

that is to say, it is equal to twice the proportional increase in output. (The prime profit increases partly as a direct result of the increase of output, partly, and to a precisely equal extent, as a result of the increase of the excess of the price over the prime cost with which the increase of output is associated.)

IV   PURPOSE OF THE NEXT CHAPTER

§ 6   In the next chapter an attempt will be made to treat in a somewhat more general way the equilibrium of an industry and the relation between changes in price and changes in output. The conclusions that will be obtained are important, but the mathematical lines of approach may be regarded purely as means to an end and do not involve any fundamental development in the realm of economic ideas.

In the first place it will be essential to investigate the conditions under which the annihilation coefficient, q, can be assumed to be a constant for a particular firm. It will be found that this assumption is usually justifiable for changes of the kind described, in § 3 of the next chapter, as conforming to type A, but not for changes of the type B. The restrictions that the assumption consequently involves are considered in § 8.

The case of an industry that consists of firms which are all identical is covered by § 4 of this chapter. In the next chapter we shall derive equations for cases that are somewhat more complicated. The firms will be supposed to differ in size and in prime cost, subject to certain simplifying restrictions, and finally we shall work out the case where some firms are working full-time or at a minimum level of output below which they will not descend.

The results are of quantitative rather than of qualitative significance. Indeed, it is only in this most complicated case to which reference has just been made, where the output of some firms is limited in an upward or downward direction, that equation (8.1) of § 2 and equation (8.3) of § 4 cannot be applied as they stand.[1] And even in the most complicated case with which we shall deal these equations are only modified to the extent of the addition of an extra term or a factor, as may be seen by turning to equation (9.15b) in § 23 and to equation (9.16) in § 25 of the next chapter. Some statistical confirmation of these equations will be found in §§ 24 and 26.

---

[1] These equations are applicable in the simpler cases as relations between the *average* values of the various quantities.

CHAPTER 9

MATHEMATICAL TREATMENT OF THE EQUILIBRIUM OF AN INDUSTRY IN AN IMPERFECT MARKET

I CONSTANCY OF THE ANNIHILATION COEFFICIENT

§ 1 In the preceding chapter there has been an understanding that for a particular firm the annihilation coefficient, q, is a constant – constant not only when the output of the single firm changes (such constancy follows at once from our assumption that over the range in question the individual demand curve is a straight line) but constant also when the prices and output of the whole industry change. Such an understanding was sufficient for its purpose. But, before it is possible to enter upon a mathematical investigation of the elasticity of supply of an industry, the constancy of the annihilation coefficient must be put to a more rigorous test.

The treatment that follows is based on the assumption of the first, and most important, case of the last section of Chapter 7 – namely, that the individual business man supposes that if he alters his price and output, his competitors' prices will remain constant. But it is not evident that either the treatment or the conclusions that emerge from it would be materially different in the more complex second and third cases.

§ 2   For the sake of simplicity it can be assumed that we are dealing with a case of pure transport imperfection. The modification that is necessary to cover the case of preference imperfection was made obvious in § 14 of Chapter 7. Then the market is divided up into a number of areas each of which deals entirely with a single firm. We will turn out attention to a single one of these areas and to the firm that produces for it.

3   Two cases, extremes of a possible continuous range, will be examined. In the first case, which will be called case A, any change that takes place in the conditions of aggregate demand for the product of the industry is located in a region that is well away from the area attached to the particular firm which is under consideration. The repercussions of such a change of course spread to this area and affect the output of the firm and its price, but the *aggregate* demand schedule of a given geographical collation of customers in the neighbourhood of the firm is unchanged.

In case B any change that takes place in the conditions of aggregate demand pervades the whole market uniformly. Aggregate demand schedules are altered in the same manner in every small strip of territory.

4   **Case A** We are going to consider the situation of the firm in two positions of equilibrium for the whole industry. In one of them let

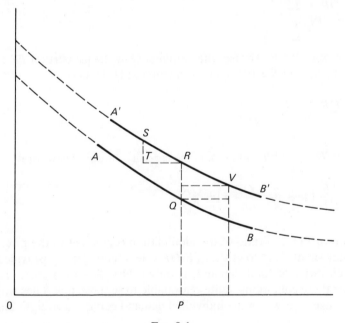

FIG. 9.1

its demand curve be *AB* (Figure 9.1) and its equilibrium position be denoted by the point *Q*. When the industry is in equilibrium in its other position, let the demand curve be *A'B'*. If now the firm were to charge a price PR, its output would be OP as before. But, owing to the fact that its price would be higher than before, the density of the effective demand in its area would be lower than before. The area which it supplies would therefore be greater than before. If now the firm were to raise its price still further, its area would contract until, at the point S, say, it became identical with its original area.[1] It will now be shown that TR is generally fairly small, so that the range over which the demand curve is assumed to be a straight line may reasonably include the point S. For the sake of simplicity it will be supposed in the proof that the demand curve *is* a straight line as far as S, but this does not, I think, render the argument circular.

The price at S is higher than the price at Q by $QR + TS$. Therefore, if e is the elasticity of aggregate demand (measured in terms of the f.o.b. price charged by the firm), the density of the demand at S is less than the density at Q by the proportion

$$\frac{QR + TS}{PQ} e$$

The output at S is less than the output at Q by the proportion TR/OP. But the area at S is the same as the area at Q. Hence

$$\frac{QR + TS}{PQ} e = \frac{TR}{OP}$$

But $TS = qTR/u$, where u is the capacity output. Therefore

$$\frac{TR}{OP} \left(1 - \frac{q}{PQ} \cdot \frac{OP}{u} e \right) = \frac{QR}{PQ} e$$

Now q/PQ, the ratio of the annihilation coefficient to the price, is usually small. It follows that TR/OP is less than QR/PQ provided e, the elasticity of total demand, is only a little less than unity. It is, under these conditions, quite reasonable to suppose that S lies within the range over which the individual demand curve is a straight line.

---

[1] The area contracts in extent, but there is, of course, no reason why it should achieve complete identity with the original area. The divergence, however, is not likely to be great, because the general interrelationship of the prices charged by neighbouring firms does not alter much between the two positions in which the whole industry is in equilibrium.

5   It remains to examine the conditions under which the annihilation coefficient is the same at S as at Q, in other words, under which the demand curves $A'B'$ and AB are parallel.

The area attached to the firm is the same at S as at Q. If the firm reduces its price by a certain small interval, the consequent increase in the area is also the same at S as at Q, for it depends only on the amount of the price reduction in relation to the costs of transport at the boundary of the area. The slope of the demand curve depends on the increase in demand that is associated with the increase in area.[1] The slope is greater at S than at Q because, owing to the higher price at S, the density of the demand is less at S than at Q. If q is the annihilation coefficient at Q and $q + \Delta q$ at S,

$$\frac{\Delta q}{q} = \frac{QR + TS}{PQ} e$$

e being, as before, the elasticity of aggregate demand.[2]
But TS is small in relation to QR.
Therefore

$$\frac{\Delta q}{q} = \frac{\Delta p}{p} e, \text{ if } PQ = p, QR = \Delta p.$$

6   To obtain a rough idea of the degree of smallness which it is necessary to ascribe to $\Delta q/q$, it will be sufficient to examine the case where most of the firms are identical. Q (Figure 9.1), as has been said, represents the position of equilibrium of a single firm in the first position. Let V represent its position of equilibrium in the second position. Let differences between the two positions Q and V be denoted by the symbol D.

Then $Dq = \Delta q$
and $Dp = \Delta p - qDf$.

The requirement is that equation (8.1) (Chapter 8, § 2) shall be capable of being differentiated as though q were a constant. It follows, then, that the second term of the expression

---

[1] For the purposes of this rough calculation, the increase in demand that is set up in the original area by the reduction of price may be neglected (particularly if the aggregate demand is fairly inelastic).
[2] Strictly speaking, e is now the elasticity of demand at the border of the area, not the average over the whole area.

$$qDf + fDq$$

shall be negligible; in other words that Dq/q shall be small in relation to Df/f.

But $Df/f = Dp/p(S)$, when S is the elasticity of aggregate supply:

$$= \frac{\Delta p}{p} S - \frac{q}{p} SDf$$

Therefore,

$$\frac{Df}{f} \left(1 + \frac{fq}{p} S\right) = \frac{\Delta p}{p} S$$

And

$$Dq = \Delta q.$$

The condition then becomes that $\Delta q/q$ shall be small in relation to

$$\frac{\Delta p}{p} \frac{S}{1 + \frac{fq}{p} S}$$

But it has just been proved that

$$\frac{\Delta q}{q} = \frac{\Delta p}{p} e$$

Finally, then, the condition is that e shall be small in relation to

$$\frac{S}{1 + \frac{fq}{p} S}$$

Now, on the assumption that q *is* constant, it will be seen shortly (§ 15) that $S = p/fq$. If q deviates only slightly from constancy, S is not likely to differ much from p/fq; and the condition for constancy of q becomes that e shall be small in relation to $S/2$.

In general the supply is highly elastic and the demand is usually rather inelastic. The condition, therefore, generally holds; and the slope of the individual demand curve of a particular firm may be assumed to be independent of the position of the curve.

7 **Case B** The course of reasoning is the same as in Case A, but it has to be remembered that in the second position of equilibrium of the whole industry (in which the demand curve is $A'B'$), the demand is everywhere greater than it was in Case A, the increase being in the ratio, say, of g to l when the prices in the two positions are the same. g is imagined to be fairly small.

Then the density of the demand at S is less than the density at Q by the proportion

$$\frac{QR + TS}{PQ} e - g$$

And

$$\frac{TR}{OP}\left(1 - \frac{q}{PQ}\frac{OP}{u}e\right) = \frac{QR}{PQ}e - g$$

The case for regarding S as lying within the range over which the demand curve is a straight line is therefore strengthened.

8 Similarly,

$$\frac{\Delta q}{q} = \frac{\Delta p}{p} e - g$$

Now

$$\frac{Df}{f} = g - \frac{Dp}{p} e$$

But, as has been stated

$$Dp = p - qDf$$

Therefore,

$$g = \frac{\Delta p}{p} e - \frac{q}{p} eDf + \frac{Df}{f}$$

Hence,

$$\frac{\Delta q}{q} = \frac{q}{p} eDf - \frac{Df}{f}$$

Or,

$$\frac{Dq}{q} = \frac{Df}{f} \left(\frac{fq}{p} e - 1 \right)$$

§ 9   The term in brackets is small when e is nearly equal to p/fq, which, as has been said, is then about equal to S. While, therefore, the condition for constancy of q is in case A that the elasticity of demand, e, shall be small in relation to that of supply, S (so that a change in price shall not have an appreciable effect on the density of the demand), in case B the condition is that the two elasticities shall be nearly equal (so that the effect of the change in demand shall be compensated by the change in price). It has been seen that in case A the condition is frequently fulfilled. But it is clear that in case B it can only be fulfilled in rare instances and then as a result of what is almost a coincidence.

§ 10   If the condition necessary to case A – that e/s is small – holds in case B, the last equation becomes

$$\frac{Dq}{q} = - \frac{Df}{f} ;$$

and differentiation of equation (8.1), instead of producing the result that

$$Dp = qDf,$$

as it does in case A, q then being treated as a constant, produces the result that

$$Dp = qDf + fDq = 0$$

It may, therefore, be said, in a rough sort of way, that the change in price that is associated with a change of output is very small under the conditions of case B compared with the change in price that ensues under the conditions of case A. The reason is that in case B the effect of the change in output is counterbalanced by the effect of the change in the degree of imperfection of the market with which the change of output is associated.

The investigations of the following pages will be based on the supposition that q can be assumed to be a constant for a particular firm. They are therefore of fairly general application in cases of the type A but will require further development before they can be applied to cases of the type B. This limitation to their usefulness is less severe than at first sight appears. It is true that they cannot be applied when a change in demand reacts directly on most of the firms in the industry. But frequently it is among the customers of only a few firms that the change has its seat; and it is just then that the results of the next pages should have a direct application. A change that is due for instance to competition from a particular area of the world or to an increase in the demand from such an area affects directly only those firms that deal with that area: the reaction on the rest of the industry occurs through a process of price-*tâtonnement* and continues until equilibrium is restored with a new complex of outputs and prices.

Moreover, some of the results that follow can be used when there is no change whatever in the conditions of demand – this is the purest possible case of type A – but where, for instance, a change in the level of prime costs reacts on the price, and so on the output.

II EQUILIBRIUM OF AN INDUSTRY

It will be convenient to set out afresh the equations that were obtained in §§ 2 and 4 of the last chapter to represent the equilibrium of a single firm. If p is the price it charges, r is its average prime cost, f is the ratio of its output to its capacity output, and q is its annihilation coefficient, then

$$q - r = fq \tag{9.1}$$

If u is the capacity output,

prime profit $= f^2qu.$ (9.2)

If the demand changes but q remains constant,

$$p = q\Delta f \qquad (9.3)$$

and

the proportional increase in output =

$$\frac{\text{change in the price}}{\text{excess of the price over the prime cost}} \qquad (9.4)$$

and

the elasticity of supply $= \dfrac{p}{fq}$ (9.5)

§ 13   If the output changes, whether as a result of a change in demand or in prime cost, the change in prime profit, and therefore in total profit, is

$$2fqu\Delta f \qquad (9.6)$$

and the proportional increase in prime profit is

$$\frac{2\Delta f}{f} \qquad (9.7)$$

§ 14   The treatment of a whole industry, which is now to be attempted, may appear clearer if it is taken in successive stages of increasing complication.

§ 15   The first stage involves no complications. The firms are all identical and the results that have just been obtained for a single firm apply to the whole industry.[1] Equations (9.1), (9.3), (9.4) and (9.5) become:

---

[1] Throughout external economies and diseconomies are being neglected.

$$P - R = Fq \tag{9.8}$$

$$\Delta P = q\Delta F \tag{9.9}$$

$$\frac{\text{Proportional}}{\text{increase in output}} = \frac{\text{Change in the price}}{\text{Excess of the price over the prime}} \tag{9.10}$$
$$\text{cost}$$

$$\text{Elasticity of supply} = -\frac{P}{Fq} \tag{9.11}$$

The supply curve is a straight line whose slope is proportional to q (*or* equal to q if the capacity of the industry is adopted as the unit of output).

At the second stage the prime costs of all the firms are equal, but their capacity outputs differ. The annihilation coefficients of all the firms are the same; in other words the slope of the individual demand curve is inversely proportional to the capacity output. It follows that the change in output that would result from a single firm changing its price is proportional to the capacity output of the firm: this seems a reasonable supposition.

But it is not sufficient to define the slopes of the demand curves. Their positions, too, require definition. The general situation is such that, if all the firms were to charge the same price, then the output of each would be proportional to its capacity output. This assumption, taken in conjunction with the preceding one, means that the separate markets of all the firms are similar in nature and are proportional in size, or in density of demand, to the capacity outputs of the firms to which they are severally attached. Again this seems a reasonable supposition.

It has just been said that, *if* all the firms were to charge the same price, then the output of each would be proportional to its capacity output; in other words the value of the ratio, f, of output to capacity output would be the same for all. But equation (9.1) demands, since the prime cost and annihilation coefficient, q, are constant throughout the industry, that, *if f* were the same for all the firms, then the price charged by each would be the same. Since, presumably, there is only one possible position of equilibrium, it is now at once clear that in equilibrium all the firms charge the same price and work at the same ratio, f, of output to capacity output.

That being the case, equations (9.8), (9.9), (9.10) and (9.11) require no modification at this stage.

§ 18   At the third stage the real complications begin. The firms now differ, not only in size, but also in prime cost. But the same type of conditions prevail as at the second stage. The annihilation coefficient is the same for every firm, and *if* all the firms were to charge the same price, then the output of each would be proportional to its capacity output. That is to say that at this stage there is no connection between a firm's market (as expressed by its demand curve) and the level of its prime cost.

Furthermore, there is no correlation between size and prime cost. In other words, the average capacity output is the same for every value of the prime cost.

In another respect also there is a random quality in the situation. The position[1] occupied by a firm in the market bears no relation to its prime cost. There is no tendency for the general level of prime cost to be less in one part of the market than in another part, as there would be, for instance, if variations in the distance from coal mines had a significant influence on the cost of fuel. The entourage of competitors surrounding every firm is of the same general constitution throughout the industry.

It may be noted in passing that if these conditions are not satisfied by a whole industry, they may still be satisfied by separate parts of the industry. Thus they are obviously not satisfied by the British coal-mining industry. But they are probably quite reasonably satisfied by the separate coal-mining districts into which, for statistical and other purposes, the whole country is divided.

Finally the conditions are still such that every firm can maximise its prime profit in accordance with equation (9.1) without being obliged to maintain on the one hand an output above its capacity or on the other hand an output less than zero.

§ 19   Let F, as before, be the ratio of the output of the industry to its capacity output. Let P now be the price that *would* rule if all the firms were working at the ratio F, which is the average of the actual ratios weighted according to the capacity outputs. Let the price charged by a particular firm be p, and let the ratio of its actual output to its capacity output be f.

---

[1] Such words as 'position', 'entourage', 'extent', etc., which retain their ordinary meanings when applied to transport imperfection, require appropriate interpretation, the nature of which is sufficiently obvious, if they are to be applied to preference imperfection.

Since the entourage of any firm is constituted in a perfectly random manner and represents the general average of the industry, it is a matter of complete indifference to the firm whether all the other firms in the industry follow out their individual policies or all work at the same ratio F and charge the same price P. It follows that its

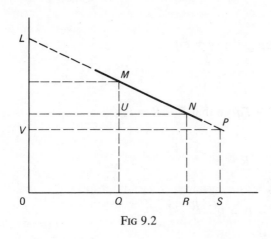

FIG 9.2

individual demand curve, LP (Figure 9.2), must be such that, if it were to alter its price to P, its output would become Fu, where u is its capacity output.

Let $OQ = Fu$, $OR = fu$ (the actual output), and $OS = u$. Then, if $QM = P$ and $RN = p$, MN is the demand curve. Then $LV = q$.

Now

$$\frac{MU}{UN} = \frac{LV}{VP}$$

In other words,

$$\frac{P - p}{f - F} = q;$$

or

$$P - p = fq - Fq$$

But, by equation (9.1), $p - r = fq$, where r is the average prime cost of the firm.

Hence,

$$p = \frac{P + r + Fq}{2}$$

and

$$fq - pr = \frac{P - r + Fq}{2}$$

Let

$$R = P - Fq, \text{ so that } P - R = Fq$$

Then

$$p = P - \frac{R - r}{2} \tag{9.12}$$

$$p - r = P - R + \frac{R - r}{2} \tag{9.13}$$

$$f = F + \frac{1}{q} \frac{R - r}{2} \tag{9.14}$$

If n is the number of firms and U is the capacity output of the industry, it follows from equation (9.14) that

$$F = \frac{1}{U} \Sigma fu$$

$$= \frac{1}{U} F \Sigma u + \frac{1}{2qU} \Sigma(R-r)u$$

$$= F + \frac{1}{2qU} \Sigma(R-r)u$$

$$\therefore \Sigma(R-r)u = 0$$

$$\therefore R = \frac{1}{U} \Sigma ru.$$

In other words, R is the average (arithmetic mean) prime cost weighted according to the capacity output.

The weighted average price is

$$\frac{1}{U}\Sigma pu = P - \frac{1}{2U}\Sigma(R-r)u \text{ (by equation (9.12))}$$
$$= P.$$

But, by definition, $P - R = Fq$, which is equation (9.8) written in terms of average values.

It follows that a firm whose prime cost is the weighted average prime cost R produces an output which is the weighted average output F at a price which is the weighted average price P: there can be little objection to describing such a firm as the 'average firm'.

Equations (9.12) and (9.13) state that the deviations of price (in the one direction) and of excess of price over prime cost (in the opposite direction) between a given firm and the average firm are equal to half the deviation of prime cost. From equation (9.14) it follows that the deviation of the ratio of output to capacity output is equal to half the deviation of prime cost divided by the annihilation coefficient.

These facts can be represented in a slightly different manner. The prefix D will be employed to represent the extent of the complete range of the different variables over the whole industry.

Then from (9.12), $\qquad Dp = \frac{1}{2} Dr$,

from (9.13), $\qquad D(p-r) = -\frac{1}{2} Dr$,

and from (9.14), $\qquad Df = -\frac{1}{2}/q\, Dr$.

These relations are important in deciding to what extent the uniformity of the first two stages can be assumed to exist in a given industry; though it will appear immediately that it is less necessary to make this decision than appears *a priori* likely.

The relation between a change in output and the associated change in price that result from a change in demand at the third stage is an extremely simple one. It has been proved that R, defined as $P - Fq$, is constant, being the weighted average of the prime costs of all the firms. It follows that

$$\Delta P = q\Delta F,$$

which is merely equation (9.8), and equations (9.9) and (9.10) immediately emerge.

In fact the relations of the first and second stages apply to the weighted averages at the third stage. This is more satisfactory than could reasonably have been expected.

§ 22   The path may grow less elegant but we now have to push our way up to the fourth stage. The only difference between the fourth stage and the third stage is that the limitations that prevent a firm from producing more than its capacity output or less than nothing now become effective. This difference is a sufficiently big one; and a whole stage may well be given up in overcoming the difficulty that it represents.

As was pointed out earlier in this essay, a firm rarely reduces its output to the neighbourhood of zero even though such a policy, from the point of view of the immediate present, may be the most profitable. In order to maintain connections, and for other reasons,[1] a firm does not reduce its output below a certain level. To render the problem reasonably tractable, we shall assume that the ratio of this level of output to the capacity level is not only absolutely fixed for a given firm, but also the same for every firm in the industry: it will be called f_0. It has, it is true, been pointed out that the amount of this kind of sacrifice that a firm will incur in the interests of a problematical future is likely to depend on the extent of its prime cost and of its losses – past, current and prospective. Firms with greater prime costs might be expected to be satisfied with smaller levels of minimum output. On the other hand, technical considerations will often be sufficient to provide us with the required stereotyped basis. Thus in cotton-spinning it is very convenient to work a full week and then to stop a full week; and for many mills the ratio of output to capacity output is 50 per cent.

If in point of fact firms do not work at a higher level of output when a lower level, or a zero output, would mean decreased losses, f_0 is equal to zero. The necessity for dealing with f_0 still remains. The whole difficulty at this stage lies in the fact that equation (9.1) leads to values of f for some firms that are greater than 1 or less than f_0 (or 0).

§ 23   Let there be a firms that are working full-time and b firms that are working at the minimum ratio f_0 (which may be zero); and let the number of the rest of the firms (working at ratios between f_0 and unity) be n. As before, F is the ratio of the aggregate output to the capacity output of the industry. P is again defined as the price that

[1] See Chapter 2, § 7.

would rule if all the firms were working at the ratio F, and now R' is defined as $P - Fq$. Then equations (9.12), (9.13) and (9.14) continue to hold for each of the n firms. For convenience they are repeated here:

$$p = P - \frac{R' - r}{2} \tag{9.12a}$$

$$p - r = P - R' + \frac{R' - r}{2} \tag{9.13a}$$

$$f = F + \frac{1}{q} \frac{R' - r}{2} \tag{9.14a}$$

The a firms and the b firms are supposed to be distributed in a random manner among the n firms. It is clear then that, since the output, relative to the capacity output, of each of the a firms is the same, the price charged by each is the same. From equation (9.14a) it can be seen that a firm whose prime cost r is such that $R' - r/2 = (1-F)q$ is just working full-time and can be placed indiscriminately in the n class or in the a class. The price that such a firm would charge is the price charged by each member of the a class. From equation (9.12a) it follows that this price is

$$P - (1-F)q$$

In the same way it can be seen that the price charged by each of the b firms is

$$p + (F - f_0)q$$

The symbol $\overset{n}{\underset{1}{\Sigma}}$ will be supposed to operate only on the n firms.

Then if U is the capacity output of the industry, so that $U/n+a+b$ is the average capacity output of a single firm,

$$fU = \overset{n}{\underset{1}{\Sigma}} fu + (a + bf_0) \frac{U}{n + a + b}$$

Then by (9.14a),

$$(n + a + b) F = nF + \frac{n}{2q} R' - \frac{n + a + b}{2qU} \sum_1^n ru + a + bf_0$$

$$\therefore q\{a(1 - F) - b(F - f_0)\} = \tfrac{1}{2}\left\{\frac{n + a + b}{U} \sum_1^n ru - nR'\right\}$$

Let the mean price, weighted according to the capacity output, be Π.

Then

$$\Pi U = \sum_1^n pu + \frac{a}{n + a + b} U\{P - (1 - F)q\} +$$

$$\frac{b}{n + a + b} U\{P + (F - f_0)q\}$$

Hence, by (9.12a),

$$(n + a + b) \Pi = (n + a + b) P +$$

$$\tfrac{1}{2}\left\{\frac{(n + a + b)}{U}\sum_1^n ru - nR'\right\} - q\{a(1 - F) - b(F - f_0)\}$$

$$= (n + a + b)P, \qquad \text{by (i)}$$

$$\therefore \Pi = P; \text{ and } P \text{ is once again the average price.}$$

From equations (9.12a) and (9.14a) it follows that the firm which works at the average ratio F sells at the average price P; its prime cost is R', but R' is no longer the average prime cost and indeed is not determined absolutely by the prime costs of the firms in the industry – it is no longer a constant.

If R' is given its value $P - Fq$, equation (i) becomes

$$Fq \{n + 2(a + b)\} = 2q (a + b f_0) - \frac{n + a + b}{U}\sum_1^n ru + nP$$

Or

$$P - \frac{n + a + b}{U} \; \frac{1}{n} \sum_1^n ru$$

$$= Fq - 2q \left\{ \frac{a}{n}(1 - F) - \frac{b}{n} (F - f_o) \right\}$$

But $\dfrac{n + a + b}{U} \dfrac{1}{n} \sum_1^n ru$ is the average prime cost of the n firms weighted according to the capacity output: this may be written R, so that

$$P - R = Fq - 2q \left\{ \frac{a}{n}(1 - F) - \frac{b}{n} (F - f_o) \right\} \qquad (9.15a)$$

This equation has to take the place of the simple equation

$$P - R = Fq$$

of former stages.

It will be more useful in the form

$$P - R = Fq \left\{ 1 + 2 \frac{a + b}{n} \right\} - 2q \; \frac{a + bf_o}{n} \qquad (9.15b)$$

If $a/n(1 - F) = b/n(F - f_o)$, equation (9.15a) relapses into the old version

$$P - R = Fq$$

The spinning of medium counts in the American section of the cotton industry provides a rough example of this type of symmetry. For an equal number of firms work full-time and half-time ($a/n = b/n = 1$) and F was about $\frac{3}{4}d$ in the middle of the winter of 1928–9.

If then q is again, as in § 3, taken to be equal to $1d$, it follows that

$$P - R = \tfrac{3}{4}d \text{ for this period.}$$

It was shown in § 5 of Chapter 6 that, for 42's weft at the end of 1927, the excess of the price charged by a standard mill over its prime cost was $0.22d$ per pound. Now a standard mill is, presumably, a sort of average mill. But we are faced with a difficulty. While p is the average price over the whole industry, R is the average prime cost only of the n firms. Since, however, the number of a firms is, in this case, equal to the number of b firms, and the differences of prime cost over the whole industry are, in any case, not very large, it may be assumed that the average prime cost of the n firms is equal to the average prime cost over the whole industry. It may therefore be concluded that, at the end of 1927, $P - R$ was equal to $0.22d$. But the end of 1927 was a period of bad trade and low margins: the Cotton Yarn Association's scheme of restriction had recently been withdrawn, and F was only about 60 per cent. Between the end of 1927 and the period of three months ending January 1929 (for which period the average production of 42's weft was 74.4 per cent of capacity), the margin on 42's weft improved by $0.5d$[1]; so that for this period of three months

$P - R$ was equal to $0.72d$.

The agreement between this figure and the figure of $\frac{3}{4}d$, just mentioned, is extraordinary, particularly when it is remembered that q was put equal to $1d$ only as a very rough approximation, based on a guess elicited with considerable difficulty from a Lancashire man who, though more qualified than anyone else to venture an opinion, obviously did not attach much value to his figure of $\frac{1}{4}d$, as the amount by which a mill working at 75 per cent of capacity would have to reduce its price in order to work full-time.[2]

§ 25   The usual step now confronts us. We have to determine the relation between a change in price and the associated change in output that result from an altered demand. If Δa, Δb are the increases in a, b and Δn that in n, then

$$\Delta a + \Delta b = -\Delta n \qquad \text{(ii)}$$

---

[1] This figure is not derived from any of the returns circularised by the Cotton Yarn Association to its members and is to be regarded as even more confidential than the information contained in such returns; see footnote to § 26.

[2] I may mention that I had written down the figure of $\frac{3}{4}d$ before I proceeded to evaluate, from the data at my disposal, the figure of $0.72d$. The closeness of the agreement is, of course, fortuitous. If a period other than the three months ending January 1929 had been examined, the agreement would not be so good. This will be obvious when we come, in § 26, to correlate changes in the output with changes in the margin.

Owing to the transfers of firms from one class to another, the mean prime cost of the n class is altered. From equation (9.14a) it follows that the firms situated near the margin between the n class and the a class (for which therefore $f = 1$), have a prime cost $R' - 2q (1 - F)$; while those situated near the margin between the n class and the b class, (for which $f = f_o$), have a prime cost $R' + 2q (F - f_o)$. The change in the mean prime cost of the n class is due to the loss of Δa firms across the one margin and of Δb across the other margin. If n is large or if a sufficient number of firms are congregated close to one of the margins, the prime costs of all the firms that are transferred across the margins may be assumed to be equal to these 'marginal' prime costs.

Hence,

$$\Delta(nR) = -\{R' - 2q (1 - F)\} \Delta a - \{R' + 2q (F - f_o)\} \Delta b$$

$$= -R'(\Delta a + \Delta b) + 2q \{(1 - F) \Delta a - (F - f_o) \Delta b\}$$

$$\therefore \Delta(nR) = (P - Fq) \Delta n + 2q \{(1 - F) \Delta a (F - f_o) \Delta b\},$$

using equation (ii) and the fact that $P - R - Fq$.

Now from equation (9.15a) it follows that

$$\Delta(nP) - \Delta(nR) = \Delta(nFq) + 2q (a + b) \Delta F - $$
$$2q\{(1 - F) \Delta a - (F - f_o) \Delta b\}$$

When the last two questions are added, this simple result emerges:

$$\Delta(nP) = \Delta(nFq) + (P - Fq)\Delta n + 2q(a + b)\Delta F$$

Or:

$$n\Delta P + P\Delta n = nq\Delta F + Fq\Delta n + (P - Fq)\Delta n + 2q(a + b)\Delta F$$

$$\therefore \Delta P = q\Delta F \left\{ 1 + \frac{2(a + b)}{n} \right\} \qquad (9.16)^1$$

This simple relation has to be substituted for the simpler one,

---

[1] It will be seen at once that this is precisely the relation that would emerge directly out of equation (15a) if it were assumed that a/n, b/n and R, the mean prime cost of the n firms, do not change. This is not remarkable, since there is no reason why there should be any firms close to the margins. Moreover, the result could scarcely depend on whether there are or are not a few firms close to the margins. But the reasoning in the text is justified by the possibility – indeed this must be the usual position – of a large number of firms being situated near one of the margins.

$\Delta P = q\Delta F$, that was deduced for the earlier stages (equation (9.9)). A given increase in output is associated with a greater increase in price when some of the firms maintain their outputs unchanged. There are two reasons, each of which is responsible for the factor $a + b/n$ which occurs doubled in equation (9.16). One reason is that the given increase in output has to be distributed over a smaller number of firms. The other reason is that the a and b class firms, although they do not increase their output, nevertheless raise their prices and so contribute to the elevation of the demand curves of the n class firms.

Equation (9.16) is the complicated version of equation (9.8). Instead of equations (9.9) and (9.10), the following are obtained by means of (9.15b) and (9.16):

$$\frac{\Delta F}{F} = \frac{\Delta P}{P - R + 2q\dfrac{a + bf_0}{n}} \tag{9.17}$$

And

the elasticity of supply

$$= \frac{P}{P - R + 2q\dfrac{a + bf_0}{n}} \tag{9.18}$$

§ 26   It will be noticed that these equations take no cognisance of the rate of change of prime cost near the margins, which, as was shown in § 29 of Chapter 6, determines the supply schedule when the market is perfect. This is a somewhat serious omission which takes its origin in the assumption made near the beginning of the last subsection: n is to be large or a sufficient number of firms are to be congregated close to one of the margins. The conditions underlying this assumption are that the market is not too perfect, so that a change of output is due preponderatingly to a change in the output rather than in the number of the n firms, or, if the market is rather perfect, that the situation is such that in a perfect market the supply would be very elastic. One or other of these conditions is often satisfied. In coal-mining the market is very imperfect, in cotton-spinning supply would be very elastic if the market were quite perfect.

The American section of the cotton-spinning industry has been working under conditions of polypoly since the end of September 1927, when the Cotton Yarn Association withdrew all restrictions. The following figures (Table 9.1) for 42's weft, are derived from the Association,[1] whose statistical work lapsed with it in April, 1929.

TABLE 9.1

Period	Ratio of output of Association's members to their capacity output as %	Average margin (corrected for changes in basis and cost to clean (in pence per pound)
Nov. 1927 to Jan. 1928	61.0	5.75
Feb. 1928 to Apr. 1928	68.4	5.8
May 1928 to July 1928	61.2	5.8
Aug. 1928 to Oct. 1928	64.3	6.0
Nov. 1928 to Jan. 1929	74.4	6.25
Feb. 1929 to Apr. 1929	68.0	5.95

It is obvious that disturbing influences have been at work, but it is equally obvious that the figures are positively correlated. While the period of one and a half years is too short for definite conclusions to be derived from the three-month averages, it is probable that the disturbing influences would prove yet more upsetting over periods shorter than three months. In any case, it is interesting to examine how the above figures fit in with our equations.

The coefficient of correlation is 0.80. The coefficient of regression of the output on the margin is 21.8 per cent per penny per pound, and of the margin on the output it is 1/34.1 pence per pound per cent. the arithmetic mean of the slopes of the two lines of regression is 28 per cent per penny per pound, and it may therefore be said that there is a tendency for a change of output of 0.028 of the capacity output to be associated with a change in the margin of 0.1 penny per pound. In other words:

$$0.028 \ \Delta P = 0.1 \ \Delta F$$

---

[1] The figures of production are contained in the private returns circulated to members, but the figures of margins were arrived at by me from data placed at my disposal during a visit to Manchester and are, I am informed, to be regarded as exceptionally confidential.

or

$$\Delta P = 3.6 \ \Delta F$$

Now a third of the mills spinning medium counts work full-time, a third work half-time, and the rest work at intermediate levels of output. Hence $a/n = b/n = 1$. Again as in § 24, $q = 1d$. Equation (9.16) then becomes

$$\Delta P = 5\Delta F.$$

The agreement between theory and practice, while not as sensational as it was in § 24, is again more satisfactory than might have been expected, particularly when regard is paid to the slenderness and apparent insecurity of the foundations on which we have built. At least it is sufficient to lend plausibility to the view that we have tentatively adopted: it would appear probable that in the spinning of medium counts of American cotton the imperfection of the market is a major influence in determining the position of equilibrium. It would seem, moreover, that mills, on the whole, adopt the individual policies that lead to minimum losses, subject to the necessity of working not less than half-time. The fact that the experimental value of $\Delta P/\Delta F$, 3.6, is less than its theoretical value, 5, may be taken to indicate that the conditions of case B of § 3 are not entirely absent. For it was shown in § 10 that, if the aggregate demand is rather inelastic, the value of $\Delta P/\Delta F$ under the extreme conditions of case B would be very small. But, on the other hand, the deviation from the value calculated for the purest type of case A is not very large; and it would, therefore, appear that the changes in the demand for cotton yarn have, on the whole, been local or sectional rather than world-wide and general.

It may be noted that our somewhat rough-and-ready determination of q as $1d$ can now be dispensed with. For the treatment of § 24 can be reversed, so as to derive the value of q from the excess of the margin over prime cost. Then this value of q, which would be roughly $1d$, could be adopted for the purposes of the above calculation. Alternatively, equation (9.17), in which q does not appear, could be employed to compare theory and fact: the result would be identical with the one that has just been obtained.

CHAPTER 10

CHANGES IN PRIME COST AND IN HOURS IN AN IMPERFECT MARKET

I SCOPE OF THE CHAPTER

1   In this chapter certain practical questions, which have been touched upon in earlier portions of the essay, will be examined in the light of the equations of Chapter 9. For the most part, the results that have already been obtained will be sufficient; but in one or two places it will be necessary to extend the methods of the last chapter a short stage further.

II CHANGES IN PRIME COST

2   So far attention has been confined to the effects of changes in demand. We shall now turn to a change in the conditions of supply, in the shape of a uniform alteration in prime cost.[1] The equations that have been obtained, culminating in equation (9.16),[2] should be capable of application to the variations of price and output of cotton yarn over the last few years, during which prime costs have remained unaltered. It is now easy to add a term that will represent the effect of such changes in prime cost as have been continually occurring in the coal industry.

At the first, second and third stages the position of equilibrium was described by the equation

[1] Such, for instance, as would be due to a uniform addition to piece-rates. The prime cost of the more efficient firm, which is less than the average prime cost R, would increase by the same absolute amount ΔR as that of the less efficient firm.

[2] So far as the numbering of equations is concerned, this chapter can be regarded as forming part of the last chapter

$$P - R = Fq$$

the symbols representing either the actual values that are the same for all the firms, at the first and second stages, or average values, at the third stage.

It follows at once that

$$\Delta P = \Delta R + q\Delta F \tag{9.19}$$

At the fourth stage $\Delta(nR)$ can be evaluated in the same manner as before, but the result must be increased by $n\Delta R$, where ΔR stands for the uniform addition to prime cost. It, of course, follows that

$$\Delta P = \Delta R + q\Delta F\left\{1 + \frac{2(a+b)}{n}\right\} \tag{9.20}$$

This equation is obviously subject to the same qualifications as were set out in the last subsection.

§ 3   It is now clear that an additional argument is available to the employers with which to attack the contention of § 6 of Chapter 6 that, when an industry is depressed, a reduction of wages results in an equivalent reduction of price. In fact, the conventional confusion between effects on output and effects on price, that was illustrated when the employers' third argument was discussed, is now seen to be not so stupid as it was then made to appear. But the long rigmarole of Chapter 6 is still necessary, because on the one hand, the employers never make use of the weapon that we are offering them – they fail to realise the implications of imperfection in the market – and, on the other hand, if they did make use of it, they would find it far too blunt for their purpose: such a reduction of losses as our equations ascribe to a reduction of wages would in most industries appear to the employers, and to the world in general, as absurdly small.

It can be seen from equations (9.18) or (9.19) that a change in price that is due to a change in prime cost falls short of the change in prime cost by an amount that is proportional to the change in output. If the demand is perfectly inelastic the two changes are equal. In general, the efficacy (in reducing losses) of a wage reduction, or the perniciousness of a wage increase, is in direct proportion to the imperfection of the market and to the elasticity of the aggregate demand.

To illustrate the orders of magnitude for medium counts of American cotton yarn, we may put $(a + b)/n$ equal to 2 and q equal to $1d$ (see § 24 of Chapter 9). Then equation (9.20) becomes

$$\Delta P = \Delta R + 5\Delta F$$

The recent award of the Court of Arbitration involves a value of ΔR of about $-0.15d$ (per lb). If as a consequence output increases by 2 per cent of capacity output, say $2\frac{2}{3}$ per cent of the actual output – this is a ridiculously extreme assumption – ΔP will still be equal to $-0.05d$. If the output increases by $1\frac{1}{3}$ per cent, ΔP will be equal to $-0.1d$.

III   EFFECTS ON PROFITS

But its effect on the excess of price over prime cost is not a sufficient criterion of the profitableness of a change. Prime profit increases not only as a result of an increase in the excess of price over prime cost, but also as a result of an increase in output. The two effects were shown by equation (9.6) to be equal, the actual increase in the prime profit of a single firm at any of the first three stages being

$$2fqu\,\Delta f$$

whether the change is one of demand or of prime cost, and the proportional increase in prime profit is by equation (9.7) $2\Delta f/f$, that is to say, twice the proportional increase in output.

As an example, a cotton mill can be taken whose fixed cost is £10,000 per annum and which is incurring an annual loss of £5,000. Its prime profit is therefore £5,000, and it follows that if as a result of a change of demand or of costs its output increases by 5 per cent, its prime profit increases and its annual loss diminishes by £500.

If the change is one purely of demand, R and r in equation (9.14) of § 19 of the last chapter are constant, while if it is a uniform change in prime cost, $\Delta R = \Delta r$. In both cases, then, it follows that $\Delta f - \Delta F$. (The output of every firm increases by the same proportion of its capacity output.)

Hence the increase in prime profit is $2fqu\Delta F$. It is therefore greater for firms with low prime costs than for firms with high prime costs. In other words, an increase in demand or a reduction of wages confers the greatest benefits on those firms which require them least.

The total increase at the third stage of prime profit to the whole industry is $2q\Delta F\Sigma fu = 2FqU\Delta F$.

§ 6   At the fourth stage it follows from equation (9.14a) of § 23 Chapter 9 that, for one of the n firms,

$$\Delta f = \Delta F + \frac{1}{2q}\Delta\ (R' - r)$$

Now $P - R' = Fq$. Subtracting this equation from equation (9.15a) we get

$$R' - R = -2q\left\{\frac{a}{n}(1 - F) - \frac{b}{n}\ (F - f_0)\right\}$$

$$\therefore\ \Delta R' - \Delta R = 2q\qquad\left(\frac{a + b}{n}\right)\Delta F$$

But, for a uniform change of prime cost, $\Delta r = \Delta R$. (If the change is purely one of demand, $\Delta R = \Delta r = 0$.)

$$\therefore\ \Delta(R' - r) = \Delta R' - \Delta R = 2q\left(\frac{a + b}{n}\right)\Delta F$$

$$\therefore\ \Delta f = \Delta F\left(1 + \frac{a + b}{n}\right)^1$$

Here, too, the output of every firm of the n class increases by the same proportion of its capacity output.

The increase in prime profit of one of the n firms

$$= 2fqu\,\Delta f$$

[1] If a/b and b/n can be assumed to be constant, this relation is an obvious one. See footnote to § 25 of Chapter 9

$$= 2fqu\Delta F \left(1 + \frac{a + b}{n} \right).$$

Again, as at the third stage, the firms which are losing less enjoy the greater decrease in their losses. But the benefit to every firm is greater, for a given proportional increase in the output of the industry, than it would be if there were no a and b class firms.

But here it is necessary to consider the changes of the profits earned by the bulk of the a and b firms, whose outputs cannot change. The prices charged by these two classes of firms were shown in § 23 of chapter 9 to be $P - (1 - F)q$ and $P + (F - f_o)q$.

The changes in these prices are, for both classes,

$$\Delta P + q\Delta F$$

and it then follows from equation (9.20) that the change in the excess of price over prime cost is in each case

$$2q\Delta F \left(1 + \frac{a + b}{n} \right)$$

The increase in the profit of an a class firm is therefore

$$2qu\Delta F \left(1 + \frac{a + b}{n} \right)$$

It is therefore precisely the same as that of an equal n class firm for which f is just under unity. This result is a little startling. A small increase in an industry's output brings no greater benefit, so it would appear, to a firm which can take part in the increase than to a firm which is already producing its maximum output, even though the firms differ only infinitesimally in respect to prime cost, output and price. The reason is that near the point where the prime profit is a maximum, its amount is independent of the precise level of the output. It can easily be shown that when output expands, the a firms, and likewise the b firms, raise their price by twice as much as each of the n firms.

The increase in the profit of a b class firm is

$$2f_o qu\Delta f \left(1 + \frac{a + b}{n} \right),$$

which is the same as that of an n class firm for which f is just a little more than f_o.

It may therefore be finally concluded that the amount of the benefit that accrues to a firm when the output of an industry increases, whether as the result of an increase in demand or of a uniform lowering of prime cost, rises uniformly with the efficiency of the firm.

§ 7   These results of course depend on the assumption that q is constant. There is a particular case, which should be mentioned, in which the reduction of prime costs takes such a form as necessarily to be the concomitant of a decrease in the value of q. Such is the case when a lowering in the costs of transport results in a decrease in transport imperfection or when an improvement of selling organisation leads to a decrease in preference imperfection.

If q is not constant, the increase in prime profit is from equation (9.2) of § 12 chapter 9, $2fqu\Delta f + f^2u\Delta q$; and the proportional increase is $(2\Delta f)/f + (\Delta q)/q$. Purely for the purposes of illustration, it may be supposed that a certain improvement in the methods of selling cotton yarn results, through its effect on the price of the finished product, in a 1 per cent increase of output. If at the same time the perfection of the yarn market is increased by only so much as is represented by a decrease in the value of q of 2 per cent (say from $1d$ to $0.98d$), profits remain unchanged (assuming for simplicity that all the mills are identical). The imperfection of the market is often a quality of a highly haphazard character, on which the operation of a small cause may produce a large effect. It must consequently sometimes happen that a reduction of the costs of transport or of marketing fail to achieve the intended purpose through the repercussions on the imperfection of the market.

It is theoretically arguable, though I know of no evidence on the subject, that the recent decrease under the late government's de-rating scheme in railway rates on coal intended for export may have involved certain mine owners in increased losses (owners, that is to say, who on the face of it should benefit from the subsidy. It is of course obvious that owners whose mines are situated close to the seaboard are adversely affected by the fall in price that results from increased competition from the inland). This is possible, for instance, in the case of a group of mines which are working short time, but which have been hitherto prevented by the high level of transport charges from selling their product outside the immediate neighbour-hood. For such a local market q is likely to be great and the price is therefore high in relation to prime cost. But if now the reduction in railway rates is sufficient to enable the mines to compete in foreign markets, q is drastically reduced in value. The increase in output may be quite small, but, in the absence of that kind of agreement that provides a basis for discrimination, it is likely to be accompanied by a substantial drop in price and increase in losses.

IV CHANGES IN HOURS

8   It has all the time been assumed that though the prime cost of the industry may change, there is no change in its capacity. But frequently a change in piece-wages (or their equivalent) or a proposal for such a change is associated with a change in the opposite direction of hours of work. There are three reasons for this. The first is that employers look upon longer hours as a path leading, like lower wages, to salvation. This type of reason was discussed above,[1] with reference to the demands of the cotton employers in January 1928. The second reason is that if workers are in a position to demand higher wages, they are also in a position to demand shorter hours. And the third reason is that by means of an opposite change in hours wage-rates can be reduced without affecting daily earnings; and similarly hours can be reduced by means of an increase in wage-rates. This reason accounts for the abolition of the seven-hour day in coal-mining in 1926 and for the objections to its restoration, though undoubtedly the first reason here too plays a part.

And of course the length of the working day may be altered without any change in prime costs. For the sake of simplicity it will be the effects of such a pure alteration of hours that will be examined. The effects of a change in prime cost can then, if necessary, be superimposed, whether the change in prime cost is due to a change in wage-rates or to a change in the average amount of the quasi-fixed elements of prime cost.

Some care must be exercised in applying our equations to a change in which the length of the working day suffers alteration. Unless it is realised that the constancy of the annihilation coefficient, q, breaks down in such a change, results of a very peculiar character will

[1] See head (3) of Section III of Chapter 6.

emerge. It has to be remembered that q measures the slope of the individual demand curve when the capacity output is taken as the unit of output; and that therefore if the capacity output increases, q increases in the same ratio.

§ 9   Provided that the conditions of the industry conform to the requirements of the third or of an earlier stage, it is quite clear that a pure alteration of hours (prime cost being kept constant) cannot exert the slightest effect on the equilibrium of the industry. The capacity output of every firm is altered, but so long as no firm is working near its capacity level such an alteration is quite irrelevant. The individual demand curves are not shifted and the prime cost curves remain in their former positions. The output and price of each firm are therefore unchanged; if more is produced in the course of each working day, the number of working days is reduced.

It is when no firm is working near its capacity level that the fullest significance can be attached to a suggestion made at the opening of Chapter 8. The capacity output is then purely a convenient unit in terms of which to measure the actual output, expressed by f or by F, and the slope of the individual demand curve, which is expressed by q. If the unit is altered, f and F on the one hand and q on the other hand move equal proportionate distances in opposite directions, and fq and Fq are unaltered. But the simplest way of applying such equations as (9.8), (9.9), (9.10) and (9.19) is to continue to measure F and q after the change in hours in terms of the capacity output before the change (or vice versa).

§ 10   When, however, firms are already working up to their capacity, the position is a very different one. Provided these a class firms are not situated too close to the margin between the n class and the a class, they take full advantage of the increase in their capacity. The output of the a class increases rather less than in proportion to the effective increase in hours. But, as a result of the general fall in prices that is associated with this increase of output, the output of the n class decreases. The aggregate output certainly increases, but the increase is less, in general it is considerably less, than in proportion to the effective increase of hours. It follows that there is, in general, a substantial increase of unemployment.

The prices charged by the n class are lowered and their outputs are decreased: they lose on both counts. The outputs of the a class are increased. But under certain conditions, particularly if the aggregate demand is inelastic, the fall in the price they have to charge may outweigh the increase in output; the a firms, too, are in such a case worse off after the increase in hours.

But when the increase in hours is coupled with a decrease of prime cost, due to a compensating lowering of wage-rates or to a decrease in the average amount of the quasi-fixed elements of prime cost, there are countervailing advantages to be set against these disadvantages. The a class are now more likely to find the change a beneficial one and it is now possible for the n class to gain as a result of it. But it is precisely when the disadvantages, due to the increase in hours, are greatest – when the aggregate demand is inelastic – that the advantages of a decrease of prime cost are least. For this reason there is a marked propensity for the double change to inflict an increase on the losses of an industry, at any rate of that section of an industry which belongs to the n class.

Unemployment is still less likely to decrease as a result of the change than are losses. It is now generally conceded that the introduction of the eight-hour day into the coal-mining industry in 1926 was the direct cause of a substantial increase in unemployment. But it is rarely admitted that a restoration of the seven-hour day would probably effect a big decrease in unemployment. The conflict doubtless originates in the fact that while it is easy to close a mine, it is difficult to reopen one. The introduction of the eight-hour day did not cause many mines to reopen, but the return of the seven-hour day would, it is felt, cause a considerable number to close. This view seems to depend on two fallacies. In the first place, a mine that is on the point of closing down must usually belong to the n class (or the b class – the argument is the same) rather than to the a class, and, as we have seen, the losses of such a mine would in most cases be reduced through the restoration of the seven-hour day. This is the case except where, as in exporting districts, the aggregate demand is rather elastic. Second, even if mines were to close down, as many probably would in the exporting districts, the demand for which these mines have so far been catering would to a considerable extent be transferred to other mines in the same district, and the increase in unemployment at one point would be partly compensated by a decrease at other points.

On the assumption that the opening and closing of mines can be neglected, the condition that the net effect of the double change, in hours and wage rates, on unemployment shall be nil is easily indicated. The change in the wage and quasi-fixed elements of average prime cost is in proportion to the effective change in hours. Consequently, average total prime cost changes in a smaller proportion. The change in output that is due to the change in hours has been seen to be also in a smaller proportion than the change in hours itself. But, if unemployment is to remain unaffected in the aggregate, the total change in output must be proportionately the same as the change in hours. It follows that the change in output that is due to the change in prime cost must be greater proportionately than the change in hours. Finally, then, it can be seen that the elasticity of aggregate demand must be greater than unity, the excess over unity originating from two quite different sources. If the elasticity of demand is greater than this quantity, which is itself greater than unity, there is an increase of unemployment as a result of the restoration of the seven-hour day; if it is less, there is a decrease.

CHAPTER 11

THE BUSINESS MAN IS NOT A TRUE ECONOMIC MAN

I FAILURE TO COMPREHEND THE MARGINAL PRINCIPLE

1   'When men act on erroneous impressions, it is the consequences of those acts which have to be reckoned with, and not the entirely differently consequences which might have arisen from acts founded on correct impressions.'[1] Now if anything is certain, it is that the attempt in the foregoing pages to trace the factors that influence price in the short period would completely fail to convince the ordinary business man. If the analysis has been correct in substance, then the business man's ideas must be regarded as distinctly erroneous. But if the business man's practice were in line with his theory, then the economist's theory of what *ought* to happen would be valueless and the business man's theory of what *does* happen would be correct.

Fortunately it is the consequences of business men's individual acts, not of their general theories, with which we have to reckon.[2] And a general theory that appears to them to be completely obvious may fail altogether to gain expression through their individual acts. But how far belief in a false economic theory, or failure to comprehend a correct one, is compatible with the standard of conduct that has to be demanded from the economic man is a matter that certainly requires investigation.

2   At the basis of the development of our whole argument has been the supremacy of prime cost and the comparative irrelevance of fixed cost, and still more of overhead cost. Many pages could be filled with

---

[1] W. H. Coates, *Appendices to Report of Colwyn Committee*, p. 65.
[2] Indeed, having exposed the errors that are latent in the business man's mind, Mr Coates bases the further treatment of his subject on an analysis that disregards such errors (but which, as Mr Robertson has shown, is itself, in respect to long-period effects, quite erroneous).

obiter dicta from the realms of industry, finance, and politics to illustrate the prevalence of the view that fixed cost influences price, even in the short period, in just the same way as does prime cost. The most obvious examples are to be derived from the discussions on de-rating, to which further reference will be made in a later chapter. Another kind of illustration was given in Section II of Chapter 4. But popular theory does not stick at technical fixed cost; financial fixed cost, too, is generally believed to play a full part in the determination of the price at which a commodity is sold. That Germany's inflation, by freeing her industry of debenture charges, enabled her to sell her goods at abnormally low prices is a view that was apparently accepted by the Dawes Committee. Professor Daniels and Mr Jewkes found that spinning margins on American cotton had risen proportionately more since pre-war days than on Egyptian cotton, and ascribed this in part to the fact that 'the American section has become burdened with large fixed interest charges which the Egyptian section has, to a large extent, avoided.'[1]

Nowhere does failure to distinguish between fixed cost and prime cost lead to greater and more dangerous confusion of thought than in discussions on the relation between output and profits. The view that the higher the level of fixed cost, the greater is the relative disadvantage of working below capacity is, of course, a common one.[2] This type of confusion is well illustrated by a statement by Professor Daniels and Mr Jewkes:

> Restriction of output could do nothing to relieve the situation, even if it did result in higher prices than would otherwise have ruled, unless the rise were greater than the increase in cost per lb.

---

[1] *Journal of the Royal Statistical Society*, Part II, 1928, p. 167. The inconsistency between the expression of this view and the support given on p. 181 to the belief that it is just the mills with high interest charges that indulge in price-cutting was pointed out in the discussion by Sir Sidney Chapman (p. 194), Mr Keynes (p. 199), and Professor J. H. Jones (p. 201). An attempt was made to remove the 'apparent conflict' (p. 204) before the paper appeared in its final form, but it cannot be said that the attempt was entirely successful.

[2] See, for an example, an article by Professor Schmalenbach in the *Vossiche Zeitung* of June 1928. It is quite true that the greater the *proportional* importance of fixed cost, the greater is the output, both under polypoly and monopoly. But this is because the average prime cost is *less* not because the average fixed cost is *greater*. The popular tendency is to look to the change in average total cost, which is equal to the change in average (if average prime cost is constant); the correct method is to look to the change in aggregate total cost, which is equal to the change in aggregate prime cost.

of yarn necessarily involved when fixed charges had to be spread over a smaller number of lbs. of output.[1]

Professor Daniels and Mr Jewkes were, of course, forgetting that the aggregate loss depends not only on the loss per pound but also on the output itself. On this piece of false arithmetic was based the conclusion that a scheme of restriction could exert little or no appeal on a large proportion of the cotton mills.

Quite consistent in their attitude, Professor Daniels and Mr Jewkes explain the action of organised short time in raising margins by saying, not that it has restricted supply in relation to demand, but that it 'has thrown the overhead costs on to a smaller total output and thus increased their weight per lb. of yarn produced'.[2] Indeed, it appears frequently to be believed that when output is altered under a scheme of restriction, the change in price is the same as the change in average fixed cost.

Thus the *Manchester Guardian Commercial* of November 18, 1926, referring to the saving that would be effected by full-time working, writes that it 'would most likely be swallowed up by the manufacturer'; and again: 'Spinners have been selling their yarns at times at a loss considerably in excess of any saving that might be effected by full-time working, and to increase production under those circumstances, even assuming the consumer would absorb the extra production, would only be to increase the gross loss.'

It must, I think, be admitted that adherence to, or at least passive acceptance of, such views as these is quite general among business men. This might be taken to indicate that business men are incapable of the act of maximising their profits, on which the conclusions of previous chapters are based. But this view is, I imagine, a mistaken one. The economic theory of a business man is based on the conception of a fair price, which covers all elements of cost of production. But, except in certain instances which will be discussed later, this fair price is not deliberately demanded by the seller of his product. The fair price is the price that in the absence of special causes ought, it is believed, to rule in the market. But each individual has to accept the best price that he can obtain. Doubtless it is pleasant to believe that the price that is charged includes a definite allowance for overhead costs. But it may be suggested that such a belief

---

[1] *Journal of the Royal Statistical Society*, Part II, 1928, p. 181.
[2] Ibid. p. 167. So that presumably in an industry where overhead costs are non-existent restriction of output would exert no effect upon the price!

represents merely an attempt to sublimate the perhaps sordid act of maximising profits. The imaginary allowance for overhead costs is nothing more or less than the difference between the price that it is most advantageous to charge and the prime cost. If it yields a surplus over overhead costs, that is so much the better. Sometimes it is much less than overhead costs; then exceptional causes must be cited in explanation. The business man's short run would be the economist's long run if it were not for these exceptional causes. For the deviations to which they give rise others are to blame – never the individual, who is compelled to follow in those vagaries of the market-place which his competitors lead.

I have had very few opportunities of going into these matters with business men of more than ordinary intelligence, but my impression on these occasions has been an invariable one. Taking as a convenient example the effect of de-rating, I have usually found a placid participation in the ordinary view. But it is not difficult, with the aid of a few figures, to demonstrate that a reduction of the burden of rates is unlikely to influence the price that a firm charges for its product. This mental revolution is accepted with a dead calm that is very disappointing. The business man reveals no perturbed intention of altering the price policy on which he has hitherto conducted his operations. The action of general economic forces undoubtedly interests him, but he would appear to believe that their sphere of action lies outside his own individual business.

§ 4   It is perhaps, then, possible to accept the view that in the mind of the business man there is combined an attempt to maximise his own profits with a belief in theories that can only be true if most business men do not maximise their profits. Admitting that a business man attempts to maximise his profits, we still have to consider whether belief in these theories is compatible with the ability to succeed in such an attempt.

Certainly, if success depended on a full realisation of the implications of the marginal principle, it would only be achieved by those whose theoretical views were economically sound. But instincts and intuitions will secure adherence to the marginal principle in action where conscious apprehension is impossible. And, failing those, we may rely on the method of trial and error; experience, embodied in rule of thumb, will often indicate how profits may be maximised. Moreover, in an industry where uniformity and publicity prevail, the individual is not obliged to rely entirely on his own experience; the experience of each firm is available for the others and a cumulative force is in operation which, while it may on occasion exaggerate the effects of errors of judgement, is likely under stable conditions to justify the assumption of an economic norm.

But that dogma has no effect at all upon practice is scarcely credible. It seems reasonable to believe that some sort of second order deviation usually results from the nature of men's beliefs. If business men really think that they are making an allowance for overhead cost when they quote a price, then an alteration in overhead cost is likely to be accompanied by an alteration in price, though a very much smaller one. In reply to a question of mine, an expert on the cotton industry stated that in his opinion spinning margins would be greater than they are if all the mills had to bear such heavy interest charges as those under which some of them labour.[1]

It is possible that the deviations between theory and practice would be more significant if it were not for the fortunate conjunction in many business men's minds of two opposing forces. On the one hand there is the feeling that an increase of output secures a reduction in the burden of overhead costs. Thus 'many American executives in key industries are being deluded by their sales and production managers into the belief that volume will reduce cost, regardless of the price level at which the volume is secured'.[2] On the other hand, it is sometimes believed that if a loss is being incurred, an increase of output necessitates an increased loss. What is not always recognised, certainly not in the cotton industry, is that one factor or the other prevails according as the price is greater or less than prime cost. A cotton-yarn salesman must frequently admit to his directors that the prices which he has obtained are incapable of yielding a net profit. Often, I am told, this admission is naively received as though it threw suspicion upon the salesman's mental state. But if next week his order book turns out to be empty, he is asked with considerable vehemence why he imagines he is drawing a salary; and he is informed that prices that their neighbours can accept can be accepted by him.

The result is that 'manufacturers, in their sales, appear to be operating on what might be called a dilemma basis. They are faced by the necessity of selling a large output around cost or less or having their production costs climb if they institute curtailment'.[3] It may be that this imaginary 'dilemma' prevents any undue influence by one

---

[1] This gentleman did not appear to share the common belief that it is the highly capitalised mills that cut prices.

[2] L. S. Horner, *Investors' Chronicle*, April 27, 1929, p. 963.

[3] Munds and Winslow's *Report on Cotton*, May 25, 1929.

error or the other, and that the position of maximum monopoly revenue, the market being an imperfect one, is secured to a satisfactory degree of precision.

II   RESTRAINTS ON REDUCING PRICES IN AN IMPERFECT MARKET

§ 6   In the next chapter we shall discuss the influence of corporate feeling in an industry. But in all its manifestations this influence also prevails in a state of polypoly, provided only that the market is imperfect.[1] In the same way, and for the same reasons, as it may be to the advantage of an industry to maintain prices in a corporate way, so it may be to the advantage of an individual to maintain prices in his own separate market. The most important reason that will be discussed in the next chapter is the reason that usually underlines monopolistic action – the simple desire to maximise profits. Its counterpart in the case of an individual who is producing for an imperfect market has already been discussed at length in the last two chapters.

§ 7   We may turn then, in the first place, to the 'objection to spoiling the market', in the restricted sense in which the term is employed by Professor Pigou. 'Spoiling the markets means selling a thing in bad times at such a price, and, therefore, in such quantities, that in subsequent good times the market is already stocked and producers cannot benefit by the then good demand. This is a state of things which can only occur in connection with goods that are, in some measure, durable'.[2] 'Each man fears to spoil his chance of getting a better price later on from his own customers'.[3] Spoiling the market, in this sense, 'means selling goods when they are cheap instead of waiting and selling the same goods when they are dearer'.[4] 'This fear of temporarily spoiling a man's special market is a leading influence in many problems of value relating to short periods.'[5]

The amount of this influence depends on a variety of factors. It depends, in the first place, on the ease with which the commodity

---

[1] The imperfection is supposed, as in the last two chapters, to take its origin in costs of transport or in buyers' preferences.

[2] Pigou, *Industrial Fluctuations*, 2nd edition, p. 186.

[3] Marshall, *Principles*, p. 374.

[4] J. M. Clark, *Economics of Overhead Costs*, p. 441.

[5] Marshall, *Principles*, p. 849.

can be stored, and on the extent to which it is in fact stored under a speculative stimulus. In the case of staple commodities storage is usually easy and the speculator is always present. But for such commodities the market is a very perfect one; it will not 'pay an individual manufacturer acting in isolation to restrict his output below the short-period norm, because only a very small part of the effect of his action in bettering future prices would accrue to his personal benefit'.[1] As Mr Shove has explained in his lectures, the market becomes less perfect as we approach closer to the ultimate consumer. But as we approach closer to the ultimate consumer, commodities become more difficult and more risky to store and speculative storage becomes more unlikely. Thus it is just when the effect itself is small that the effect of spoiling the market is concentrated on the individual producer who is responsible for the effect.

Second, speculative storage is only likely when there is some likelihood that the price will rise in the fairly near future. If the depression is expected to last a long time or if prices are expected never to rise again, there can be no spoiling of the market. It is therefore not unreasonable to suggest that, while this fear of spoiling the individual market may have a marked effect in retarding a downward fall of prices, its effect is generally small in a period of prolonged depression and stable prices.

8   The second factor that may restrain a producer from reducing his price is the knowledge that 'a cut in price may actually check demand, because buyers think that it portends a further cut for which they wish to wait'.[2] This factor can only arise in the case of commodities of which surplus stocks are available or whose use can be postponed. Here again, the influence is significant rather at a time of falling prices that after a period of some degree of stability.

9   Third, the producer sometimes has to take into account the possibility that a reduction of prices may shake

the purchaser's faith in the fairness or economic necessity of the previous level of prices. He [the purchaser] comes to think of the lower prices as fair, and judges that they are made voluntarily; and therefore he may be resentful when they rise, and may even be provoked into a 'buyers' strike.[3]

[1] Pigou, *Industrial Fluctuations*, p. 186.
[2] Pigou, *Industrial Fluctuations*, p. 188.
[3] J. M. Clark, *Economics of Overhead Costs*, p. 442.

This factor is only of importance in the case of a commodity whose price is absolutely fixed over a fairly long period of time. But it may then be of the utmost importance; the more so because it is precisely for this type of commodity that the subdivision of the market into separate markets is likely to be very marked.

§ 10   The system of fixed prices rules over a great part of the realm of retail selling, particularly for branded goods. But it is by no means confined to this region. It often prevails when specialities of one kind of another are sold, and it is usual in that type of contract work of which printing is a good example.

The reasons for the maintenance of fixed prices are various. The most important lies in the convenience that they provide, convenience to the buyer and convenience to the seller. Manufacturers of branded commodities often insist on a fixed retail prices to prevent their goods finding disfavour with retailers who are afraid of destructive competition. Then the force of tradition cannot be overlooked. Where it is strong, customers would be unable to accept a state of affairs in which prices fluctuated with the intensity of the demand.

Where suspicion is likely to be engendered in the minds of customers, price fluctuations are unlikely. The actual price becomes something much more like the long-period price. A tailor or printer who tried to maximise his revenue at a rush period would be accused of extortion, and would lose most of his customers; if he were to offer cut prices at a slack season, these might subsequently be used as precedents against him. But in the case of regular seasonal fluctuations, it may sometimes be possible to employ a firmly established system of 'off-season discounts'; the only proviso is that the customers must appreciate the reason.

Even a change in demand to which some semblance of permanence is attached may fail to react on the price, or only react after a considerable time-lag. For if a manufacturer reduces his price in small stages, his customers will become agitated. But if the imperfection of the market is not complete the full reduction of the price of one firm must await the reductions of all the other firms; the price of each firm, if it is to be reduced at all substantially, must be reduced in successive stages. It follows that a substantial change of price can take place within a short period of time only if all the firms act simultaneously. In the absence of some kind of agreement or of corporate feeling, the change of price may have to await a sudden or very rapid change in another factor. For instance, a rapid change in the cost of labour or of raw materials may provide the stimulus, and at the same time the pretext, that is necessary to overcome the stickiness inherent in a system of fixed prices. It required the Great War to alter hairdressers' tariffs, which now, for the most part, rest at the precise level to which the war elevated them.

Thus, for the first time in this essay, a certain element of arbitrariness creeps into the process by which prices are fixed.

III   EFFECT OF FINANCIAL FIXED COSTS IN THE COTTON INDUSTRY

It is often said that the troubles of the cotton industry are in part due to the fact that mills with heavy interest charges reduce their prices lower than they would if they were free of this burden. Statements to this effect appear with monotonous regularity, whenever the ills of Lancashire are under discussion; and more occasionally the same reasoning is applied to other industries. It is into the possibility and nature of this effect that we must now enquire.

But at the outset it may be mentioned that the cotton experts whom I have consulted do not appear to participate in the view that 'the intolerable burden of fixed interest charges . . . has been chiefly responsible for the disastrous "weak-selling" of the last seven or eight years'.[1] They agree that there is some such effect, but it is a small one; and, in the opinion of at any rate one of these experts, the effect may be overweighed by the influence of a high level of fixed cost in restraining price-cutting.[2] It seems probable that the role of scapegoat was originally designed for the recapitalised and refloated companies on grounds that were mainly moral. Even though the orgies of 1920 may be now forgiven and partly forgotten, it is too late, because the role has become a traditional one.

The effect that we are considering is usually referred to as though its nature were quite self-evident. Thus, 'the necessity of meeting these heavy interest payments has been the chief cause of the frantic scramble for orders which has persistently been draining away the resources of the mills'.[3] The plain meaning of this sentence, which is a typical reference to the matter, is that mills that have to meet heavy interest payments are more anxious to do profitable business than

[1] *Economist*, August 3, 1929, p. 210.
[2] See § 5 above.
[3] *The Times* leading article, December 21, 1928.

mills whose financial liabilities are small. But, on the whole, it seems probable that even the more fortunate mills do not overlook any opportunity of reducing the heavy losses with which they are confronted. Some more subtle explanation must be sought; several are worthy of examination.

§ 12   (1) Two have already been suggested.[1] One is that desperate mills neglect the work of repairs and renewals, thus effecting a saving in prime cost; the other, due to Professor Sraffa, is that desperate mills exclude prime depreciation from prime cost. For the first explanation there appears to be no evidence; the second falls to the ground if we are right in our presumption that *all* mills exclude prime depreciation from prime cost.

§ 13   (2) Having rejected the plain interpretation of these frequent references to the effect of high interest charges, we may fall back upon an interpretation that is only a little less obvious. When it is stated that 'in mad eagerness to appease creditors mills have sold mountains of yarn below cost',[2] the emphasis is perhaps laid on the sale rather than on the manufacture. 'Bang goes the stock of any old price', I have known an Oldham manager to put it. The implication would then be that, in order to meet their liabilities, mills have to reduce their stocks. But the process of reducing stocks cannot continue for very long; and, in any case, this explanation would not be applicable at a time like the present when stocks stand at a very low level.

§ 14   (3) The most satisfying explanation lies in the probability that the difficulty of meeting interest charges induces, or compels, firms to ignore the restrictions that – by agreement, tradition, or corporate sentiment – are usually regarded as binding. To a firm on the verge of despair the attraction of what may be called 'blackleg profit' is sometimes irresistible. It is interesting, then, to note that after the discussion on the paper by Professor Daniels and Mr Jewkes to the Royal Statistical Society had brought out an apparent inconsistency,[3] Professor Daniels stated that 'actually our second statement refers, in particular, to the position when the short-time policy was in operation'.[4] But, according to my information, it was precisely the Royton spinners who, guiltless of 'the unholy goings on of the boom period' and consequently free of all interest charges, pursued such a

[1] See end of Section VI and Section VII of Chapter 3.
[2] G. W. Armitage, *Problem of the Cotton Trade*.
[3] See footnote to § 2 above.
[4] *Journal of the Royal Statistical Society*, vol. 91, pt II, Part II, 1928, p. 204.

grasping policy that the Cotton Yarn Association's scheme of restriction had to be abandoned in September 1927 after an unhappy life of only five months. Moreover, in an article in the *Economic Journal*, published at a time when polypoly was rife, Professor Daniels and Mr Jewkes stated without any qualification that 'the probability is that many of these refloated concerns must sell in order to meet fixed interest charges and consequently create difficulties even for those concerns which still retain the designation of "original" companies';[1] and similar statements appear in the columns of *The Economist* and *The Times* even now, when agreements have disappeared, tradition has been forgotten, and corporate sentiment is simply non-existent.

5   (4) We are forced, then, onto an explanation which is, perhaps, the correct one, even though it is rather curious. Such, I am told, is Lancashire mentality that frequently no attempt is made to accumulate funds for interest payments until only a few days before the day of reckoning itself. Then, when payment becomes due, it can only be effected by selling out yarn at whatever prices it will fetch. These prices are likely to be definitely unprofitable, perhaps even below prime cost. This extraordinarily lackadaisical method of business results in a greater loss on the year's working than would be incurred under a less short-sighted policy. It would appear, then, that some of those mills which are bound in any case to incur exceptionally great losses pursue a policy that makes the loss greater than it need be.

This phenomenon, almost ridiculous if our explanation is correct, only occurs because interest becomes due at rare intervals, perhaps half-yearly. If interest had to be paid as regularly as wages and the cost of raw material, its amount would not, on the basis of this explanation, influence the selling policy of a single mill.

---

[1] *Economic Journal*, March 1927, p. 46.

CHAPTER 12

THE CORPORATE INSTINCT

§ 1 'Whatever might be the natural effects of unchecked competition, business has evidently developed checks sufficient to protect its necessary earnings, taking good and bad years together.'[1] 'Since unchecked competition is suicidal and cannot continue, can anything continue which deserves the name of competition? . . . The answer appears to be that business rivalry still exists, subject to checks in the way of understandings and standards of fair tactics, enforced partly by the group ethics of the business community, partly by a lively sense of the need of common self-preservation, which is at the bottom of a deal of the group ethics, and partly by the discipline exercised by the larger and stronger concerns.'[2]

The subject of this chapter therefore comprises those important corporate feelings which range from Marshall's 'fear of incurring the resentment of other producers'[3] to something far more altruistic on the one side and to something rather more selfish on the other side; and these feelings may be experienced in varying degrees of consciousness. We have to consider a state where competition would still, in common parlance, be said to prevail, but where polypoly no longer exists. Cases of organised restriction are excluded from our treatment.

The small amount of space that is devoted to the subject in this essay is perhaps an indication rather of its difficulty than of its importance. At the same time, it is not unreasonable to argue that undue weight is sometimes attached to these influences, particularly in comparison with the imperfection of the market. Certainly in the industry of American cotton-spinning to-day they are almost entirely absent: I am told that no 'spirit of gentlemanliness' can be said to exist.

[1] J. M. Clark, *Economics of Overhead Costs*, p. 447.
[2] Ibid, p. 435.
[3] Marshall, *Principles*, p. 374.

2   Professor Clark describes four different varieties of 'fear of spoiling the market'.[1] Three of these, in slightly different guise, were applied in the last chapter to the case of polypoly in an imperfect market;[2] not much more need be said of them here.

The fear of causing an accumulation of stocks in the market is doubtless the most important of these three varieties. Where consumption and supply are both rather inelastic, a small volume of surplus stocks may, as Mr Keynes has shown, exert a depressing influence on demand that is serious and long-lived. But here again, as discussed in the last chapter, this influence cannot be of importance when conditions have become fairly stable.

The fear that buyers will hold off a falling market, in the expectation that prices will fall further, is even more limited in its application. Finally, the fear of shaking the buyers' 'faith in the fairness or economic necessity of the previous level of prices' must be rare in its corporate aspect. Resentment against a single firm is often expressed in a refusal to buy its goods; but a 'buyers' strike' among the customers of a complete industry is a rare occurrence.

3   We may turn, then, to that most general and most significant form of corporate instinct which originates in the mere desire for a level of prices above the level that would persist under polypoly. The usual view is that this type of force is not noticeable so long as conditions in an industry are normal; it is when there is a tendency for prices to become depressed that corporate instinct is provoked into action.

> There is a vast difference between reducing net earnings from 12 per cent to 8 per cent, and reducing them from 6 per cent to 2 per cent. The total amount lost is the same, but the latter cut is destructive, and is resisted with far more energy and with a real sense of moral reprobation.[3]

According to this view, the corporate spirit becomes mobilised just when it is most urgently needed. But this is scarcely sufficient to explain why it is not exerted in an attempt to maintain prices above their normal level. It is possible to suggest two further reasons, which apply equally to the somewhat analogous case where monopoly power exists in an organised form. In the first place, it is usually

---

[1] *Economics of Overhead Costs*, pp. 439 to 443.
[2] Chapter 11, §§ 7, 8 and 9.
[3] J. M. Clark, *Economics of Overhead Costs*, p. 440.

recognised that an abnormally high level of prices will rapidly serve to draw new competitors into the industry. The second reason originates in the attitude of public opinion in respect to business ethics. A scheme of restriction that is intended to reduce the losses of a depressed industry is generally welcomed as being in the best interests of everyone – it need not even, so it would appear, come within the scope of the American anti-trust laws;[1] but an attempt by means of an identical scheme to earn abnormally high profits has attributed to it all the worst aspects of profiteering. In just the same way, when a corporate instinct raises prices above a normal level, it is a vice; but it is a virtue if it prevents prices from falling below the normal level.

§ 4   The corporate instinct would be far less effective if it were not aided by the conception of a fair price that is current among business men. To accept a price that does not afford a full contribution to overhead costs as often regarded as akin to dishonesty. So long as output does not fall conspicuously short of capacity, this feeling may be sufficient to maintain the industry in a fairly profitable condition.

The business man's outlook becomes focused yet more sharply on the fair price when there are available figures of standard costings prepared by some central organisation. Even if he does not cling rigidly to these suggested standards, they do not usually fail to influence him when he is making a quotation. To those business men who are incapable of calculating their own costs such standard costings may appeal as the one piece of firm ground where all else is treacherous.

§ 5   But when the depression is serious, prices do not usually fail to fall to levels that are unremunerative. The corporate instinct is still a restraint on price-cutting, perhaps a stronger one than ever, and the fair price is still an objective, even though an unattainable one. An important problem is how an alteration of fixed cost, as a result, for

---

[1] L. S. Horner, writing on the 'Advantages of "A Firm Price with a Profit" Policy', says: 'There is a great wave of understanding of this general plan spreading through our business world, for which the US Department of Commerce, with Mr Hoover's vision of the past seven years, blazed the way. Now the Chamber of Commerce of the United States, through Dr Baker's Trade Association Department, is ready to advise how properly to set up an association. The Government departments – Federal Trade Commissions and the once-dreaded Attorney-General's department – will be found sympathetic and helpful. Industry needs to realise that honest cooperation is better than bitter competition. Industry in general in America is sick, and a price with a profit is necessary to restore health and future progress (*Investors' Chronicle*, April 27, 1929, p. 964).

instance, of de-rating, affects the operation of these forces. There are three different aspects to be considered:

(a) A reduction of rates reduces *pro rata* the value of the fair price, which would yield a normal profit. If the actual price is really related to the fair price through the intervention of some kind of corporate feeling, a reduction in the fair price may result in a reduction of the actual price.

(b) A reduction of rates reduces the losses that an industry incurs. There is, it appears, a definite relation between the strength of the calls that are made upon the corporate spirit and the seriousness of the industry's position. By alleviating the seriousness of the position, de-rating reduces the intensity of the psychological restraints on price-cutting. In this respect, too, it leads to a lower price.

Aspects (a) and (b), therefore, both face in the same direction. But aspect (a) is the important one when the corporate instinct reacts directly on the price that a manufacturer quotes for his goods, aspect (b) when it reacts directly on the volume of production that he places on the market.

(c) But even though corporate sentiment grows stronger as conditions become more desperate, a point may be reached, as we saw in the last chapter,[1] at which the temptation to alleviate the position by ignoring corporate sentiment grows too violent. If this point has been reached, de-rating, by reducing the seriousness of the situation, may restore some of the power of the corporate instinct, and so, somewhat paradoxically, result in a *higher* price.

[1] Chapter 11, § 14.

CHAPTER 13
DE-RATING

§ 1 The late government's scheme for relieving productive enterprise of part of the burden of rates provides a useful example by means of which to summarise our conclusions as to the effect of fixed cost in the short period. We are not concerned with long-period effects. That the system of local taxation exerts an important influence on the flow of new investment is, of course, quite obvious. But it may, in passing, be suggested that from the long-period point of view it is their variability from one part of the country to another rather than their average weight that renders rates an uneconomic form of taxation. The scheme of de-rating has certainly reduced absolute differences between districts, but relative differences will be almost as great as before.

The manifest purpose of the scheme is to relieve unemployment, and it is often praised on the grounds that the greater part of the benefit is extended to those sections of industry that are most distressed. For these depressed industries the short period is a very long one. It is, therefore, not unjustifiable to enquire in what manner de-rating relieves unemployment in the short period.

§ 2 The view to which we at once run counter is that it enables firms to reduce their prices by an amount corresponding to the reduction in rates. This view is, of course, very common and has been continually expounded as though it were quite obvious by multitudes of Conservative speakers and writers. But, to avoid any suspicion of political partisanship, I prefer to quote from the Report of the Liberal Industrial Enquiry, which was published shortly before the Conservative Government made their first public announcement of their intention to reform the system of rates:

> A business must pay its rates whether it earns any profits or not; it must therefore include an allowance for rates in the prices which it charges. Thus rates, unlike income tax, enter directly into the costs of production, raising the cost of living and diminishing the competitive power of our industries. Our industrial leaders are constantly asserting, and with truth, that local rates are now, by

174

reason of their effect on selling price, a serious handicap to our exports.[1]

The strength of the conviction on which this passage insists is sufficiently indicated by the ribald reception that greeted Lord Passfield's exposition of a different view.[2] This is the view which throughout this essay, though subject to modifications, has in principle been upheld: whether under conditions of polypoly or of monopoly, in a perfect market or in an imperfect market, a firm that is engaged in production will not lower its price as a result of a reduction in fixed cost. To the modifications we shall return shortly. But meanwhile the general principle can be regarded as so important as deserving, at the cost of some redundancy, a simple proof by *reductio ad absurdum*. Let x be the output of a firm per unit of time, p the price at which it sells its product, C its total cost per unit of time. Then its profit per unit of time is $px - C$. Now let the burden of rates be reduced by R; and suppose that if everything else in the industry were to remain unchanged,[3] it would be profitable to lower p to p', so that x would become x' and C would become $C' - R$. It follows that

$$(p'x' - C' + R) > (px - C + R)$$

Therefore

$$(p'x' - C') > (px - C)$$

It follows that a reduction in price is only profitable after the reduction in rates if it was already profitable before the reduction in rates.

---

[1] *Britain's Industrial Future*, p. 433. Compare the passage quoted above in Chapter 4, § 2.

[2] House of Commons, November 28, 1928. I venture to suggest that the speech of Mr Sidney Webb, as he was then, was somewhat wanting as a scientific treatment. He failed to draw any distinction between the long-period and the short-period effects and omitted to draw attention to the serious reservations to which his main thesis must be subjected. Regarded as an exposition rather than as a scientific treatment, the speech clouded the issue by its subsequent references to the inelastic nature of most demands – as, for instance, of the demand for coffins – (*Official Report*, col. 448). Moreover, it contained an implication that rates are only without direct effect on price when trade is slack (col. 447). (I am not aware that anyone else, besides Lord Passfield, has, in public, passed this kind of criticism on the scheme.)

[3] It is only if there is a stimulus towards a change on this assumption, that a change will actually occur.

§ 3　　So much for a firm that is actually producing: a reduction in its fixed costs exerts only a secondary influence. But when we come to consider the possibility of a firm closing down, temporarily or permanently, the level of fixed cost becomes, as we saw in Chapter 3, § 9, and as is, of course, quite obvious, a factor of great importance. Here exists an opportunity for de-rating to exert an influence on the volume of unemployment. This influence is the more important because a large volume of unemployment is due to the actual closing down of productive enterprises, as opposed to the working of short-time; particularly is this the case in coal-mining and the heavy industries. But it has to be remembered that some of these enterprises have closed down permanently and that in the case of others the costs of reopening are very heavy.[1] It follows that in this respect de-rating is more effective in preventing an increase of unemployment than in stimulating a decrease.

In general, firms that close down are the less efficient firms. It follows that in so far as de-rating prevents firms from closing down, it is likely to hold up that process of concentrating the output of an industry on to the more efficient units on which so many place their hopes of industrial salvation. There is here no ground for criticising de-rating as a means of relieving unemployment. This is merely one aspect of the opposition that generally exists between the reduction of unemployment and the introduction of all that is covered by the word 'rationalisation'.

§ 4　　Apart from certain repercussions, which are discussed below, it appears from what was stated in Chapter 3, § 8 and proved later in that chapter that a reduction of rates can only increase output by preventing firms from closing down or by encouraging them to produce, not for the sake of prime profit, but for the sake of maintaining connections. It is with this possibility of production at under prime cost that we must now deal; and only with the case where marginal prime cost is not equated to the price. It follows from Chapter 3, § 10 that a reduction in rates is not likely to result in an increased output under these conditions, except when the prime cost is much greater than the price. In any case, it would be more important in maintaining the level of output in the face of a declining

---

[1] A touch of piquancy has been added to the situation in Glasgow inasmuch as 'the Inland Revenue authorities have objected to derating being applied to idle plant', *The Times*, September 27, 1929, thus blocking up the one obvious line of approach up which the late Government's scheme can tackle the problem of unemployment. But 'in every instance the Appeal Court has given industry the benefit'.

demand than in restoring the level of output after the demand has been depressed for some time.

5   We turn next to those repercussions that were discussed towards the end of Chapter 3. In the first place, de-rating may partially overcome those restraints on output that are sometimes set up by financial embarrassment (resulting in lack of working capital, and so on).[1] Second, it may encourage expenditure, or reduce the necessity of retrenchment, on organisation, maintenance, and renewals.[2] The effect on output is likely to be a favourable one, but it only becomes important after the lapse of time, and then not always unless output has increased for other reasons.[3] In so far as firms in our depressed industries are being prevented through lack of resources from maintaining their plant in good condition or are intending, with an eye on future prospects, to allow portions of their plant to decay away completely, de-rating will exert a significant influence on unemployment in the near future.

But if it is an increase in the *prime* cost portion of the costs of maintenance and renewals that de-rating encourages, the *immediate* effect on output and employment is precisely the opposite.[4] Prime cost is increased and output is diminished as a result of de-rating. But prime cost is prevented from increasing in the future, as a result of deterioration of plant, so fast as it otherwise would, and consequently de-rating may result in a higher level of output in the future than would otherwise be obtainable.

In much the same way, if, as a result of the improvement in their financial position, firms are encouraged to include part of the actual prime depreciation in their price cost,[5] or more of it than they were previously including, de-rating has a depressing influence on output. But in this case, as opposed to the case of an increase in the prime cost portion of the costs of maintenance and renewals, there is not necessarily a countervailing benefit in regard to output in the future.

6   These last two cases are merely particular applications of a general rule. Whenever low prices in an industry can be ascribed to financial embarrassment, caused for example by high interest charges,[6] de-rating, by alleviating the financial position, causes prices to rise and

---

[1] See Chapter 3, § 15.
[2] See Chapter 3, §§ 16 to 26.
[3] See Chapter 3, §§ 19 and 26.
[4] See Chapter 3, § 28.
[5] See Chapter 3, Section VII.
[6] See Chapter 11, § 11.

must, at the same time, cause output to decrease. There is one exception to this rule. If the low prices are due to a progressive reduction of stocks rather than to a high level of output,[1] de-rating restrains the process of throwing stocks on the market, and the higher prices encourage a *higher* level of output.

§ 7   If on the other hand there is a tendency, due to erroneous thinking on the part of the business man, for the level of fixed cost to be dimly reflected in the price,[2] then a reduction of the burden of rates results in some reduction in the price and to some increase in the output. If the business man really *does* believe that prices will fall as a result of de-rating by the full equivalent of the relief, then possibly de-rating *will* cause a very slight fall of prices.

§ 8   Finally, de-rating may produce an effect through the medium of the corporate spirit. The effect is most important when the corporate spirit manifests itself in the shape of a 'fair price', to which producers aspire, even if unavailingly.[3] A reduction of rates leads to a fall in this fair price. The effect is in the same direction, though probably smaller, if the improvement in the financial situation that sets in with de-rating leads to a weakening of corporate sentiment.[4] But, of course, if de-rating, by withdrawing firms from the verge of despair, permits them to pay greater attention to the promptings of the corporate spirit,[5] the effect on output is once again a depressing one.

§ 9   These various considerations qualify, but do not alter the fundamental importance, of Lord Passfield's appraisal of the late Government's scheme: 'It is, in effect, a gift to the employers, a gift to their profit and loss – notice that – in all productive industry.'[6] And again: 'It will make no difference at all to their business.'[7] Though the editor of *The Economist* may quote 'the whole weight of authority (including that of the Colwyn Committee)'[8] against Lord Passfield, it is difficult to avoid the conclusion that in principle he is right, or would be right if he were to specify that he is thinking of the short period. When we have to part company with Lord Passfield is when he goes on to signify his approval of Sir William Beveridge's dictum: 'The problem of unemployment – this is a point which cannot be too strongly

---

[1] See Chapter 11, § 13.
[2] See Chapter 11, § 5.
[3] See Chapter 12, § 5, factor (a).
[4] See Chapter 12, § 5, factor (b).
[5] See Chapter 12, § 5, factor (c).
[6] House of Commons, *Report*, November 28, 1928, col. 444.
[7] Ibid, col. 446.
[8] *The Economist*, December 1, 1928.

emphasised – is insoluble by any mere expenditure of public money.'[1] The whole point is that an *unconditional* subsidy, such as a reduction of fixed costs by means of de-rating, is ineffectual. But the same amount of money spent in a *conditional* way, i.e. so as to reduce prime costs, might achieve much (particularly if the subsidy were directed towards the utilisation of surplus fixed plant in exporting industries for whose product the foreign demand is fairly elastic). Of this nature are the subsidies in aid of wages proposed by Professor Pigou[2] and by Lord Melchett, and the relief of unemployment insurance contributions suggested by Miss Susan Lawrence as an alternative to the relief of rates.[3]

Nothing short of a complete failure to realise the fundamental difference between the effects of a reduction of fixed cost and of a reduction of prime costs can explain the utterances in the House of Commons of two members of the late Government. According to the report in *The Times* Sir L. Worthington Evans, speaking on November 12, 1928, said 'the reduction of wages was not in the mind of the Government in the least. Their aim was to reduce the cost of production and so to enable our manufacturers to compete in the markets of the world.' The confusion was even better expressed by Sir Boyd Merriman who was referring on November 27 (to quote again from *The Times*) to the allegation that the Government were 'putting the burden back through the petrol tax'. 'That was true', he admitted, 'in a sense . . . They were substituting a burden which bore direct relation to the amount of production *and therefore to the profits*, which rates did not.' With the omission of the words that I have underlined it would be difficult to devise a more concise and striking indictment of the scheme fostered by the Government of which Sir Boyd Merriman was a member.

But the real heights of absurdity were attained by Captain T. J. O'Connor, in replying to Mr Sidney Webb's onslaught. 'In my opinion' he said, 'the bargaining power of the trade unions is amply sufficient to ensure that an industry which by reason of its prosperity increases its profits under this dis-rating scheme shall have to disgorge for the combined benefit of those engaged in the industry, any increased profits which accrue to it.'[4] In other words one of the

---

[1] House of Commons, *Report*, November 28, 1928, col. 450.
[2] *Economic Journal*, September 1927.
[3] House of Commons, *Report*, November 15, 1928.
[4] House of Commons, *Report*, November 15, 1928, col. 479.

advantages of a reduction of fixed costs lies in the likelihood that it will lead to an increase in prime costs!

§ 10　　But not every supporter of the late government has been equally dogmatic. In particular Mr Winston Churchill has shown considerable discretion in asserting the benefit of de-rating. Thus, 'the best and surest help we can carry to productive industry, and through productive industry to employment, is by a reduction of the burdens which enter directly into the cost of production, or *which deplete the capital accumulations upon which in modern times industry can alone develop.*'[1] It seems probable that Mr Churchill would attach particular importance to the words that I have underlined; and it is to this aspect that we must now turn for a moment. To do so we must leave the boundary of the short period a small distance behind us. The short period is in general very long in the case of a depressed industry. But it need not necessarily be long. Complete reorganisation and re-equipment may sometimes be profitable even when an industry is working at a loss; and the short period, with its disagreeable associations, may be brought to a premature close. This it is that appears to characterise the processes of 'rationalisation' by which Germany restored some of her depressed industries. Two barriers stand in the way of these processes of new investment: lack of incentive and lack of capital. De-rating does something to lower each of these barriers; and it is particularly helpful to those industries of which the banks and the ordinary investors fight shy. These considerations must have been in the mind of Viscount Furness when, referring to the scheme of de-rating, he made this cautious statement. 'It is not too much to say that the unfortunate financial condition of many collieries and manufacturing companies is largely due to the drain on their resources by demands that have been made from local authorities, and the efficiency of the works and employment of labour have suffered in consequence.'[2] In the same way it has been stated by Sir M. W. Jenkinson of the Vickers-Armstrong concern, that 'the present parlous position of many British industries could be attributed to the fact that sufficient reserves had not been made in the past to provide for obsolescence.'[3] De-rating may have little effect in the short period. But it may do something if not very much, by reducing the drain upon capital and by increasing the stimulus towards new investment, to bring the short period to an end.

[1] Budget speech, April 15, 1929.
[2] General Meeting of South Durham Steel and Iron Co., December 19, 1928.
[3] *The Times*, March 9, 1929.

11   It is on this note that we may not inappropriately close. Consideration of the short period is necessary to clear thinking, but it is not by itself sufficient for the solution of industrial problems, even when the industries are depressed. The long period, on the other hand, is too long: in it profits, wages, and employment are all normal, and there are no major industrial problems. The modern industrial world is highly dynamic: the essence of it is change. These all-important changes, not yet visible in the short period and fully completed before the long period may commence, can receive that attention which is undoubtedly due to them only through the investigation of some kind of longer period.

BIBLIOGRAPHY

ARTICLES AND BOOKS BY RICHARD KAHN

1931

'The Relation of Home Investment to Unemployment', *Economic Journal*, June 1931, pp. 173–98; reprinted in (RFK) *Selected Essays on Employment and Growth* (1972) pp. 1–27.

1932

'The Financing of Public Works: A Note', *Economic Journal*, September 1932, pp. 492–5.

'Decreasing Costs: a Note on the Contributions of Mr Harrod and Mr Allen', *Economic Journal*, December 1932, pp. 657–61.

1933

'Public Works and Inflation, *Journal of the American Statistical Association*, Supplement, March 1933, pp. 168–73. Papers and Proceedings of the Ninety-fourth Annual Meeting of the American Statistical Association (edited by Frank Alexander Ross), held at Cincinnati, Ohio, December 28–31, 1932; reprinted in *Selected Essays on Employment and Growth*, pp. 28–34.

'The Elasticity of Substitution and the Relative Share of a Factor', *Review of Economic Studies*, October 1933, pp. 72–8.

1935

'Some Notes on Ideal Output', *Economic Journal*, March 1935, pp. 1–35.

'Two Applications of the Concept of Elasticity of Substitution', *Economic Journal*, June 1935, pp. 242–5.

1936

'Dr Neisser on Secondary Employment: a Note', *Review of Economics and Statistics*, August 1936, pp. 144–7.

'Mr Paine and Rationalisation: a Note', *Economica*, August 1936, pp. 327–9.

Review of A. D. Gayer, *Works on Prosperity and Depression*, *Economic Journal*, September 1936, pp. 491–3.

Review of 'Report of the Committee of Investigation for England on Complaints made by the Central Milk Distributive Committee and the Parliamentary Committee of the Cooperative Congress to the Operation of the Milk Marketing Scheme', *Economic Journal*, September 1936, pp. 554–9.

English translation of K. Wicksell, *Geldzins und Güterpreise* (*Interest and Prices: A Study of the Causes Regulating the Value of Money*, London: Macmillan, 1936).

1937

'The Problem of Duopoly', *Economic Journal*, March 1937, pp. 1–20.
'The League of Nations Enquiry into the Trade Cycle', Review of *Prosperity and Depression: A Theoretical Analysis of Cyclical Movements* by G. Harbeler, *Economic Journal*, December 1937, pp. 670–9.

1938

'A Rejoinder', (to some comments on Mr Kahn's Review of *Prosperity and Depression*) *Economic Journal*, June 1938, pp. 333–6.
Review of E. Lundberg, *Studies in the Theory of Economic Expansion*, *Economic Journal*, June 1938, pp. 265–8.

1939

Review of J. E. Meade, *World Economic Survey: Seventh Year, 1937–8*, *Economic Journal*, March 1939, pp. 96–8.
Review of E. G. Nourse, *Industrial Price Policies and Economic Progress*, *Economic Journal*, June 1939, pp. 321–3.

1947

'Tariffs and the Terms of Trade', *Review of Economic Studies*, no. 1, 1947, pp. 14–19.

1948

'The 1948 Budget: An Economist's Criticism', *The Listener*, May 6, 1948.

1949

'Our Economic Complacency', *The Listener*, February 3, 1949.
'Professor Meade on Planning', *Economic Journal*, March 1949, pp. 1–16.
'The International Bank for Reconstruction and Development', *Economic Journal*, September 1949, pp. 445–7.
'A Possible Intra-European Payments Scheme', *Economica*, November 1949, pp. 293–304.

1950

'The Dollar Shortage and Devaluation', *Economia Internazionale*, February 1950, pp. 89–113. Reprinted in *Selected Essays on Employment and Growth*, pp. 35–59.
'The European Payments Union', *Economica*, August 1950, pp. 306–16.
'An Approach to Economic Development in the Middle East', Review of *Final Report of the United Nations Economic Survey Mission for the Middle East*, *Economic Journal*, September 1950, pp. 634–5.

1951

'Home and Export Trade', *Economic Journal*, June 1951, pp. 279–89.
'The Balance of Payments and the Sterling Area', *District Bank Review*, December 1951, pp. 3–17.

1952

Review of 'Oxford Studies in Price Mechanism', *Economic Journal*, March 1952, pp. 119–30.

'Comments' (on monetary policy and the crisis) *Bulletin of the Oxford University*, April and May 1952, pp. 147–53.

'Britain's Economic Position', *The Listener*, July 3, 1952, pp. 18–22.

'Comments' (on monetary policy again) *Bulletin of the Oxford University*, August 1952.

'Monetary Policy and the Balance of Payments', *Political Quarterly*, July–September 1952, reprinted in *Selected Essays on Employment and Growth*, pp. 60–71.

Review of B. Ohlin, *The Problem of Employment Stabilisation*, *American Economic Review*, March 1952, pp. 180–2.

'International Regulation of Trade and Exchanges' in *Banking and Foreign Trade*, Fifth International Banking Summer School, Oxford 1952 (London: Institute of Bankers, Europa Publications, 1952).

1954

'Some Notes on Liquidity Preference', *Manchester School of Economic and Social Studies*, September 1954, pp. 229–57; reprinted in *Selected Essays on Employment and Growth*, pp. 72–96.

(With D. G. Champernowne), 'The Value of Invested Capital: a Mathematical Addendum to Mrs Robinson's Article', *Review of Economic Studies*, 1954, no. 2, pp. 107–11. (Reprinted as Appendix to J. Robinson, *The Accumulation of Capital*, London: Macmillan, 1956).

1955

(RFK), 'Short Term Business Indicators in Western Europe', in United Nations, Economic Commission for Europe, *Economic Bulletin for Europe*, November 1955, pp. 34–78.

1956

'John Maynard Keynes', *The Listener*, May 3, 1956, p. 540.

'Lord Keynes and the Balance of Payments', *The Listener*, May 10, 1956, pp. 591–3.

'Lord Keynes and Contemporary Economic Problems', *The Listener*, May 3 and 10, 1956, reprinted in *Selected Essays on Employment and Growth*, pp. 103–23.

'An Answer to the Capital Question', *Westminster Bank Review*, August 1956, pp. 1–26.

'Full Employment and British Economic Policy', *Nihon Keizai Shimbun*, 1956, reprinted in *Selected Essays on Employment and Growth*, pp. 97–102.

1957

'Doubts about the Free Trade Area', *The Listener*, February 28, pp. 331–3.

'A Positive Contribution?', *Bulletin of the Oxford Institute of Statistics*, February 1957, pp. 63–8.

1958
'Memorandum of Evidence' submitted to the Radcliffe Committee, in Radcliffe Committee on the Working of the Monetary System, *Principal Memoranda of Evidence*, pp. 138–46, reprinted in *Selected Essays on Employment and Growth*, pp. 124–52.
'Evidence', submitted to the Radcliffe Committee, Q. 10938–11024, in Radcliffe Committee on the Working of the Monetary System, *Minutes of Evidence*, pp. 739–46.
'The Pace of Development'. Lecture delivered at the Eliezer Kaplan School of Economics and Social Sciences, *The Challenge of Development*, pp. 163–98; reprinted in *Selected Essays on Employment and Growth*, pp. 153–191.

1959
'Exercises in the Analysis of Growth', *Oxford Economic Papers*, June 1959, pp. 146–63; reprinted in *Selected Essays on Employment and Growth*, pp. 192–207.
'Sur l'analyse de la croissance' in *L'accumulation du capital*, Colloques Economiques Franco-Britanniques, pp. 51–69.

1961
Organisation for Economic Cooperation and Development, *The Problem of Rising Prices*, report by William Fellner, Milton Gilbert, Brent Hansen, Richard Kahn, Friedrich Lutz, Pieter de Wolff. OECC, 1961.

1964
(With R. Cohen, W. B. Reddaway, J. Robinson) 'Statement submitted to the Committee on Resale Price Maintenance', *Bulletin of the Oxford Institute of Statistics*, May 1964, pp. 113–21.

1965
United Nations Conference on Trade and Development, *International Monetary Issues and the Developing Countries*, New York: UN, 1965. Report of the Group of Experts (RFK was one of the twelve members).
'Un confronto fra la politica inglese e guella italiana' in G. Fua (ed.), *Programmazione economica: confronti italo inglesi*, Urbino, Argalia editore, 1965.

1966
United Nations Conference on Trade and Development, *Payments Arrangements among the Developing Countries for Trade Expansion* (Geneva: UN, 1966). Report of the Group of Experts (chaired by RFK).

1969

United Nations Conference on Trade and Development, *International Monetary Reform and Co-operation for Development* (New York: UN, 1969).

1971

'Notes on the Rate of Interest and the Growth of Firms' (1971) reprinted in *Selected Essays on Employment and Growth*, pp. 208–32.

1972

Selected Essays on Employment and Growth (Cambridge: Cambridge University Press, 1972).

1973

'The International Monetary System', *American Economic Review*, May 1973, pp. 181–8.

'SDR and aid', *Lloyds Bank Review*, October 1973, pp. 1–18.

1974

'Plans for a Monetary System to Replace the Bretton Woods Agreement', in Fatemi, N.S. (ed.) *Problems of Balance of Payments and Trade* (New Jersey: Rutherford, 1974), pp. 199–266.

(With M. Posner) 'Cambridge Economics and the Balance of Payments' in *London and Cambridge Economic Bulletin*, July 1974, pp. 19–30.

'On Re-reading Keynes', Keynes Lecture delivered on November 6, 1974, *Proceedings of the British Academy*, vol. LX, 1974, pp. 361–92, Oxford: Oxford University Press, 1975.

(With M. V. Posner) 'The Effects of Public Expenditure on Inflation and the Balance of Payments' (London: HMSO, 1974).

1975

'Oil and the Crisis', IEA Occasional Papers, 1975, no. 43, pp. 34–8.

1976

'Thoughts on the Behaviour of Wages and Monetarism', *Lloyds Bank Review*, January 1976, pp. 1–11.

'Inflation: A Keynesian View', *Scottish Journal of Political Economy*, February 1976, pp. 11–16.

'Political Attitudes involved in teaching Economics', *Oxford Review of Education*, 1976, pp. 91–5.

'Unemployment as seen by the Keynesians' in Worswick, G.D.N. (ed.) *The Concept and Measurement of Involuntary Unemployment* (London: Allen & Unwin; and Boulder, Colorado: Westview Press, 1976), pp. 19–25.

'Historical Origins of the International Monetary Fund' in Thirlwall, A.P. (ed.) *Keynes and International Monetary Relations*, pp. 3–35 (London: Macmillan, 1976).

1977

'Mr Eltis and the Keynesians', *Lloyds Bank Review*, April 1977, pp. 1–13.

(With M. V. Posner) 'Inflation, Unemployment and Growth', *National Westminster Bank Quarterly Review*, November 1977, pp. 28–37.

'Malinvaud on Keynes: Review Article', *Cambridge Journal of Economics*, December 1977, pp. 375–88.

'A Comment' in T. W. Hutchinson, *Keynes versus the 'Keynesians'* (London: IEA, 1977), pp. 48–57.

1978

Review of J. Hicks, *Economic Perspectives: Further Essays on Money and Growth*, *Manchester School of Economic and Social Studies*, March 1978, pp. 83–5.

'Some Aspects of the Development of Keynes's Thought', *Journal of Economic Literature*, June 1978, pp. 544–59.

1984

The Making of Keynes's General Theory (Cambridge: Cambridge University Press, 1984).

1985

'The Cambridge Circus' in *Keynes and his Contemporaries*, The Sixth Centennial Keynes Seminar held at the University of Kent at Canterbury, 1983, ed. by G. C. Harcourt, London: Macmillan, 1985.

1987

'Rostas, L.', entry in *The New Palgrave. A Dictionary of Economics*, ed. by J. Eatwell, M. Milgate, P. Newman, vol. IV (London: Macmillan, 1987) pp. 222–3.

'Shove, G. F.', entry in *The New Palgrave: A Dictionary of Economics*, ed. by J. Eatwell, M. Milgate, P. Newman, vol. IV (London: Macmillan, 1987) pp. 327–8.

LETTERS TO THE PRESS AND ADDRESSES TO THE HOUSE OF LORDS

1946

'Exports and Manpower', *The Economist*, December 14, 1946.

1947

'Trade Make-Believe', *The Economist*, January 4, 1947.

'The Saving Campaign', *The Times*, August 25, 1947.

'Marshall Aid and the Dollar Gap', *The Times*, December 30, 1947.

1948
'Civil Service Examination', *The Times*, March 30, 1948.
'The Volume of Exports. Need to Raise the Level', *The Times*, October 28, 1948.

1949
'Disinflation continued?', *The Economist*, March 19, 1949.
'Devaluation and Sterling Markets', *The Economist*, October 15, 1949.

1950
'Marshall Aid', *The Times*, November 1950.

1951
'The Budget', *The Economist*, May 5, 1951.
'Manpower Control', *The Economist*, December 15, 1951.

1952
'Manpower Control', *The Economist*, January 5, 1952.
'Investment', *The Economist*, December 6, 1952.

1953
'Living with the Dollar', *The Economist*, January 1, 1953.
'The Dollar Gap: Our Precarious Balance', *The Times*, February 23, 1953.
'Living with the Dollar', *The Economist*, March 14, 1953.
'Equipment for industry', *The Times*, April 20, 1953.

1954
'The Convertibility Risk', *The Financial Times*, September 10, 1954.
'The Case for Cheap Money', *The Financial Times*, June 3–4, 1954.

1957
'Doubts about the Free Trade Area', *The Listener*, February 28, 1957.
'Doubts about the Free Trade Area', *The Times*, March 21, 1957.

1961
'The Budget I should like to see', *The Financial Times*, April 13, 1961.
'A Reasonable Doubt: Government Views on Wages Policy', *The Times*, October 31, 1961.

1962
'Policy on Wage Rates: Annual or Actual Increases', *The Times*, May 16, 1962.

1963
'Economic situation', *The Times*, January 24, 1963.

1965
'The Problem of the British Economy in 1965', *The Financial Times*, January 1, 1965.
'The Budget I Would Like to See', *The Financial Times*, April 5, 1966.
'The Problem of the British Economy in 1966', *The Financial Times*, December 31, 1965.

1966
House of Lords, *The Economic Situation*, July 28, 1966.
House of Lords, *The Prices and Incomes Policy*, August 3, 1966.

1967
House of Lords, *European Economic Community*, May 8, 1967.

1968
House of Lords, *The Economic Situation and Public Expenditure*, January 24, 1968.

1973
House of Lords, *Economic and Industrial Affairs*, November 6, 1973.
House of Lords, *Counter-Inflation (prices and pay code) (no. 2)*, November 20, 1973.
House of Lords, *Economic Policy and Fuel Supplies*, December 18, 1973.

1974
House of Lords, *Industrial and Economic Situation*, February 6, 1974.
(With M. Posner) 'Challenging the Elegant and Striking Paradoxes of the New School', *The Times*, April 17, 1974, reprinted in *London and Cambridge Economic Bulletin*, July 1974, pp. 19–23.
(With M. Posner) 'Theory Dogged by its Assumptions', *The Times*, April 18, 1974, reprinted in *London and Cambridge Economic Bulletin*, July 1974, pp. 25–9.
'What Keynes Really Said', *Sunday Telegraph*, September 22, 1974.
'The Mini-budget and the Crisis', *Sunday Telegraph*, July 28, 1974.
House of Lords, 'The Economic Position', July 30, 1974.
(With M. Posner) 'Why an Incomes Policy Remains Essential', *The Financial Times*, August 22, 1974.
'Is a Dose of Sir Keith's Horrible Medicine the Only Way to Bring Britain to its Senses?' *The Times*, September 16, 1974.

1975
'Erosion of UK Competitive Position', *The Times*, March 5, 1975.
'Reducing the Rate of Inflation', *The Times*, July 4, 1975.
House of Lords, *The Attack on Inflation*, July 30, 1975.

1976
'Public Expenditure Cuts', *New Statesman*, February 2, 1976.

1977
House of Lords, *The Economic Situation*, January 26, 1977.
'Inflation and the Unions', *New Statesman*, August 1, 1975.

INDEX